Arc of the Journeyman

Muslim International

Sohail Daulatzai and Junaid Rana, Series Editors

With Stones in Our Hands: Writings on Muslims, Racism, and Empire
Sohail Daulatzai and Junaid Rana, Editors

Foucault in Iran: Islamic Revolution after the Enlightenment
Behrooz Ghamari-Tabrizi

Arc of the Journeyman: Afghan Migrants in England
Nichola Khan

ARC OF THE JOURNEYMAN

Afghan Migrants in England

NICHOLA KHAN

Muslim International

University of Minnesota Press
Minneapolis
London

An earlier version of chapter 2 was published as "The Taste of Freedom: Commensality, Liminality, and Return amongst Afghan Transnational Migrants in the UK and Pakistan," *Journal of the Royal Anthropological Institute* 20, no. 3 (2014): 466–85. Portions of chapter 3 were previously published as "A Moving Heart: Querying a Singular Problem of 'Immobility' in Afghan Migration to the UK," *Medical Anthropology: Cross-Cultural Studies in Health and Illness* 32, no. 6 (2013): 518–34.

Published by the University of Minnesota Press
111 Third Avenue South, Suite 290
Minneapolis, MN 55401–2520
http://www.upress.umn.edu

ISBN 978-1-5179-0961-1 (hc)
ISBN 978-1-5179-0962-8 (pb)

Library of Congress record available at https://lccn.loc.gov/2020024757

Printed in the United States of America on acid-free paper

The University of Minnesota is an equal-opportunity educator and employer.

UMP BmB 2020

For Yuen Miu Ling

journeyman . . . ORIGIN late Middle English: from journey (in the obsolete sense "day's work") + man; so named because the journeyman was no longer bound by indentures but was paid by the day

—*Oxford Dictionary of English*

. . . a traveling aspirant, who tours around various locales over a number of years while he learns his trade.

—George Sand

CONTENTS

PRELUDE

From the Red River to England's Shores

"It's true, I swear," Zmarai insisted. Sitting in front of the fire in my family home in Sussex in England, its flames crackling low, he prodded the kindling and insisted I write everything down.

Zmarai's tale begins in the Battle of Jalalabad in the spring of 1989,[1] during the time that civil wars ignited Afghanistan after the Soviets had withdrawn in deep winter after ten years of occupation. All across the country, mujahideen groups planned to attack provincial towns and cities, and to take down President Mohammad Najibullah Ahmadzai's Soviet-backed Communist government in Kabul. Pakistan, keen to secure a land route through Afghanistan to the former Soviet Central Asian republics, supported a Pashtun government that would have its provisional headquarters in Jalalabad.[2]

United by their common opposition to the Soviet Union, the U.S. ambassador to Pakistan and the Pakistani prime minister Benazir Bhutto planned to capture Jalalabad and defeat Najibullah's forces there. They successfully mobilized thousands of mujahideen and Arab fighters[3] loyal

1

to the factional leaders Gulbuddin Hekmatyar, Abdurrab Rasul Sayyaf, and Pakistan's intelligence services director Hamid Gul,[4] against the forces of Rashid Dostum, Mohammed Fahim, and Najibullah's army. The Afghan army, assisted by intensive artillery and air power, flew high-altitude bombers that could circle the sky and evade the mujahideen's Stinger missiles, and dropped cluster bombs intensively over the battlefield.[5]

After several rounds of offensive and counteroffensive they captured the supply road to Kabul and sent reinforcements. By May the Afghan army and government had prevailed in an unexpected and humiliating defeat for the mujahideen that left twelve to fifteen thousand civilians dead, and many more fleeing on foot to Kabul or to the city of Peshawar over the border in Pakistan, where they queued to be registered as refugees in the city and camps there.

Zmarai was born in 1974 in Kabul. Each winter before the freezing weather became too treacherous, his family would shift from the capital to their home on less unyielding ancestral lands near Jalalabad. In that spring of 1989, Zmarai's cousins, uncles, and elder brothers fought for Hekmatyar there. Zmarai, young and forbidden by his father to fight, took to wandering in the fields nearby the battleground close to their home. That such wanderings were dangerous became clear one day when a bomb swooped low and fell close by him. Certain he had been deliberately targeted, he turned in terror and ran as far as he could, for what felt like miles, until with pounding heart and bursting lungs he collapsed in exhaustion. Yet there followed no reprieve—just, incredibly, the mocking wail of another falling bomb whose scream ripped through his eyes and ears as it fell to the ground nearby. Running for safety, he mused while recounting this memory, was a deception, a trickery, like the story of his life.

Fearing they would be killed by Najibullah's troops, the family fled to Kabul soon after. Zmarai became separated—or perhaps, he realized later, he was deliberately left behind in order to make the journey alone with an aunt, to increase her chances. Just the two of them, they slept at night at a watering trough for cattle and in other shelters, walked endlessly until their feet were numb, and rode in trucks with many women. He absorbed his aunt's paralyzing fear—of death, violence, and the drivers who would transport people along the road in exchange for payment but also, they heard whispered, for sex with women chosen at random from the trucks.

After a week, the two of them reached Kabul, which had remained peaceful. During a short, pacific lull, Zmarai rejoined his school and his wrestling club. Too soon, however, the shroud of war engulfing the country enveloped the city as well. After Najibullah's government fell in 1992, the city imploded, destroyed by fighters, described by people as resembling crazed dogs tearing over flesh—or perhaps this was the passionate love that burns and compels mujahideen to kill and sacrifice themselves, and anyone around.

Zmarai's father crossed the border into Pakistan and found them a house to rent in Peshawar city. The family all followed, again fleeing, now grateful to be refugees. Some years later, after England had honored the new Taliban emirate (1996–2001) by offering asylum to all comers from Afghanistan while it waged the "fourth Anglo-Afghan war" there (2001–14)—oblivious to the paradox in the "host who kills"—Zmarai and his cousins left Peshawar. They crossed through Russia across Europe to London to take their chances, promising to work hard and send money so they might regain their family's riches and build a home once again, find peace and perhaps, they dreamed, even farm cows one day in Jalalabad's fertile valleys.

On this cold evening, close to this shore where Zmarai, his relations, and many others had made landfall, crossing the cold Channel to find what others called refuge, he recounted his tale, which had become a kind of myth or fable about the battle, told him by his elder brother, and that was now passed onto me that winter's night in Sussex.

The story begins in Afghanistan's civil war during the deadly battle of Jalalabad in 1989. It then journeys with the story's protagonist and his family to Pakistan as refugees, and ends in England with a family fable relayed in turn to me. In lyrical prose form, it recounts the story of an aged nomad woman, a mother figure not fully human, who lived in the deepest part of the Jalalabad battlefield and cooked bread on a woodfire every day for the mujahideen who fought the Afghan army there. It ties cycles of life to the storyteller's longing for return, for a sense of home, for a time when he was protected by the idealized love of women, to the difficulties of a reality in which he must provide for them. It also evokes his personal fears of aging, of his aging mother's death, and the forms of living death that follow on the vicissitudes of war. This leads us on from deaths on the Red River in Jalalabad to the fluvial undercurrents of living death that shape the heavy economic burdens of war and its aftermath borne by remitting taxi-drivers in England.

Over the red dust of British troops dead in Jalalabad for a hundred years, now when Afghanistan had turned on itself like a rabid dog, many sad and impassioned men, Arabs and mujahideen, fought the government. When they died, the Red River (Surkh Rōd)[6] bathed and feasted on their prayed-over corpses, fattening its banks.

Within a wide swelling of dry mud walls over this arid expanse of death smoke a single nomad, a *koch,* no longer wandering, fixed herself to the earth. All sensible life had fled the killing there—how strange, how fecund her rooting! Adey,[7] her walnut-ridged face, arms fleshless, fingers and knees now gnarled, her backbone an ancient tamarisk.

She, centenary mother, sexless widow, or wiser virgin, she this watchful fairy, this *khapeyrey,* scorns your fear, you and I now looking back from the future, of that blistering gunfire, those screaming bombs, that burning mud.

Like brightly torn flowers or sons, each evening at sundown mujahideen rose as from deep within the mortal earth for the fresh flatbreads, *de tabaiy dôdey,* which she cooked like a man, like hot magic, on a wood fire. The commander assisted her.

As from nowhere she handed him a pile the size of a hero. He returned for yet another. Daily she nourished them all. Daily they rested, miraculously still alive. All loved her like a mother. "I am Adey," she vouched simply. "If you are tired, or injured, rest beside me."

Undoubtedly Adey was a fairy, a genie, a jinn, or an angel, a *malaika,* or some other supernatural creation. After she died, in that battle zone with her smile of an angel, the mujahideen washed her in the river and buried her there.

She had told them, "I have no need of white *qaffin* [funeral cloth], just wrap me in a man's shawl, a *patoo,* wash me three times in the river, and bury me like a soldier, like a man. I have no need of women to wash my corpse. Women these days are no good."[8]

Fairy queen, mother of life and bread, only a mother can feed a man's soul, and sacrifice her body for her sons in this untrustworthy war. What Stygian couplings that produce the burden of children, mothers, and families, ensnaring noble sons in the relentless appetites of hungry kin that have become alien, in a new world that looks like filicide.

Yes, by some inky divination I shall make a story of your mother, too, on this page—your mother who exchanged the red dust and fat pomegranates of Jalalabad, her black hair and wedding gold, for the alien concrete of Peshawar city to feed her filial army, her sons now faraway bread-makers, that fertile lapping river now an English road, those cold rifles pointed toward the future now become English taxis.

Your mother is living but dead. "Make bread!" she says. "Send us money, more money! We need you, our flesh and bone, to live. We will feast on your body."

And so the spent and wandering corpses of children, mothers, and fathers, now build crude dams and furious bridges across time zones and oceans.

Underneath the Red River's muddy caul—now become the tarmac patternings and road signs of an English city's careful grid—there menace unstoppable undercurrents and eddying losses, long-ago surgings and disorientations, lost mappings and stagnant pools that spume out the bloody effluent of delusory progress. We are more than history or mere parchment, insist the crying corpses—we are human! Bring us alive! We are not yet dust.

Why are you telling me this?

In this place where life and writing, and your life and my life meet, are standing your mothers, my mother, two wars, and many more. In the shared story of transoceanic argonauts who sailed from war to London, my own ghostly mother appeared in the

rearview mirror of your taxi. Your waxen image in my mother's
war. In hers the demonic hunting boots of anti-British Japanese
soldiers satisfied their rage on the body of her father. Her mother
dropped the baby. In front of the children's eyes.

Years after, in England, her heart thickened like a jalousie.
Your mother, my mother, like a hollow banyan. You are right,
separation from one's homeland is difficult—*musaferi sakhta
khwareeda*—if *musaferi* is about deaths, dying, or discovering that
one has become the living dead.

And so in this dialectic of woeful rivers and imploring souls, of
newly dead migrant arrivals on Acheron shores begging to enter
the underworld, of reuniting body fragments with dead children,
there may be words, but no wholeness, no ultimate grasping, no
healing, no marvelous crescendo, no fully formed sentences. Just
openings, banal madness, half utterances, unpolished fragments,
separateness, and a curtainous silence.

We, the children and grandchildren of rivers and seas, of the
flotillas of dead people and the boats of refugees, are now become
wordy sailors ourselves, and we chart the waves' cruel curl and
memory pull. Sea creatures writing the stories of sea creatures.

So I have asked, ten thousand times, "How and who are you?"
And with hesitant fingers pressing onto English phone keys, you
answered:

"*Ze narogh yum, ze khapa yum, ze intizar kaom; khoob na razi;*
I am ill, I feel down, I can't move; I am waiting; I can't sleep; I
can't work; I will sleep; I am ill; I am ill; I am ill; I can't move; I am
waiting. I need money not a doctor; I feel bad; I am sleeping since
yesterday; everything is going bad; I am not sleeping."

"See a doctor," I reply. "Sleep then; I am sorry you feel bad;
you can't drive a taxi if you are ill; you need a doctor, not money;
take care; come to us if you want food; you look ill; I'm sorry it's
difficult; stop fighting with people; you should live your own life; I
am not your mother."

And so between landlocked Afghanistan and the isles of the
British, the seabeds crack with alluvial fragments, littoral tales,
dead feelings, tectonic plates, and the transitoriness of life—with
the very point of it all. Words and oceans apart. If not on the

Argo, Lemnos, in Trobriand, if not with Ulysses, or in the genealogy of your fathers' tombs, how then to follow anew these shiny,
English four-wheeled chariots?

In a transmigration of sleep maybe, in resting from the world
and in slumber thick and eternal, might God restore marvelous
souls to dead taxi-men, sleepy journeymen who would be king.
"Do not bury me in London!" you cry. "I will build a vast
house in Jalalabad, in green fields grown over the dead."

Regarding ways anthropology may intertwine professional life, personal experiences, and the lives of our informant friends (Stoller 2007,
179), the mother–son analogy in Zmarai's story bears on the variegated
losses of both our mothers' care in experiences of war, displacement, and
migration. My mother was orphaned as a child when she witnessed her
parents killed in their home during the Japanese occupation of Hong
Kong in World War II—her father by murder, her mother by a bomb.
As an adult, she migrated to England, the imperial homeland. For Zmarai, the analogy bears on his mother's loss of her sons to foreign lands
from where they sent home money so that she, her daughters-in law, and
grandchildren might live. It also ties cycles of life to a sometime mythic,
lyrical mode of storytelling that invokes his longing to return to the cer-
tainties of childhood when he was protected at home by the idealized
love of women—his mother and his elder brothers' wives—and the difficult reality of an adulthood in which he must provide for them (hence
"women these days are no good"), and continues to feel abandoned as he
is charged to ferry them to safety through Afghanistan's burning ground
(the journey with his aunt, continuing war).

While neither mothers, mothering, nor my story are the focus of
this book, the analogy intruded at various acute moments during this
fieldwork—for example, when I felt charged with helping Zmarai with
his suicidal feelings, desires to die, to sleep for days, but I could not. Thus
it bears, too, on the human relationships that constitute fieldwork, and
the limits of what ethnography can do to assist with, alleviate, or represent suffering. It also demands reflections on ways that stories, dreams,
longings, and rememberings can intimate another kind of life, and another kind of anthropology—one that is both personal but also centrally
about the ways anthropological knowledge is formed eclectically out of

exchanges, dialogue, and shared sufferings that make up the relationships, and stories of what people agree on, and the desires, dreams, facts, and imaginings by which they make sense of what is strange or difficult to bear.

Zmarai's story about Adey also communicates some themes of irrevocable life-change. Uncovering its meanings in the silences, arrested expressions, and oblique symbolisms of what is communicated brings us, further, to scrutinize Zmarai's desires for sleep: deep sleep that will mercifully erase all possibilities of returning to himself, anesthetize remembering, and deliver release. In sleep he is confronted with memory images or a subjectivity that lies somewhere between life and death, remembering and consciousness. Sleep and its correlate dreaming also invite questions about a condition of wonder about a world that can transform young soldiers into blackened tree husks, and the home, country, and insomniac time into an empty dystopia, where corpses line the riverbanks of Jalalabad. Sleep also points us away from ideas centered around the politics and rationality of the neoliberal or progress project toward a half-waking, dreaming space where other kinds of knowledge and truth about one's life and history can be encountered. In doing so it intimates a particular storied kind of ethnographic attentiveness that can invite new possibilities of startling revelations where, "within an utterance, a word suddenly swells up in intensity to convey a completely different meaning from what the conversation seemed to have been about" (Das 2018, 547).

The story about Adey and Zmarai's and his family's flight to Pakistan was narrated in English and Pashto and subsequently interpreted by myself in this writing style. It reflects my attempt to capture the sense of myth, wonder, dreamlike sense of reality, and idealization of the mother figure that I felt Zmarai wanted to convey within his telling by way of this spoken realm of half English and half Pashto we shared, wherein neither of us had achieved fluency in the other's language.[9] Over the years, I occasionally asked Zmarai about this story, wanting to understand whether Adey was human, spirit, angel, or ghost. He invariably replied that she was a fairy, a *khapeyrey*—a beautiful fairy in visible form. Such ideas about fairies draw from Afghan folkloric culture, but also a patina of Islamic ideas of the spirit or supernatural world that precede the human world, and from divisions between humans and spirits (*ins* and *jinns*).

Correspondingly, this book also raises questions about ways the ethnographic condition of storytelling may occupy a shared, intersubjective or "in-between" space of possible repair, imagining alternative futures, or allaying the present. The anthropological project of dealing in losses, inevitably, is also one of dealing in rage, the violences that caused and are repeated in those losses, and with the dreams and fantasies of escape or oblivion that follow. Therefore, there is also anger in Zmarai's story, offered freely, of a man fully embedded in the movements of migration and taxi-driving but wanting to stop moving. It is universal, too, insofar as I, and millions of others, share a different but similar family history of war, killings, and migration. To cite Claude Lévi-Strauss, the anthropologist "acquires a kind of chronic rootlessness; eventually he comes to feel at home nowhere, and remains psychologically maimed" ([1955] 2011, 55). Here, Lévi-Strauss might usefully conjoin the book's topic with my position as anthropologist, and provoke a broader analogy between the ethnographer's condition and the migrant who understands him- or herself in motion and through otherness, and who must confront feelings about deracination, loss, and belonging.

INTRODUCTION

Life as a Moving Form

Magkh de zre ayna da—The face is a mirror of the heart.

Ghār ke tsoomra jig da pe sar lārlaree—No matter how high the mountain, there will be a track over the top (i.e., you'll find your way along).

This book is about ways that forty or so years of continuous war in Afghanistan since the Soviet Invasion of 1979 permeate the movements and encirclings of labor, kinship relation, and the everyday lives of migrants—including Zmarai and his relatives from the once-proud Pashtun Ghilzai tribes that fought the British—who became British taxi-drivers living transnational lives between Britain and Pakistan. This particular perspective on Afghan refugee migration, occurring against the backdrop of border, nationality, and territory disputes between British India, Afghanistan, and modern-day Pakistan, disrupts many conventional views on Anglo-Afghan relations. Given that Pakistan is the largest host country for Afghan refugees, it also brings the political territory of Afghanistan firmly into the fold of South Asia. Thereby it extends the fold of South Asia to a more trans-global perspective on Britain's legacies of empire, war, and movement.

The book develops the interface between social anthropology, mobilities research, the historiography of Anglo-Afghan relations, and the anthropology of migration from Afghanistan. These foci shift us toward some fresh starting points. They are developed through an analysis of the ways that movement and mobility are organized through the following frames: language and life, historical and temporal transformation, and the time clock of migrant taxi labor.

First, following many stories I heard like Zmarai's, the book provokes questions regarding the forms that relations of language and experience may take in ethnographic writing and storytelling: on the ethics, limits, and potentialities of translating violence into words; the troubled relation of language to life; and the point at which people's suffering or "failures" arising from events involving war and migration, or from fearing and witnessing deaths, might reach their unbearable threshold and enter into lyrical prose or myth, poetry, or languages of suffering, trauma, or silence. At what point does language falter at the task of remembering painful experience? This is not a problem of expression in Pashto or English. Rather than a lexicon of words, it points to ways that suffering might express itself as staccato breaks, quavers, or rests—like punctuation points, or full stops, semicolons, pauses, sharp inhalations, and breaks—behind which thoughts and feelings are racing, and take the form of symbolic images, metaphors of drowning, an alluvion of blankness, the loss of speech, or arrested lucidity.

Second, the book maps some new connections in the shared history of Britain, the subcontinent, and Afghanistan. Rather than telling the story of Anglo-Afghan relations through the historical travels of British armies, explorers, and anthropologists who journeyed from the center of the British empire to its frontiers in Afghanistan, its perspective is the contemporary one of Afghan migrants who traveled to Britain to claim asylum starting in the nineties. Building on the historical traces of earlier exchanges between England, Afghanistan, as well as the Raj and its North-West Frontier, the English county of Sussex is an apt field site to explore these connections. The coastal village of Rottingdean near the city of Brighton was home to the colonialist Rudyard Kipling (1897–1902), the British writer born in the Raj who wrote extensively about British India, including Peshawar. In 1895 the Afghan prince Nasr Allah Khan (1874–1920) made a visit to Brighton, where he was struck by the Chinese style of the Royal Pavilion there[1] and, upon returning to Kabul, decorated one of his new palaces, the Koti Londoni (i.e., London Palace), in a fusion-inspired pastiche of English and European influences (Wide 2014, 6).

The perspective of Afghans in England can also usefully unsettle imperial binaries (between there and here, then and now) and reorient the persistent fixed gaze of the colonial ethnographer in shaping new understandings about Afghanistan and Pashtuns, war and exile. For example, it can disrupt critiques of persistent "West helps the rest" ideologies that have long weighted asymmetrical concerns with Afghanistan as humanitarianism's deserving subject, and a primal traumatic scene of refugee migration, or the origin of Europe's immigration problem: from an Orientalist view of a backward nation in permanent chaos and crisis, to modernist queries about its incorporation into a liberalizing civilizing mission, and to war.

Next, the book's focus on living history underpins the examination of some imperial ruins in the real-world workings of Afghan refugee migration, its psychosocial harms, and the political and economic rationalities working through it. It draws attention to ways idealized bonds of honor, self-sacrifice, and loyalty regarding the Pashtun family become recast in migrant subjectivity as sources of impossibility and impasse. It additionally explores the deep personal predicaments of those who fail to settle their wives and children, but must continue to remit everything they earn—and who cease to function, or in mobility terms to "move." While migrant lives are permeated with the history of colonial and postcolonial contestations over Afghanistan's borders, and with war and migration, the book also shows how individual territory for some is diminished to the inside of a taxi, or found in the ability to sleep, dream, or otherwise create moments of pleasure on the road.

In examining ways that the burdens of war and exile fall unforgivingly on Afghan families and their remitting sons, and following migrants' travels through life ethnographically, the book also seeks to integrate ideas of freedom and suffering in some original ways. For many migrants, such inner conflicts implicate asylum as no experience of safety and freedom, but rather a carceral burden of familial obligation, political and legal constraint, the inability to fit in or forget—and enduring struggles that, after years living in Britain, still enrich a rich inner archive of dreams, fears, and anxieties. Thus, rather than focus on the regimes of war, migration, and bordering that have governed four decades of "refugee crisis" as a series of radical disjunctural moments in Afghan, Pakistani, and British history, my focus is downward—into what Das (2006) would term a descent into the ordinary, and into ways that *in* ideas of the ordinary also reside ideas of movement and mobility that can assist thinking about migration.

I emphasize migrants' everyday struggles, some ways they cope with losses that outweigh profit, and the false promise in narratives of security, healing, or even progress. I bring this to anthropology's remit to render intelligible the migrant and even human condition. This involves questioning what limits of freedom and endurance are found in the logic of exchange that impels the migrant to cross the world in hopes of renewal, as well as ways that people remain in ambivalent relation to their primary ties, affines, and cultural attachments while moving through life. This is the book's departure point over an analysis of historical events and culturalist readings of tribal codes of honor and *pietas* such as characterize the dominant colonially derived, Euro-American paradigm of studies of the Pashtunwali (i.e., "the way of the Pashtuns"). These relations are not confined to a specific time period. They draw historically, phenomenologically, and intersubjectively on national, cultural, and personal pasts and presents. They shape everyday labor and survival, material and social relations, the sacrifices of sons and mothers, their unfulfilled longings, and dreams of death or peace. They also return us in new ways to subjectivity, feeling, and love, reminding us of Rousseau's distinction between *amour de soi* and *amour propre*—or tensions between the pursuit of self-love or personal interests, and the love that binds (marriage, family, nation) but which can also destroy.[2]

Ethnographies of the *longue durée* have observed that tensions have always existed in Afghanistan and among Pashtuns—as elsewhere—between nation, territory and diaspora, center and periphery, duty and desire, marriage and love, conservation and new invention, outward appearance and interior imaginings, political transformation and stagnation (Ahmed 2004; Barth 1959a, 1959b; Canfield 1988; Caroe [1958] 2006; Lindholm 1982; Malik 2016; Marsden and Hopkins 2008). Thus, while this study focuses on Pashtuns—and specifically Pashtun networks of labor, kinship, and sociality—its address to history and to ideas of time for transformation also invites a recognition of a plurality of multiple Afghan pasts and presents. This implicates ways some historical dialectics of Pashtun anticolonial resistance, ethnic conflict in Afghanistan, the settlement of millions of Afghan refugees in Pakistan, and long-standing Afghan migrations across the globe contribute to new migrant positionings in contemporary geopolitical, economic, and cultural spaces. It also bears on ways cultural codes of the Pashtunwali[3] *do* still signify—for example, for contemporary Ghilzi[4] tribesmen—but do not determine their behavior or experiences, all the while their ideas of culture, tradition, and genealogical provenance are transformed, fragmented, and challenged in diasporic contexts.[5]

Third, the book prioritizes the theoretical lens of movement. Analyzing the local and transnational movements of migrant taxi-drivers can mobilize some fresh understandings of ways that cultural knowledge is contingently constituted and dissolved within movement. This opens up questions about the multivalent labor of moving through life, of being *in* the world, and about migrant life as a source of contradictory and difficult knowledge. It highlights some ambiguous ways that lives unfold between given views of reality, and cultural codes governing the expression of emotion within the imperative of survival and progress. It also points to the material importance of mobile money—as remittances—in creating new lines and limits, or borders of autonomy and obligation between migrants and their families.

This allows us to move from a "fixed" culturalist reading of Pashtun "tribal" structures of kinship, custom, and monetary and emotional exchange and to, for example, newly engage Fredrik Barth's long-standing call to analyze "conditions of change" by which structural organizations became transformed in community action (1959b, 20). This shift in perspective can also highlight some ways that the movements of taxi labor affect their families as they move through, or become stuck in, the impasses of globalization. It reaffirms afresh the argument that geographical and political borders can no longer be equated with national territories (Balibar 2002; De Genova 2017; Wilson and Donnan 2012). Thereby it disrupts the order of Western imperial cartography with its notions of linearity and progression that fail to capture the roundabout and circuitous path of the East or the Global South.

Hence, *mobilis in mobili*. The book seeks possibilities in that which moves. It does not, however, rigidly relinquish the static map in favor of the moving line, or the classification for experience. These ideas are offered as tools, or departure points for trying to apprehend how fluxes between conventional oppositions absorb migrant journeymen taxidrivers' efforts to make progress. They are brought to the task of finding a new social, ontological, and theoretical cartography that can interlace a topographic view with a roadside view—and properly institute ideas of mobility in ways, for example, that Afghans themselves make sense of Afghanistan's past (Green 2015a), themselves as strangers, and in ways that ideas of Afghāniyat (Afghanness) become imprinted on Afghans through travel (Wide 2013a) as, in this case, the journeyman taxi-driver moves through the vicissitudes of life. These ideas should be read both with and against the Eurocentric record.

Afghan Transnationalism

Present-day Afghanistan is still under-researched in many aspects. This is due, partly, to the embargo placed on fieldwork in Afghanistan by many universities since the eighties. Political and geopolitical transformations during this period were key to shifting anthropological foci from nomadic pastoralism, tribe, and ethnicity in the seventies, to refugees and diasporas after the eighties, to nongovernmental organizations, state, supra-state, and military forces as well as policy concerns after 2001 (Monsutti 2013; Oeppen and Schlenkhoff 2010). A few native and foreign researchers are distinct in having worked in Afghanistan since the seventies and eighties. They include Baily, Barfield, Centlivres, Dupree, Edwards, M. J. Hanifi, Neamatollah, and Shahrani. During the Taliban regime of the nineties, Afghanistan acquired a global notoriety that propelled researchers into the spotlight, while the difficulties of conducting research also resulted in a heavy reliance on the imperial archive (Edwards 1994). In October 2001, the U.S.-led invasion of Afghanistan in a war for "Enduring Freedom" against "global terrorism" and the Taliban regime[6] revitalized many imperial axioms in both academic and political discourse. The global war on terror (GWOT) hence also serves as a valuable site for forensic thinking about some contradictory, difficult reversals, or counterflows of migrant movement and mobility within larger Western imperial modes of movement, particularly as they create new forms of ordinary everyday labor, and enable and block movements for taxi-drivers—as in some cases, men without alternatives.

Twenty-first-century studies began emerging through Hamid Karzai's presidency (2001–14) to the partial withdrawal of international troops and Afghanistan's mooted transition to democracy. This occurred alongside increasing instability and violence under President Ashraf Ghani

Ahmadzai, a Columbia University–trained anthropologist. Studies questioned why fifteen-plus years of international military presence failed to achieve either peace or democracy (Coburn and Larson 2014); why tens of billions of dollars of international money spent on development failed to achieve the goals of development (Coburn 2016); problematized ways the privileging of gender in international humanitarian action results in obstacles to either acknowledging or understanding the experiences of Afghan men and women (Daulatzai 2006); problematized the rhetoric of absolute reversal from an old brutal order to a new one characterized by "democracy," "the rule of law," and "gender justice" (Billaud 2015); and explored the deep cultural, religious, and historical links between sacrifice and suicide bombing in Afghanistan (Edwards 2017). They further examined, inter alia, dynamic cultural, political, economic, and juridical transformations, "distance" methodologies, the movements of traders, village chiefs, money, "displacees," development specialists, judicial praxis, biopower and beauty, and jihadists;[7] diverse political, cultural, and economic experiences of exile;[8] demonstrated ethnographically how the cultural, economic, and political territory of Afghanistan is both global and transnational (Monsutti 2010b), characterized by strong relations between the objectives of integration and transnationalism that had previously been considered as opposites (Oeppen 2010); and contested the confines of the categorization of refugee (Hanifi 2000).

Marsden's (2015) study of Afghan global commodity traders in Central Asia, the post-Soviet states, and Europe, for example, draws out connections and connectivities across networks of regional and long-distance trade, while examining the diverse impacts and transformations these traders make in those areas in which they trade. Through connecting Afghan traders to historical and wider networks, he rightly contests the relevance of the category of refugee to explain their worlds. The Afghans I mostly conducted research with live within the constraints of local driving regimes, and inhabit social and economic networks that are more geographically limited than those Marsden researches. For them, the refugee category matters because of the specific transnational political matrix in which they are embedded—because they officially entered Britain seeking asylum and refuge, and particularly because of the harsh situation facing Afghan families as refugees in Pakistan.

Rather than debate classificatory differences between ambiguous terms such as refugee, economic migrant, or forced voluntary and return migration from Afghanistan—which for Afghan and other migrants to Europe certainly have their obfuscatory and cruel political effects (De Genova 2017)—researchers of Afghanistan and its people now tend to prioritize understandings of the ways social and transnational networks based on kinship, ethnicity, economic relations, faith, and party politics facilitate, protect, and sustain large refugee populations over long periods of time. This is unsurprising given the fact that Afghan migration long predates recent crises, and that for over three decades Afghans constituted the world's largest refugee population.[9]

Although Pakistan is the largest host country for Afghans, it did not ratify the 1951 UN convention on refugees. In addition to around 1.5 million documented Afghan refugees holding Proof of Registration cards, an estimated one million undocumented Afghans are living in Pakistan (UNHCR 2015), with around three quarters of them born there (UNHCR 2012). After concerted government efforts to return or deport Afghan refugees, by 2017 at the close of this fieldwork the number of registered Afghans in Pakistan was estimated at around 1.3 million (UNHCR 2017).

"Mohajir" (refugee) status in Pakistan has been one of long-term temporariness, and offers no pathway to citizenship, although it does provide rights to remain, as well as rights to mobility, employment, and protection (Alimia 2014). During the Soviet–Afghan War (1979–89), between four and five million Afghans settled in Pakistan, over two million in Peshawar district; between 1979 and 1984 around two million Afghans from mostly urban areas settled in camps in Khyber Pakhtunkhwa and Balochistan.[10] During the eighties, around one million refugees from Afghanistan settled farther south, in Karachi, and in terms of labor and business consolidated Pashtun power in the city, particularly in land and transport economies (Khan 2010; Malik 2016).[11] Further in-migrations of Pashtuns from Pakistan's tribal areas after 2004 led Karachi to become the world's largest Pashtun city, with more Pashtuns living there than in Kabul, Kandahar, or Quetta (Rehman 2017). Around three million Afghan refugees also settled in Iran, with significant numbers migrating to western Europe, North America, the Middle East, Russia, and China (UNHCR 2005). When Pakistan's North-West Frontier Province

(NWFP) was renamed Khyber Pakhtunkhwa ("Khyber side, land of the Pukhtuns") in 2008, debates from the sixties and seventies revived around the movement for an independent Pashtunistan, the status of the 1893 Durand Line which drew the long contested borders between Afghanistan and British India (Caroe 1958 [2006], 436), and the distribution of natural resources, especially water (Leake 2017; Malik 2016). Afghanistan repeatedly rejected the Durand Line agreement under the U.S. "Af-Pak" foreign-policy strategy of the 2000s; and in the subsequent decade, Pakistan sought to fortify the porous border physically, politically, and socially in order demarcate its territory and population as separate and different from Afghanistan.

The enormous presence of Afghans in Pakistan pushes us to rethink how we theorize Pakistan, and Pakistani labor; and to engage a politics of difference that is not attended to in the literature where both "Afghan" and "Pakistani" become catchall terms. Rana (2011) examines the racialized "Muslim" as a global racial entity, through analyzing Pakistani labor diasporas, and the working-class Pakistani migrant experience in post-9/11 America. Drawing parallels between colonial systems of servitude, contemporary transnational migrant labor conditions, and the predicament of a nexus of terror, terrorism, and being terrified, he shows how the doubly racialized "Muslim migrant" is subject to aggressive state-legitimized violence that led many, terrified, to return to Pakistan, or to be deported as terror suspects.

Attending to Afghan migrant labor from Pakistan can challenge Rana's work in productive ways, forcing a reconceptualization of transnational racialized labor and social class through highlighting the contradictory position whereby Afghan refugee families in Pakistan, for example, are subjected to chronic conditions of instability and insecurity but their sons, as British passport-holders and global citizens, enjoy greater freedom of movement and earning potential than most Pakistanis. These occur, as Rana stresses, within larger structures of imperial, colonial, and postcolonial domination that criminalize, police, and deport the figure of the potential Muslim terrorist. De Genova (2017) likewise argues that the situation of Afghans and many other refugees seeking new futures in Europe is deeply shaped by both an indisputably European colonial past, and a U.S.-dominated, global colonial present. Their migrations are shaping a new Europe both "fortified by very old and new morbid cruelties" (18) and the unsettling of the complacent notion of "Europe" as a discrete totality.

Since 2001, alongside the GWOT and the U.S.-led NATO invasion and occupation of Afghanistan, the situation of Afghan refugees has deteriorated in Pakistan. While Afghan refugees were welcomed into Pakistan during the Soviet–Afghan War, their presence usefully serving the geopolitical interests of the United States and its allies, the situation generated by the GWOT characterized a volte-face. Between 2001 and 2015 around 3.9 million Afghans were forcibly expelled or voluntarily repatriated, with mass detentions, deportations, and tactics of harassment increasing steadily since 2010.[12] A critical turning point for attitudes toward Afghan refugees was an attack on an army school in Peshawar by the Pakistan Taliban in December 2014 that resulted in around 150 deaths. During 2015 and 2016 Prime Minister Nawaz Sharif issued repeated expulsion orders, rescinded and extended settlement permits, and declared that all Afghans should leave by March 2017. In the tense summer of 2016, which saw shots fired across the Torkham border, up to 730,000 registered and undocumented Afghans left or were forcibly expelled, among them the iconic "Afghan girl" Sharbat Gula, photographed for the *National Geographic* magazine by Steve McCurry in 1985.[13]

In February 2017 Sharif extended permits only through the end of the year.[14] Legal rulings calling for deportations increased each time permits expired, in 2013, 2015, and 2016. The forced movements of refugees over the border, the cat-and-mouse extensions and revocations of Afghan permits, and the disruption to international trading by the protracted closure of the Chaman and Torkham borders in 2017, directly demonstrate ways mobility and immobility are used as tactics of states' regulative power in regard to migration policies and regimes, the hospitality of host states, and international relations. While in September 2018 the incoming Pakistani prime minister, Imran Khan, announced he would grant citizenship to registered Afghan refugees in Pakistan, this promise remains unrealized.

In Britain it is not clear how many Afghans who successfully claimed asylum were refugees from Pakistan, as asylum in the UK depends on proving circumstances in Afghanistan. The first wave of asylum seekers fleeing the Communist regime arrived in the eighties, followed in the early nineties by refugees fleeing the mujahideen, and subsequently the Taliban. The 2011 national census registered 62,700 Afghans in the UK, including 37,680 in London. These numbers subsequently swelled in the European "refugee crisis" when 2.5 million asylum claims were made in Europe in 2015 and 2016, by applicants mostly from Syria, Afghanistan, and Iraq. Minors made up one-third of those figures (Eurostat 2016a, 2016b, 2017).[15] At the end of 2018 the Office for National Statistics estimated seventy-three thousand Afghans living in the UK.

While the southern English coast is home to many Afghan and other asylum seekers, with the latter concentrated geographically due to processing centers in Kent and Croydon, and the town of Hastings long used as a dispersal center, research into social and cultural change in the area linked to race, migration, and class has largely been neglected (Burdsey 2016). In the coastal city of the southeastern county of Sussex that constitutes my principal field site, Afghans estimate that they number around 400–450. Ethnic Pashtuns constitute around half, mapping ethnic compositions in Afghanistan, while bearing in mind that population statistics in Afghanistan are disputed (Misdaq 2006, 7). More than one hundred of these individuals are taxi-drivers whose families live in Afghanistan, or as refugees in Pakistan or Iran. Many such "double refugees" have British citizenship. Many others have permanent residence permits, or "leave to remain." Most arrived during or after the nineties. While increasing numbers have since settled their wives and children, others still send remittances to support families in Pakistan or Afghanistan. These differences usefully point to ways ethnic and national categories do not have the same meaning, are used differentially within migrant communities, and play out in different and complex ways for people in everyday life. Given that new Afghan and Pashtun refugee and migrant groups across Western countries are living within similar social structures, burdens, and restraints, this in-depth study of a particular community, city, and region also addresses a wider international picture.

Fieldwork and Methods

The core group of my interlocutors are Pakhtun (a regional appellation;[16] see Hanifi 2013 for a history of language variations in Pashto) migrant taxi-drivers originating from southeastern Afghanistan (Nangarhar,

Logar, and Laghman provinces) and Kabul, with some having families living in extended family households as refugees in Pakistan, mostly in the city of Peshawar.[17] They do not constitute a geographically limited or discrete community of Pashtuns, of the kind characterized in historical literatures and popular discourse, but are fully immersed in relations and friendships with Afghans from different backgrounds, with British authorities, and with taxi-drivers, customers, and people from all parts of the world. They also maintain everyday relations and friendships with kin from the same tribal, descent, and ethnic groups. Their wider Afghan community and friendship groupings include ethnic Tajiks, Hazaras, Nooristanis, and Pashtuns from other tribes and regions in Afghanistan. I have known several migrant families for almost two decades. This study analyzes networks of their kin and friends who work mostly as taxi-drivers in Sussex as well as in London, where their kinship networks number several hundred—and also extend out across other locations around the globe (for example, to Dubai, Canada, Moscow, and other European countries, as well as to Peshawar and Karachi in Pakistan, and across Afghanistan).

This fieldwork was conducted in several periods between 2009 and 2017 in Sussex, London, and Peshawar. It develops first on Monsutti's (2005, 246–47) proposal that anthropologists need to develop fluid, peripatetic ethnographies to reveal the existence of multi-local families and communities and transnational networks, and jettison the idea that Afghan societies and networks are based on integrated territorial entities. In doing so, it combines multi-sited ethnography (Marcus 1995) with mobile and multiple qualitative methods, including life-history work, dream sharing, and historical, literary, poetic, and imaginative research in order to capture the "feeling" of movements (also blocked, potential, and imagined movements) pertaining to labor migration, transnationalism, exile, and displacement (Büscher and Urry 2009). It also employs a storied ethnographic approach (Stoller 2007) in order to develop reflections on ways lifeworlds become storied in motion, through waxing or waning, wherein nothing is static or fixed (Jackson 2013, xv).

Practically, I gathered stories through the use of mobile techniques that involved driving around both purposively and aimlessly, taking planned and unplanned trips, mobile tours, excursions and picnics, attending weddings, Afghan community and local council meetings, musical and cultural events, or eating, cooking, and sitting in homes, including my own. Gaining access and trust was difficult in the beginning, as other scholars of Afghan migrants in Britain have noted (Schlenkhoff 2010). From the outset, research with men was easier than with women. The men I conducted research with were not from an educated elite, as typifies a younger, newer influx of Afghan students in Britain, but have low educational levels, literacy, and English. Working in the public sphere as taxi-drivers, restaurateurs, cooks, car-washers, kitchen porters, and in other jobs around the city, they were initially more accessible than the city's married Afghan women, whose lives were more circumscribed—indeed, by these very men.

I began this fieldwork with those Afghan Pashtun refugee families I had known since the millennium, and with families who had migrated earlier during the Soviet war. As a British woman of mixed Asian origin who has lived in Pakistan and traveled in Afghanistan, I established a fairly easy rapport. I had previously conducted fieldwork in Karachi with male militants[18] and been used to conducting research predominantly with men. Like these Afghans, I also had family and personal connections in Pakistan. When I first met these Sussex Afghans, who became my core interlocutors, they were waiting out the four-year probationary period on their refugee visas (increased to five years since 2006) so they could apply for indefinite leave to remain and visit their families in Pakistan, while I was waiting for my then husband in Pakistan to be granted a visa to come to England. These processes involved surmounting the hurdles of labyrinthine bureaucracies and many delays for us all. Hence, I shared struggles with these men who hoped to settle their wives, or to marry and start families in England, and these were key in my decision, some years later, to begin this research.

These men introduced me to other Afghan drivers, both Pashtun and not, and to their friends and contacts in and outside the city. I met other drivers myself either by using taxis, or visiting places where they worked—and followed up by arranging to meet and talk, perhaps on the seafront, in cafés, or if in London in chai or biryani shops, but most often in their taxis. I wanted the research benefits to involve reciprocity. As I got to know taxi-drivers better, they would ask me for assistance, typically with official letters and documents.[19] I booked their taxis, for example, to travel to and from the airport, and in cases where they insisted on no payment I either did pay, or paid in kind with gifts upon my return.

Such activities strengthened fieldwork relations. Drivers began to stop me on the road to offer a lift, exchange pleasantries, invite me to forth-coming events, or to tell me about what they had been doing. Those I knew better, I accompanied on business or personal trips, and later two return visits to Peshawar. All drivers spoke more freely with me indi-vidually than if in groups, for example at the taxi rank or in restaurants. Some were wary to be seen publicly socializing with a woman; others were anxious, in the earlier years of intense war in Afghanistan especially, that this could lead to accusations of spying. To mitigate worries that a "friendship" with me might also be construed as immoral, in some cases I did not meet brothers together. Unlike friends, they maintained the ob-ligation to "do Pashto"[20] in front of one another—and were censorious of a brother having a friendship with an unrelated women in the highly networked, very public space of a small city where taxi license plates daily circulating within its parameters meant drivers were easily identifiable to one another other, and also to me. In other cases, these boundaries did not apply. While driving along in their taxis, drivers usually spoke openly about their families, ambitions, business plans, settlement or visa cases, difficulties living in England, their holiday or marriage plans, and hopes for the future. I recorded these conversations in my notebook while driv-ing around, or else soon afterward.

Regarding language fluency, I acquired a Pashto good enough to ser-vice everyday conversations about business on the road. Like the course of fieldwork, conversations and interactions flowed, halted, and stopped as they were conducted in English, Pashto, or sometimes Urdu (common to our shared experiences living in Pakistan) as I and my interlocutors code-switched, or quoted in Pashto and then translated their concepts instructionally, or we jointly sought the correct word in both languages.

Navigating through fieldwork, "following," "shadowing," interviewing, or informally talking, I thus inevitably also "moved," became stuck, and inched along between the roles of friend, passenger, "doctor," "teacher," and many tricky cultural and gender boundaries regarding behavior in the facilitative privacy of moving cars, or public space.

Aside from innumerable taxi rides, I exchanged hundreds more mo-bile phone conversations and messages with drivers between jobs while they drove around and between cities, or else struggled to, or waited in taxi ranks—and I conducted fifty-four variously detailed life-history interviews in Sussex, London, and Peshawar. Drivers' narratives often took the form of instructional vignettes full of jokes and imparted wisdom. These gesture to a strong Pashtun oral tradition of *qissa* or folktales (Dupree 1973). The tale of Adey with which the book opened describes one such example.

Proverbs *(matalun)* were used liberally throughout my research. Proverbs, poems, and aphorisms are valued Pashtun rhetorical tools for negotiating everyday relations, prestige, and moral authority, as well as for conveying societal codes of conduct. Those transliterated in this book— which were commonly employed as media of instruction, emphasis, or explanation in my fieldwork—express ideas of progress, blockage, and flow in the movement of life. The Pashto phrases, proverbs, song lines, and quotes I present reflect the colloquial style of speaking among taxi-drivers, rather than formal or classic language form, and have been transliterated into the Roman alphabet phonetically as spoken—in close consultation with my interlocutors and other Afghan Pashtuns.

One advantage of conducting fieldwork over immersive periods is that I gained trust through simply being visible in the city to taxi-drivers over a long period of time. While most requested anonymity, others chose pseudonyms or were keen to have their names and voices heard. Where necessary I changed names and distinctive identifying features. This research also challenges any sexist notion that women should only research women. Sexism is still prevalent in academia, and also among many Afghan men. Indeed, one peer reviewer rejected a journal article I submitted partly on the grounds that it was unfitting for a British women to be traveling about with Afghan men.[21] Indeed, I struggled with many such disciplinary biases, orientalist imaginaries, and the staples of colonial anthropology (e.g., honor, shame)—as well as everyday incidences of sexism during my fieldwork—that apparently render problematic the prospect of a lone women researching a group of male Afghans. Notwithstanding, this study shares company with several comparative examples of women doing ethnographies of men in other settings. Noteworthy studies include Cassidy's (2002) work on horseracing in Newmarket, Allison's (2013) study of corporate masculinity in Japan, and Prieur's (1998) study of male transvestites in Mexico City.

Although the research may have challenged strict notions of doing Pashto, or gender propriety, it represented a highly valuable, positive learning experience for me, and I hope for my participants, too. Hence the book also involves some myriad dilemmas of a woman conducting research mostly with men, and the ways the observer's presence alters the topic under investigation. Crossing borders and boundaries of Pashto and presumptively fitting behavior revealed that the closer these Afghans are in kinship terms, the less open they can be. The further the social distance, the more open conversations can be. It is my belief that the intimacies and confidences I became privy to, and which I present in this book, would not have been solicited had I been a male researcher. It is *because* the research occurred within the alternative, transgressive, interstitial spaces outside convention and propriety that this book takes its particular form.

I also formed close relationships with women in Pashtun and Afghan student societies, Muslim and Afghan community organizations, and female relatives of my informants. I conducted workshops with women at Afghan organizations, and collaborated with Afghan Pashtun women to found a nongovernmental organization for migrant Muslim women. Their perspectives are also included in these pages.

MUSAFERI AS STORIED LIFE

The following sections engage some relevant theoretical arguments and literature on Afghan migrant movement, mobility, and *musaferi* (travel; separation or exile from one's homeland). First is the frame of language and life. To what extent do Zmarai's broken utterances, syntax, and fragments of speech reflect the broken life? Zmarai's story is not representative of my informants. Not all witnessed deaths and killings, or experienced bombings firsthand, terrifying flight, or life-threatening crossings to Europe. Nonetheless Zmarai's story is important for its ability to highlight the stakes of life and death that are frequently glossed over in Afghan men's public life; or in Afghanistan studies as a way of rightly avoiding the crude tendency to interpret all migrant experience through the hegemon of trauma, and the categorization of refugee.

Concerning language, the dissolution of empire in the twentieth century witnessed the fixed relation of language to reality or experience fragment, and overflow its borders of nation, race, and class difference. Along with the illusions of the "first world" of security, so, too, dissolved the modernist idea that language reflects rather than constitutes the world. Into the dust of imperial ruins swept post-structuralist and postcolonial critiques about language and oppression, governmentality and subjection, classification and romantic resistance, narratives connecting ancient, modern, and contemporary histories of an imagined West with a fictitious Eastern counterpart (Ahmad 1992; Bhambra 2010; Rose 2017; Said 1987; Subrahmanyam 2004); ways that imperial divisions are promoted by Afghans driving Western development agendas (Kalra, Ibad, and Purewal 2013, 180); or how putatively incompatible elements may coexist, as in the paradox of the "medieval" Taliban's sophisticated internet propaganda, and the movement's infra-red, missile-powered, "modern fundamentalism" (Rashid 2000; Shahrani 2002).

Other critiques have questioned what of life, its violence and awfulness, might inhabit the gaps, interstices, slips, games, silences, affects, and interruptions of language (Arendt 1958; Scarry 1985)[22]—wherein "language becomes involuted or fantastic, and memory distorted—victims often imagining they are responsible for their own pain. In such situations of social death, storytelling all but ceases" (Jackson 2013, 174).

Anthropologists have variedly addressed the problem of linking the subject to the world, the limits of language to express suffering, and the problem of how to recover violence in words (e.g., Das 2006; Jackson 2013; Pandolfo 1997; Rosaldo 2014). Bringing a dialogical focus to the gap between life and its representational forms can reveal ways that Anglo-Afghan relations are moved temporally and imaginatively by shared and singular histories of migration. Dialogue here implies according serious expression to practices marginalized or suppressed by imperialism and colonial authority. This does not mean simply substituting one language for another—for example, replacing the dominant with the "minor discourse" (Kapferer 2013, 823),[23] or unnecessarily seeking to "decolonize" the Anglo-Afghan analytic landscape (Caron 2016)—but rather recognizing ways ruins of war and empire "saturate the subsoil of people's lives" (Stoler 2008, 192). To illustrate a literal example from Afghanistan, the unmitigated failure of an American foreign development dam and irrigation project on the Helmand River in the 1950s created an artificial salt lake and a residue of salted soil that provided perfect conditions for cultivating opium (Chandrasekaran 2012).

Certainly, in the travel of Anglo-Afghan, or indeed any other migrant relations, to the imperial homeland, coloniality runs through every aspect of everyday postcolonial life and labor, people's bodily encounters with loss, their accommodations and resistances to the hardships of low-paid migrant labor in the imperial "homeland"—and their enduring fear of the "never fully achieved conversion from Otherness into Sameness" (Napolitano 2015, 5). Retaining a focus on ways that coloniality insinuates into the everyday present, and everyday sites of eruption, can also link the madness of the state and individuals, collective and individual memories, repressions and remembering (Good 2012). It can denote constructions of threats to order, force our attention to the often violent ways that political, moral, and epistemic orders are established, and shape the modernist equation of "disorder" in opposition to ideas of colonial and postcolonial order (518). Correspondingly, in those places where this book addresses the trope of "madness," it neither emphasizes a discrete psychological category, nor an experience interior to the psyche. While it attends to these aspects, it gives priority to ways that experiences of extreme suffering are existentially produced within and through suffering as *possibilities* of what life might, or might not, be (Das 2015).

Such approaches infer a psychosocial subject who is embedded economically, polysensorially, historically, and contemporaneously within mobile contexts of colonialism, commerce, and capital. Developing this epistemological stance in relation to Afghan refugee migration requires more than a single unified mode of inquiry. Here I have been drawn to anthropologists who have, inter alia,[24] inspired existential questions about migrant's condition in Europe as one of madness and a desire to "fight" off forces that threaten to overwhelm (Mapril 2011, 293); ways the refugee condition is shaped by "a landscape of mistrust, suspicion and militaristic control" (Besteman 2016, 97); and elucidated an imaginary of wariness and paranoia that threatens to engulf the migrant as he wanders through the streets of London, for example, without fully grasping who and how to be (Jackson 2013). Others have highlighted stories and poetic renderings in the historical and colonial imagination in southern Morocco (Pandolfo 1997); conflicts between traditional and modern forms of knowledge in the madness of psychotic raging against the helplessness of the mother (Pandolfo 2008); linked violence in political life to rich anthropological writing on madness (Lovell et al. 2013); and queried how to grasp deep experience, finely tuned subjectivities, and conscious and less visible aspects of coloniality, trauma, and violence (Good 2012).

Such works also point toward the frontiers of what a mind can bear—in crossing frontiers of nation, endurance, and familiarity—before it enters worlds of terror, madness, insomnia, nightmare, and dreaming. More than simply disrupt the blunt heuristic of trauma, or Afghanistan's disordered condition as chronic and lifelong (a view that frustrates or restricts what is analytically and practically possible), they raise important questions about ways that Afghan lives buffet up against the edges of empire, civilization, European borders—and help challenge simple divisions between history and the present, fantasy and reality, sanity, and madness.

Drawing connections to contemporary Pashto literature also offers many diverse and useful cultural archetypes and images of madness—from feverish dreams, to symbolic oppositions between the figure of the king and the filthy unwashed mendicant, the rabid diseased dog, and the maddening conditions of war and exile in Pakistan (Widmark 2011, 169). As an innovator, lover, and person operating outside recognized boundaries of the everyday, the Afghan madman is a useful figure who can bring strange experiences from outside and make them familiar (Baily 1988a, 134). He also represents a useful tool for the transformation of anthropological knowledge; for drawing connections between motifs from Pashto literature, Sufi expressive poetry, and music, with those European Romantics who wandered around the imperial landscapes crazy with hashish and broken hearts.

While madness in the Pashtun literary imagination has been constructed as a "mode of resistance against authority, society, imperialism, occupation, war, and the pressures of the world" (Caron 2009, 219), it is important that we neither romanticize nor overplay elements of agency and resistance in analyzing people's suffering, or feelings or fears of madness, which certainly describe no uplifting experience of autonomy or freedom. This is not an inevitably pessimistic position. The movement of difficult experience through networks of knowledge relations, institutions, and stories also involves ways of trying to reestablish new norms, of allowing the person to buffer themselves against a fragmenting reality, and to exist more cathartically both in, yet also outside, the world they inhabit. In short, while dream stories may admit unwanted revelations from other worlds outside reality, and invite new anthropological styles of telling, this inquiry into Afghan refugee migration finds a rich invitation from the worlds of fairies *(khapeyreyān)*, kings *(bādchaiyān)*, madmen *(lewanaiyān)*, witches *(sheeshakān)*, as well as ghosts and spirits *(peyrān, jinns)* to think, move, drive, and also to dance with.

HISTORICAL AND OTHER TIMELY TRANSFORMATIONS

The book's second organizing frame of historical transformation seeks to *move,* or to vitalize, some political histories of Afghanistan through the lived experiences of refugee migrants. Migrants did affirm their political positions on the war, for example, or other news events, by listening to Pashtun nationalist music, or Taliban *tarānas,* at home or in their taxis. *Tarāna* means ballad, song, poem, aria, melody. It refers to chanting unaccompanied by instruments (and therefore not "music," which the Taliban considered un-Islamic). The secular national anthem, military songs, and school songs of Afghanistan are also called *tarāna.* They may have religious content, with frequent reference to *shahids* (martyrs) killed fighting anti-Taliban forces (Baily 2015). This *tarāna,* which I first heard played in a taxi, became popular in 2007, following the summer of 2006 when the UK took lead of the International Security Assistance Force expansion into southern and eastern Afghanistan (i.e., Helmand, Zabol, Kandahar, and Oruzgan): "Afghans, the English are walking on your land / Just as they did in the past / The very same your grandfathers chased away / Are today walking like masters of your soil / They come talking friendship / Of building your country / These are not guests but traitors / Since long past these enemies have been here / Again, today, they have attacked your soil / They have made plans to kill you / Afghans, be careful they don't trick you / Don't let them divert you from your mission."[25] Other examples are more pithy, as in this *landay:* "Without the Taliban, Afghanistan would be London" (Griswold 2015, 116).[26]

Afghanistan's modern history has been framed in terms of diverse ideological and political shifts: from regional imperialism, to conflicts between the former Soviet Union and United States, territorial disputes following the creation of Pakistan's borders along the Durand Line, wholesale failures of democracy, peace, and development, and crises of war, refugees, communism, fundamentalism, and misogyny. Such all-consuming explanations of history risk reproducing the same conventions of coordinating power as those under scrutiny (Benjamin [1937] 1968). They also tend to gloss over the complexity, uncertainty, and fragility of unfolding relations and experience that living within such "conditions" entails—and ways the evasive history of empire disappears into other appellations, not in a fixed way, but as vital processes of becoming in people's lives that prevent it being bracketed off into a *passé composé* (Stoler 2008, 194–95).

By integrating forms of migrant experience into oral history, memoir, and storytelling, this book inevitably offers a partial historiography of Afghanistan's modern history. Nonetheless, even briefly traversing the historical territory of contemporary Afghanistan and South Asia with regard to the ebb and flow of movements of imperial expansion, and military and ideological struggles to secure Afghan territory and rights, can provide salient understandings of ways that regions of the past are shifted and transformed by migrants in the present. It can set the ground for migrants' stories to explode chronological time, and the dominant historical view of Anglo-Afghan relations, to contain and understand more deeply the reality of the historical event, and also upturn the Aristotelian idea (expressed in his *Poetics*) that a story should follow the temporal structure of a beginning, a middle, and an end.

Afghanistan's modern and older history may be studied in numerous key texts (see, inter alia, Ali 1964; Barfield 2010; Bayly 2016; Caroe [1958] 2006; Dupree 1973; Gommans 1994; Green 2015a; Hanifi 2011, 2019; Hopkins 2008; Misdaq 2006; Rashid 2000; Rubin 1995). Of particular relevance are ways that several attempts of various rulers to turn Afghanistan into a modern constitutional nation-state met with the priority given by Pashtuns to tribal autonomy, the fragility of the state, and Afghanistan's vulnerability as a strategic geopolitical entity to external forces (Misdaq 2006). These tensions date back to Ahmad Shah "Baba" (Father) Durrani's founding of the Pashtun Durrani empire in 1747, which resisted the incursions of Mughal, Persian, and British rule.[27] In 1709 Ahmed Shah was supported by the eastern Pashtun tribes who rose up against Persian rule in Kandahar. In these first national struggles for independence from the Mughals emerged the mythic sentiment the "Pashtun seeks freedom, not slavery" (Misdaq 2006, 39). The period also witnessed the ascendancy of the Afghan–Persian language Dari as the administrative and cultural language of the Persian-centric Mughal empire (Caroe [1958] 2006, 4).[28] This position was later consolidated in British colonial accounts and colonial politics in Afghanistan (Hanifi 2016). Its promotion by successive Afghan governments inaugurated long-standing antipathies over language that have continued to this day. Notably, the Afghan rulers from 1747 to 1978 have always been Durrani Pashtuns. Pashtuns enjoy a particularly privileged place in Afghan society, and they constitute around half the ethnic composition of the population. Relatedly, in thinking about anticolonialism in Afghanistan and as an analytic stance of this book, it is important to account for differences produced by ethnic hierarchies, Afghanistan's own hierarchies, and a modern situation of internal colonization that harmed other ethnic groups, and also Pashtuns not in line with the ruling Pashtun elite—that is, to neither collapse Pashtuns and Afghanistan, nor to homogenize the experience of what it means to be Afghan.

British expansionist ambitions in Afghanistan were famously thwarted in three Anglo-Afghan wars, most spectacularly when Elphinstone's army sustained cataclysmic losses to Ahmad Shah in 1842 at Gandamak near Jalalabad—referred to in the Taliban *tarāna* on the previous page. Relevant to this study's emphasis on movement, the period of 1860–76 was characterized by the British policy of "masterly inactivity." This eschewed Britain's hitherto costly "forward" policy of military engagement for one of prepared watchfulness. It was abandoned over British failures to persuade Afghanistan to cooperate in securing its borders against Russian influence (Bayly 2016, 241–42). Following the British defeat in the Second Anglo-Afghan War at Maiwand near Kandahar (1879–81), Afghanistan's transition from a segmentary to a unitary state accelerated under the "Iron Amir," Abdur Rahman Khan (1880–1901). Khan signed the Durand Line agreement in 1893, which drew the boundaries between the Raj and Afghanistan.[29]

When British India was decolonized fifty-four years later, Pakistan's new borders followed the Line, in a kind of "second partition" of contested Afghan territories—separating Pashtun tribes, and inaugurating the contentious seeds of what would later become the "Pashtunistan" issue.[30] The Third Anglo-Afghan War in the summer of 1919 reaffirmed the Durand Line boundary, and Afghanistan's independent right to minister its foreign affairs. Glossing over the period, the next sixty years were relatively peaceful.[31] In the light of the subsequent fractures that would result from the chaos created by Daoud, the Communists, mujahideen groups, and the Soviet invasion, the forty-year reign of King Muhammad Zahir Shah (1933–73) is remembered as a golden age and a time of unity (Misdaq 2006, 170).

Afghanistan's four decades of war began on April 27, 1978, when the People's Democratic Party of Afghanistan (PDPA)—a small, splintered Marxist–Leninist party—launched a coup and killed President Muhammad Daoud Khan.[32] The twentieth century witnessed Russia's ascendancy and Britain's replacement by the United States as a superpower. These events, well rehearsed in the literature, occurred within the living memory of many of my informants. The Soviet–Afghan War (1979–89) saw the twentieth-century superpowers transform Afghanistan into a "jihadist" front line of Cold War intractability (Giustozzi 2000; Rubin 1995). During this period the Russians safeguarded the interests of Hazara and Uzbek minorities against the Pashtuns. Language issues became so contentious that even the Pashtun President Najibullah gave interviews in Dari (Misdaq 2006, 195).

Civil war followed the Soviets' departure in 1989. These battles were prolonged by the involvement of Pakistan, Iran, Saudi Arabia, India, the United States, Russia, and the post-Soviet Islamic republics, who sponsored different factions (Rashid 2000). By winter 1992 Najibullah was forced to resign. He was succeeded by the Islamist Burhanuddin Rabbani (1992–96) who, with his northern commander, Ahmed Shah Massoud, and PDPA Parcham forces, held off the resistance parties. These included the Pakistani-sponsored factions of Rabbani's Jamiat-i-Islami, Hekmatyar's Hizb-i-Islami, Abdurrab Rasul Sayyaf's Ittehad-i-Islami, and four minor groups: Hizb Islami (Younous Khalis), Mahaz Milli Islami, Jabhyi-Nejat Milli, and Harakat-i-Inqilab-i-Islami. Kabul, an increasingly Tajik city, was eventually destroyed in months of intense street-to-street fighting and bombing—during which Gulbuddin Hekmatyar earned the epithet of "Butcher of Kabul."[33]

Hekmatyar was not exclusively to blame for Kabul's destruction. After his attempts to persuade Massoud not to bring war into the city failed, Junbish-i-Milli and "Shumali" (i.e., Northern) fighters seized Kabul. They took control of the airport, jet fighters, Balahisar, Naqlia base, Mukoriyan, and Bibi Mahru hill, and forced Najibullah to take refuge in the UN compound. In July 1992, Dostum commandeered several strategic areas. Hekmatyar—supported by Pakistan, Saudi Arabia, the United States and other countries—began fighting, as did other factions. Systematic atrocities were committed by the Iran-controlled Shia Hazare Hizb-i-Wahdat forces, Massoud, and Sayyaf's forces—supported by Saudi Arabia, indirectly by Pakistan, and by other countries as well. The 1992–94 "Battle of Kabul" resulted in around fifty thousand deaths and the large-scale exile of refugees to Pakistan and Iran, including large numbers from the eastern tribes, as well as of my informants and their families.

In Pakistan, Pashtun mujahideen leaders of the seven factions sponsored by the Inter-Services Intelligence (ISI) established strong followings in Peshawar and its refugee camps (e.g., Kacha Garai, Nasir Bagh, Shamshatoo, Worsak, and Jalozai).[34] Refugees in Peshawar were required to join a party in order to be eligible for aid. For example, Shamshatoo and Kacha Garai camps were mostly affiliated with Gulbuddin Hekmatyar (who twice became president of Afghanistan, in 1993–94 and 1996), and the Jalozai camp with Abdurrab Rasul Sayyaf. These leaders built schools in the camps, where several of my informants grew up. While those of my informants who grew up in Afghanistan learned to speak Dari as their second language, and then Urdu in Pakistan, those born in Pakistan do not tend to speak Dari or to know, or be interested in, as much about Afghan politics as their Afghan-born counterparts.

Over the next four years, the Taliban movement took over 90 percent of the country: in 1994 the Taliban took Kandahar, in 1995 Herat, and in 1996 Jalalabad and Kabul, where they killed Najibullah and hanged his body in the streets for two days (Rashid 2009), and reportedly stuffed a cigar in his mouth and American dollars and alcohol into his pockets. Under Mullah Omar's leadership, they used their knowledge of mujahideen groups that had fought the Soviets to defeat the warlords, apply one of the strictest interpretations of sharia ever witnessed, and to establish the Islamic Emirate of Afghanistan from 1996 to 2001 (Rashid 2009). Notwithstanding, interpretations of the Taliban's puritanism downplay foreign interests in the region's gas and oil reserves, the flows of money, and the trade and transport networks they established in Central Asia (Canfield 2010; Giustozzi 2012; Rashid 2000; Shahrani 2002). Massoud—who took support from the West, Russia, India, and Iran—was killed two days preceding the 9/11 attacks.

On October 7, 2001, U.S. President George W. Bush ordered the invasion of Afghanistan, and in December the Bonn Agreement installed Hamid Karzai as head of an interim government. The war's early phases involved systematic massacres on all sides.[35]

Following the 2001 defeat of the Taliban, the West's policy of arming warring factions, and a highly ethnicized new National Army, while simultaneously pursuing humanitarian agendas, weakened and corrupted the state, and created a highly militarized society with precarious prospects for peace (Suhrke 2011). The partial withdrawal of troops and official "transition to democracy" in 2014 saw President Ghani struggle to establish an inclusivist government, all while major development initiatives were initiated between China and officials of the resilient Taliban.

Controversies surrounding Afghanistan's future shaped Kabul's reconstruction, symbolized in the luxurious, ultramodern City Center shopping mall opened in 2005, the ambitious "City of Light Development Project," and other futuristic malls. Such dreams appeared overtaken (or temporarily immobilized) in the lead-up to the 2018 presidential elections, which saw the new U.S. president, Donald Trump, bomb Nangarhar province in April 2017 with the "mother of all bombs," and which ushered in a tense and weary sense of déjà vu as the now Russian-backed Taliban and surviving members of the old mujahideen vanguard (e.g., Hekmatyar, Dostum, Sayyaf) moved to align themselves in national oppositions that also centered around Russian and American tensions in Afghanistan, and devastating suicide truck bombs exploded in Kabul—belying the shaky international narrative promoted since 2014 of the GWOT's success. Bombs, violence, and fighting between the Taliban and government security forces continued throughout Ghani's presidency.

Unmooring

In pursuing the frames of stories and motion, I next turn summarily to the British historical record from the nineteenth century, which bequeathed a peculiarly fixed view on Anglo-Afghan relations, deriving from the lenses of empire and colonialism. British accounts of the Pashtun tribes of the North-West Frontier of British India largely prioritize the travels, wars, and military–political endeavors and defeats of the British in Afghanistan. Vicissitudes of the Great Game[36] engaged strategic military, intelligence, and political rivalries between Britain and Russia over Afghanistan and other territories during the late nineteenth century. The Great Game literature established the colonial knowledge basis of understandings of Afghanistan's people and its tribes through a gaze that explained the short-circuiting of nineteenth-century British colonialism via fixed tropes of a turbulent polity, a resistant anachronistic tribal tradition, the "graveyard of empires," and ideas of honor and revenge (Barfield 2010; Burnes 1834; Caroe [1958] 2006; Connolly 1838; Elphinstone [1815] 1992; Greenwood 1844; Hanifi 2016, 2019; Hopkirk 2006; Marsden and Hopkins 2011).

The period was also heavily romanticized in British novels, travelogues, poetry, and literature of the time. British officers, political governors, agents, spies, explorers, and surveyors (also including Pottinger, Burton, and Kipling) strategically mapped the local geography. Their intriguing tales of the fierce Pathan thrilled Victorian audiences at home, inspiring a generation eager to join the imperial front lines. Martin Bayly (2016) locates the genesis of the colonial story of Afghanistan in a handful of "knowledge entrepreneurs" and explorers, in figures such as Rudyard Kipling (a "chief myth-maker" who never actually visited Afghanistan), Mountstuart Elphinstone, Alexander Burnes, Charles Masson, and Henry Rawlinson. He discusses ways their prejudices created a form of epistemic colonialism, but also became translated into concrete policies and negotiations with the rulers and peoples of the region. Shah Mahmoud Hanifi (2016, 398) by turn calls for emotional and intellectual antidotes to persistent "colonially induced afflictions of Afghanophilia and Pashtophobia," and to the lack of Pashtun voices in the literature about Afghanistan's Pashtuns.

Throughout the twentieth century the Great Game paradigm was reproduced in resistant temporal scripts that described a barbaric backwater resistant to change, such as in a *National Geographic* article titled "Afghanistan Makes Haste Slowly" (Williams 1933), or that implied Afghanistan, like many postcolonial societies, is unable to move (at all, or quickly enough) out of the racialized, uncivilized, anterior time of the West's past (Gupta 2004). These discourses reprised the tenacious axiom that the "unconquerable Pathan" is driven by timeless tribalism, ethnic discord, and geographic isolation; and nostalgia about Afghanistan as a place to observe past time in the present (Green 2013, 69). Chatwin's

(1990, 286) "Lament for Afghanistan" inveighed against the "hippy occupation" of the sixties by Western travelers who "wrecked" Afghanistan's timeless beauty—while in 1961 the Afghan Ministry of Planning
published a tourist brochure equivocally titled "Ancient Land of Modern
Ways." The twentieth and twenty-first centuries reprised many regressive
populist stereotypes for new audiences, and adapted several films from
literary classics to critical acclaim, as Western audiences projected domestic anxieties about disintegrating social, political, and imperial orders
onto a caricatured, distant landscape.[37]

Unsettling the colonial moorings of such literatures on Afghanistan
created fruitful dialogue between historians and anthropologists. Authors
emphasize that modern Afghanistan is, far from an immobile or sedentary land, a British cartographic creation of contested porosity whose
boundaries have included present-day India, Iran, and Pakistan (Hanifi 2011; Hopkins 2008). Accounts of constant mobility among Afghans,
including of nomads and displaced people, now definitively supersede
neat narratives of exodus, return, and refugee migration (Centlivres and
Centlivres-Demont 2012; Marsden 2008). As the modern battleground
for competing colonial and imperial powers, Afghanistan experienced
the constant dislocation of its population internally and across its borders
in conflicts encompassing colonial frontiers, disputed national borders,
territorial blocs of occupation, and forced or restricted movement.

Hanifi (2016, 389) emphasizes the significance of long history in the
ways that manifold manifestations of nomadism and sedentarization
provide evidence of "'back to new' forms of nomadism" among Pashtun
communities both within and outside Afghanistan, not least in multiple
varieties of "in, out, to, through, internal and return migration/s." Indeed
the historical record also thoroughly debunks the notion of an impene-
trable terra incognita, and shows that Afghanistan has accommodated
the Buddha, Sufi saints, Alexander, Darius the Great, Genghis Khan, Ta-
merlane, traders, kings, Anglo-Russian rivalries in the Great Game, three
Anglo-Afghan wars (1879–81, 1842, 1919)—four including the UK's involvement in the 2001–14 war—and numerous migrations of Afghans
across the region.[38] While foreign saints, kings, invaders, and armies all
traveled to Afghanistan, Afghan nomads, traders, cameleers, students,
and exiled royalty in turn sortied across the globe (Ali 1964; Edwards
2002; Gommans 1994; Hopkins 2008). In 1928 King Amanullah made an

official visit to England and undertook a thrilling circular flight around the city of London, whereupon he reflected on the possibilities of the London Underground as a blueprint for Kabul—unaware that Afghan communities would flourish around stations such as Shepherds Bush, Ealing, Wembley, Kilburn, Harrow-on-the-Hill, Edgware, and many more a century later.

Historical Afghan settlements exist as far afield as Calcutta, Singapore, and Ukraine—and "Afghan," "Cabul," and "Kandahar" street names in Asian cities may represent memory traces of settlements long disappeared. Between 1850 and 1900, teams of Afghan camel-drivers comprising Pashtun tribesmen (Ghilzis, Durranis, Afridis, Balochis) assisted in the large-scale development of Australia's interior (Stevens 1989). After the end of the First Anglo-Afghan War in 1842, during which Afghan nomads had assisted the invasion of Afghanistan through supplying camels to transport the British, these nomads fell out of favor with the Amir Dost Mohammed Khan and relocations occurred. Afghan nomad traders had previously introduced British goods to Afghanistan and Central Asia during the 1830s (Husain 2018). Certainly Anglo-Afghan diplomatic, cultural, and intellectual relations in the nineteenth century provide evidence that far extends the priority accorded to wars between the two countries (Green 2015b). Afghan mobility has also provided a rich source of sociopolitical critique, for example in Rabindranath Tagore's 1892 story about the itinerant Afghan trader titled "Kabuliwala," which criticized the suspicion of foreigners in Bengali society.

Regarding contemporary studies of migration, some notable ethnographies build outward from the detailed stories of individuals to a larger transnational mapping of Afghan migration. Monsutti's book *War and Migration* (2005) about Afghan Hazaras in diverse sites of migration emphasizes that Afghanistan's contemporary political and cultural territory is both fully international and transnational. Migration and war do not inevitably de-structure societies but paradoxically open up spaces of freedom to establish adaptive migratory networks, forms of autonomy, and social relations between even distant places that may nonetheless be intense (246–47). Whereas Monsutti's book rejects the literature on the "mobilities turn," which he argues constructs schematic pictures of anthropology's history, and views of movement as either anomalous or pathological regarding Afghan refugees or political and economic migration (23), I argue that Afghan migrant taxi-drivers in Britain have a unique and multiplex vantage point on mobility's nuances, structural interconnections, and contradictions.

Rogaly (2015) provides some useful insights into contours of the debate about mobilities within migration studies. He revisits criticisms that the mobilities turn reduces everything to mobility; caricatures ways people are expected to occupy particular mobile or immobile positions according to social categories of class, gender, ethnicity, et cetera; and overemphasizes human movement across space. He argues that retaining the analytic interrelationship between mobility and fixity can valuably illuminate ways migration reproduces class and racial inequalities, as well as everyday mundane, habitual mobilities (528–30).

Monsutti's later book *Homo itinerans: La planète des Afghans* (2018) is more sympathetic toward mobility's analytic value in uncovering migrants' and experts' co-imbrication in relations of power and global inequality. It focuses on ways Afghan society has been marked indelibly by war and the exodus of a great part of its population, but equally by numerous NGOs and foreign armed forces on its soil. He juxtaposes remitting migrants' circulations across the globe with the circulation of highly paid experts on Afghanistan, drawing examples from the Afghan mountain villages, an ex-pats' soirée in Kabul, an aid program in Abu Dhabi, and the Jungle Camp in Calais.

Next, Baily's study (2015) is similarly transnational and distinct insofar as he expands on fieldwork in Afghanistan over four decades. Like Monsutti, he focuses in detail on a small sample of individuals, and in his case links specific detail on musicians who synthesized Indian classical, Khorasanian, and Pashtun musical traditions at the courts of Kabul's rulers (amirs) in the nineteenth century, to the establishment of originary musician communities in Kabul's Kucheh Kharabat quarter, with portraits of hereditary Afghan musicians singing about the harsh conditions of exile in Peshawar, Hamburg, Australia, and California.

Fragments, Words

Following these literatures, this book asks how migrants' worlds can be understood or represented in ethnographic writing more deeply as forms of life. How can we complicate rubrics such as "colonial legacy" in relation to Afghanistan that fail to capture the re-appropriations and re-positionings of exposure to the damage of "imperial ruins" within the politics of the present? (Stoler 2008, 196). How to keep in view ways that zones of ontological, social, and economic dislocation are inhabited by Zmarai and others from Afghanistan living at once in Britain and Pakistan, and ways they differ from other imperial histories of war and migration lived out in Britain?

In order to tackle these questions, and to introduce a view on mobility that can shift political, economic, and migrant life from its fixed meanings, I am drawn to anthropologists of broader contexts and traditions who have developed analyses of fragments, borders, edges, itineraries, flows, lines, atmosphere, affects, traces, liminality, tidemarks, and phantoms (e.g., Donnan, Leutloff-Grandits, and Hurd 2017; Ingold 2011; Jackson 2013; Napolitano 2015; Navaro-Yashin 2009).

For example, Napolitano's (2015) study of Mexican migrants in Rome prioritizes an apprehension of affect which, she argues, "animates and stops the heart in different forms of migrant itineraries" (11–13). In her account, affective histories derive "from a feminist and psychoanalytic tradition that has focused on alterity, Lacanian gaps, and Freudian symptoms in religious imagination, including the embodiment of experience and limitations of official histories and language" (15), and illuminate lingering histories or itineraries of anxiety, hope, and difficulty in subjective experience (106). Napolitano inspires reflection on ways that Anglo-Afghan relations are, likewise, moved by the labor of migrants moving from the peripheral to fully human, the outer edges of Western civilization to its center (2–3), and by the entanglement of multiple pasts and histories in migrants' hopes, dreams, and ideas about England, and what belonging and being Afghan in England will entail.

Next, Jackson (2013) draws from existential and phenomenological anthropology and philosophy to develop his concept of the "lifeworld." His starting point is that the meaning of any human life cannot be reduced to conceptual languages of culture or identity to render it intelligible (7). He emphasizes "the sense of a social field as a force field *(kraftfeld)*, a constellation of both ideas and passions, moral norms and ethical dilemmas, the tried true and unprecedented, a field charged with vitality, and animated by struggle" (7). Regarding migrations that follow war and violence, it is insufficient, he argues, to cast the migrant simply as an exemplar in search of global modernity. Rather than reducible to history, his struggle first expresses the human condition that everywhere "entails a perplexing indeterminacy between our confused longings, imaginings, desires . . . [and] realising these longings and integrating them with the longings of others" (165). Next, while national conditions of violence may change, he rightly emphasizes that violence still lives on irrevocably, terribly, in torn and fractured lifeworlds (116). Indeed, far from being heroic or brave, those who know the terror of war, displacement, and flight may show "no bravado" at all, "but only a desire to avoid and appease" (149). Jackson inspires attention to the migrant's way of enfolding himself like a second skin in his story of customs and traditions, wherein we find no essential, natural characteristics of unyielding culture—but instead the displacee's experience of everyday failure, abjection, fractured and fracturing selfhood, smallness, and being left behind (161). The paranoia invoked by the migration experience is also attended to by Navaro-Yashin (2007, 82), who analyzes in psychoanalytic terms the politico-legal affects of fear and rushes of panic precipitated for an irregular Turkish–Cypriot migrant in London by the arrival of a Home Office letter on his doormat, affects derived from the state apparatus so powerful that, not daring to bring it home, he requests a refugee help center to keep his paperwork in a filing cupboard at their office.

In building a critical epistemology of Afghanistan, other scholars have emphasized the ways that Afghan histories are nonlinear, decentralized, fragmented, itinerant, and counter-hegemonic, and interrupted regularly by war, revolution, and exile (Green 2015a, 49). They have usefully conceptualized this stance in terms of "fragments" (Marsden and Hopkins 2011), "border thinking" and "border historiography" (Caron 2016), and "borderism"—including borders between prose and poetry that reinstate Pashtuns at the center in a Persian-dominated polity (Widmark 2011, 17); accorded priority to Afghan ink over the colonial pen (Green and Arbabzadah 2013); and the nationalist poetry of the Taliban over the travelogues of Kipling and Churchill (Strick van Linschoten and Kuehn 2012); and Pakistan's frontier tribal area as a "defiant" border that has remained important to policy making across the world since the end of World War Two, disproportionately so given its size and geographical distance from the global centers of power (Leake 2017, 6).

Synthesizing historical and anthropological perspectives, Marsden and Hopkins (2011) bring ideas of fragments to scholarship on Afghanistan's borderlands with Pakistan. They build on socially, historically, and politically interwoven fragments of understanding in order to resist, first, unified narratives of a unified tribal hinterland, as conceptualized by a confluence of local, colonial, foreign, and international powers (2); and second, the imperial genealogy of the North-West Frontier as an in-between space or buffer zone for the Raj. Their book compellingly reveals ways that small fragments of regional and localized difference "signal major differences in culture, religious life and political disposition" (3). In the book, Hopkins (2011) reveals inefficient management processes in British imperial rule that fragmented the already-disunified frontier into zones of customary "tribal" rule. Complicating polarities between tradition and modernity, he shows how "the colonial state was at one and [the] same time fundamentally a European creature of modernity *and* a 'premodern' South Asian polity" (63; emphasis added). Disrupting notions of the North-West Frontier as a zone for Pashtun isolationism and religious militancy, Marsden (2011) prioritizes trans-regional forms of mobility—through bringing ethnographic detail to the ways that mobility assumes importance in how people shift between different everyday registers of being Muslim in contexts of war, globalization, and geopolitical change (175).

Other historians develop a distinctive and influential literary focus in challenging the Great Game paradigm, and in revisioning the historiography of Afghanistan. Hanifi (2016, 389) debunks the "tautological reasoning about the country that traps one into believing Pashtuns are somehow exclusively responsible simultaneously for making and breaking the state because of their ethnicity," whose origins he locates in pervasive, damaging British colonial military frames of reference. Green (2015a) in turn focuses on the history of Afghanistan's literary traffic in order to disrupt in valuable ways some spatial and ideological confines in understandings of the nation-state project. By developing a definitively "Afghan" view, Green reveals that internal versions of Afghan history are divided, fractured, and "equally if not more oppressive than external colonial or neo-colonial models" (3). Green also offers an interesting reversal of direction in his study of six Iranians who traveled to "Jane Austen's London" in 1815 (2015b). He details much more besides—scholarly, evangelical, and diplomatic friendships and cooperations in a fascinating exposition of London, Oxford, and southern England at the time.

Combining multiple forms of Afghan "history as text," Green (2015a, 12) establishes a geographical history of "overlapping empires, mobile persons, and inter-regional languages." Importantly, he emphasizes that "the history of historical writing in Afghanistan was never one of linear developments" (49), but interrupted regularly by war, revolution, and exile. Rival versions of the past, he argues, reveal the intelligentsia as just as fractious as the more familiar image of warring mujahideen, and the historian as a crucial political player in modern Afghan history. He argues for a dialogical historiography that can illuminate Afghan interactions with non-Afghans, internal and external factors, "through the recognition of cross-border networks, dialogical developments and deep regional dynamics" (50). Green's work is important not only in challenging the primacy of colonial or singular ethnically focused sources, but for rebuffing the tendency to center Western colonialisms as the starting point and epistemology for studies of the East.

Likewise emphasizing the mobility of Pashto literary forms, Wide (2013b) elucidates the development of Pashto written literature in shaping a self-consciously Afghan identity vis-à-vis a perceptibly cosmopolitan Persianate power over a parochial Pashto and Pashtun majority in the region. He argues that Pashto literature, like Pashtun peoples, was far from geographically bounded, but traveled freely across the 1893 borders, at the same time as being inseparably connected to British imperialism and the shaping of Russian, Pakistani, and Indian regional power (92). Caron (2013, 139) shows how internet and electronic audio and video sharing via mobile phones reveals an inheritance of oral and written genres of Pashto poetry, songs, activism, and literary criticism that can travel freely across the world's borders through cyberspace, requiring neither high levels of education nor literacy. Caron (2016) develops the notion of "border historiography," using *tazkiras* (biographical dictionaries) and autobiographies from the Afghan–Pakistan Frontier since 1900, and juxtaposes these with wider social science scholarship on "border thinking" in order to disrupt some old perspectives on imperial bordering, and to connect historical scholarship on Afghanistan with wider theoretical work on language, intertextuality, and mobility (2016, 327).[39]

Continuing the literary focus, the anthropologist Zuzanna Olszewska (2015) studies organized poetic activities among Afghan refugees in Iran ethnographically. She draws from writing on margins and borders to reveal paradoxes in the Islamic Republic's maxim that "Islam has no borders," and the fact of national exclusions around state bureaucracy, a restricted labor market, legal marginalization, and social, economic, and immigration rights (5–8). Refugees' oral poetry in Iran expresses "a melancholic, liminal, and ambivalent disposition; a feeling of being incomplete, and neither fully Afghan nor Iranian" (33). Olszewska does important anthropological work in detailing how migrant personhood, social change, and identity in exile emerge through active involvement with a poetry organization. She and I both uncover a sense of melancholy and liminality among our informants. However, while her informants make identity claims to improve their lives through the formation of a refugee intelligentsia, I locate the importance of storytelling among semiliterate Pashto speakers, and in taxi-driving as a quotidian and mundane setting that also provides valuable information on the lives of Afghan migrants. Further, rather than draw distinctions between literacy, illiteracy, or restricted literacy, I find helpful Street's (2006) conceptualization of "multiple literacies" that posits literacy as a primarily *social* practice rooted in conceptions of knowledge, identity, being, and power. Multiple literacies comprise interacting modes of communication and, importantly, attribute meaning to shifting understandings of history, globalization, and locality in everyday forms of oral and textual exchange.

These works usefully analyze the faceted, prismatic production of words as life, and they establish the ways that Afghan literary forms travel as and through migrant life. They also speak to broader works that can complicate how we think about borders, nations, diasporas, and the border terrains of self, psyche, culture, and community (Anzaldua 2012), ways the refugee serves as a living border concept (Agamben 1994), which switches flexibly between forms or classifications of personhood or citizenship imposed by conventional state regulations on movement, and the mobilities and temporalities generated by them (Donnan, Leutloff-Grandits, and Hurd 2017; Donnan 2015). Thus, letting words wander and playfully overturn the boundaries of existing knowledge, shifting from Anglo to Afghan, historical to contemporary, fixed to nomadic, and genealogical to motile epistemologies, can introduce unexpected incursions of critical disruption to the historical archive, and offer a different view on the present.

I develop and bring this orientation to living words, ethnographically, in the form of unprivileged, minor, and fragmented voices, and to wider anthropological scholarship about mobility, exile, and violence. This approach implicates oral history forms, but also oblique, controverted, and disrupted narratives, dream stories, and the less coherent imprints of nebulous memory. Rather than reveal any triumphant arrival on the "world stage," or a warrior Pashtun culture thrust into the present, it offers instead a way into everyday lives with language—and into various reprisals, renewals, and struggles that move in and out of words. Such struggles are not exclusively Afghan. They apply to conflicted shapings of relationships between race and nation for other immigrant groups (Maghbouleh 2017; Thangaraj 2015), and to refugees and "first-generation" migrants in Western cities everywhere (Besteman 2016; Kalra 2000; Napolitano 2015; De Leon 2015).

As a heuristic device, I use fragments to usefully disrupt the fixed genealogy of Western cartographies of knowledge about Afghanistan and to point to the diversity of Afghan migrant experience—particularly to the fragmentation of selfhood, suffering, and forms of impasse that arise from the failures of mobility to bestow its promises and new wherewithal for life. The putative exchange of war for the oppressions of freedom and refuge also underlines a certain impasse or impossibility of inscription. It provokes long-standing anthropological questions regarding the languages we work with, and ways that narrative gaps, fragments, and silenced memories and events implicate an immenseness of life beyond the storyteller and ethnographer. By expressing its faithfulness to an incomplete and fragmented epistemology, and to the discordant voices of migrant journeymen, this book follows a movement in which the map, the journeyman, the anthropologist, and the place are all displaced, and turn along with the tracking, temporality, and circumvolution of their own movement. The focus on worlds of Afghan mobility and the connectivities this establishes beyond dominant reasoning about Afghanistan, and Afghan bordering practices of culture and history, also stands in "counterpoint to imperial fragmentations, even if this counterpoint enjoys less global visibility" (Caron 2019, 447).

I also experiment with writers of prose poetry and ethnographic snapshots, in order to align the book's style with its focus on mobility and fragmentation of experience. For example, Berlant and Stewart (2019) riff conceptually on ideas of the new ordinary—using short poems, prose excerpts, punctums, and thought experiments to "follow the impact of the things (words, thoughts, people, objects, ideas, worlds)." This book's approach—like theirs—also seeks to dispense with the map, to allow knowledge about ordinary life to emerge through fragments that intimate their own gestalt, in the time and speed of their own creation, on the move. It describes an ethical commitment to come closer to experience that is not easily mapped out, or dishonored through cartographic distortion, and represents an attempt to capture the varied pulses and tempo of the simultaneously lucid and enigmatic proximity of migrant life on the move that stops, judders, stalls, lurches forward, detours, or coasts along unthinkingly.

MOVEMENT AND MIGRATION

The book's third organizing frame adds the perspective of movement to the broad brushstrokes of a historically fixed cartography. This involves questioning studies that neglect how mobility was a central feature of many premodern societies, drawing continuities between past and present to critique the notion of the contemporary "refugee crisis"—arguably better conceived as the contemporary refugee normality—and others for whom it is not possible to stay where they are and therefore seek a better life in Europe.

Indeed, many analysts have argued that Afghan spatial mobility and dispersion are long-standing economic and political "strategies" linking mobile people for whom return is neither feasible nor desirable (Monsutti 2010a, 185–88). This is where smuggling agents, asylum, and visa regimes turn the capacity to move into a class distinction, and movement becomes a privilege. Being a migrant is one of the most convincing or appealing ways of being able to do something about one's life; a practical means of having "choice" in the world is having an EU or British passport, even while the liberal idea of full choice over one's life is not possible. Refugees en route must become experts in navigating agents, trainlines, roads, lorries, and guides, forming what some scholars call "migration-specific capital" (De Leon 2015). Migration also constitutes an interesting way of navigating the world, via a particular mobile experience. It concerns growth, expansion, and the way mobile people, including refugees, are a force for change—akin perhaps to the course and flow of a river; but one that also involves painful fractures of attachments and a sense of place in the lives and minds of migrants.

The perspective of movement also involves a more philosophical perspective. In the endeavor also reside ideas about time, and the way time moves. Rabinow (2007) emphasizes the way contemporary time is contingent, and the ways its multiple elements combine and move through nonlinear space. That is, while time may have historical connotations, it cannot be reduced to prior elements and relations. Relatedly, taking a contingent, creative, and multisided approach to moving time we can confound explanatory lines and mappings, and rehearse a more kinetic approach to Afghan migration.[40] It can allow an approach to history as a contingent, living temporality that is backward- and also forward-looking in subjective experience. For Afghan refugees and migrants this might describe, in the form of "nostalgia for the future" (Battaglia 1995), a generative forward movement that elucidates possibilities of being into the future, as well as a conscious turn to undertake a journey into colonial resistance and those places and events that placed limits on one's pathways through life. It can prioritize people's dialectical relationship with time: from ways time is intentionally shifted, or stands still, to time endured waiting—for peace, or a new future, or people's fears that the past should stay confined to dreams and not ooze into the relentless present. This shifts us in turn to a view of time as a moving entity or space of possibility—and conjoins frames of time and mobility to Bergson's (2002) argument that in the creative movement of life, which forever overtakes ends that are created and pursued, lies the essence of time.

The perspective bears on the epistemology of genealogical versus motile forms of knowledge.[41] Many robust critiques have challenged false equivalences drawn between theory and practice, the ideal and reality, lineage and alliance, symbolic and actual affines, the map and the moving border, the fixed representation versus the fluvial flow of life, and the assumed isomorphic relation between words and life. For example, James Clifford (1997) distinguished between traveling-in-dwelling and dwelling-in-traveling. While the former refers to the adaptive, negotiated circulation of cultural narratives and representations, the latter refers to maintaining life through the constant and simultaneous constitution of mobility and stasis, dwelling and traveling. These readings on motile logic are important. They problematize dominant cartographies that privilege

Western ways of knowing and living, and ways that understandings of movements of assimilation and enculturation demand a certain type of linearity that Afghans both incorporate and refuse. They can keep in view for us ways that knowledge emerges in movement as we go along, and history produces itself in "the track of things," in the possibilities residing between fragments of relations of past and present, time and space, dreamworlds and awakening (Benjamin 1999).

If the history of anywhere cannot be read as a straightforward narrative of linear development, the motif of movement helps us think afresh about migration from Afghanistan. It can add complexity to fixed representations of linearity, center–periphery circulations, charts of migratory strategies, flows of refugees, remittances, and returning migrants. That is, it can assist in addressing the problematic in the flow of the chart whose direction is confounded by continually needing to be redrawn as circumstances change. The question speaks to the ways that forms of "genealogical imposition" have dominated in accounts of Pashtun tribal structures that carefully enumerate descent groups, origins, and tribal regions, and depict in maps and diagrams the formal relations of the tribe to *qaum* (a segmentary kinship group contained within a tribe) to *khel* (a patrilineal descent group) and specific oppositions contained therein (Ahmed 1980, 2004). It can thus complicate and expand on schematic typologies of tribal behavior that highlight the cultural bases for feuding, loyalty, refuge, and revenge, and the extensive reliance on charts, illustrations, and maps in creating knowledge about Afghanistan. It aligns rather with approaches that emphasize *qaum* as a highly plastic organization enfolding Islamic, regional, and linguistic ties, and dynamic alignments to business and political networks in shifting terrains, for example of war and globalization (Ahmed 1980; Shahrani 2002)—one that influences but does not determine action.

The book's analysis of Afghan transnationalism, migration, and the everyday movements of migrant taxi-drivers links to several insights from developments at the nexus of migration and mobility studies. Mobility's genealogy in anthropology parallels comparative developments across the social sciences and humanities in the "mobilities turn."[42] Developing methodologically on moving phenomena can overturn binary extremes in phenomena we normatively think of as mobile, and vice versa—for example, the idea that geographical movement generates social and economic mobility, or that mobility links with freedom, progress, modernity, and profit, and immobility with the inverse (Dean 2016). Specifically, a study of taxi-driving and mobility can reveal infrastructural, networked, and communicative labors, occasions of comings and goings, and multiple potentialities, not always economic, which are actualized in transient and permanent ways. Rather than a rooted sense of dwelling, or community building, it can show here that what is at stake are contracts around mobile money, market relationships on the road, social, class, and ethnic difference. As migrants move through the world's ebb and flux, these relations transform the weighty morphology of the historical record, and assumptions about what moves or not in migration, at least theoretically.

Importantly, ontologies of suffering only tell part of this story. This book also attests to many pleasures of friendship among kin abroad. The focus on sociality reveals many relations of kinship that are less burdensome and demanding than with kin back home who require remittances. It also helps us to integrate the positions of freedom and suffering together in interesting ways. It brings to the fore desires, connections, and moments of joy that we see start to surface in movements of dance, excursions, picnic trips, and the back and forth of humorous banter on the road.

Traffic

Pashtun oral traditions are rich with examples of commentary about contemporary issues such as the separation of families, the freedom of the road, and the cruel enticements and entrapments of mobile capitalism. Consider, for example, this *landay*: "Oh God curse the German who invented the car, that carried my lover away so far" (Griswold 2015, 47), which suggests a bitter separation from an exiled lover, and alludes to the driving jobs that many remitting migrants undertake in Europe. Next, take these lines from the 1973 Pashto film *Orbal* (lit. "a flick of the hair") starring the superstar Badar Munir, which celebrate the culture of life on the road: "I am a truck driver / Today in Peshawar, tomorrow Lahore / In an hour I'll be leaving behind the city neighborhoods / On the way there will be lots of good food stops / For chicken and rice dishes / I am a truck driver."[43] Third is a quote from John Ruskin's essay *Traffic*: "There is no wealth but life" ([1866] 2015). Here Ruskin reflects on the demonic relations of capitalism, knowledge, and morality, and the pessimistic proposition that in the body in motion resides the loss of all received wisdom, knowledge, and reason (34)—a view contradicted by Afghans' hopes of taxi-driving, but which in reality may appertain.

Transport has long been intrinsic to Afghan business networks: from trade networks established by nomadic Pashtun tribes *(kochiyān)*, to the Afghan monopoly on seasonal fruit trades from eastern Afghanistan to British India in the late nineteenth century (Hanifi 2011, 128–41). It continues in Pakistan's large urban fruit and vegetable trading centers; in Pashtun trucking and lorry transport companies operating between Pakistan, Iran, Europe, and Afghanistan; and in the smuggling of people from Afghanistan and Pakistan to Europe. Pashtuns are prominent in taxi-driving and transport businesses across Pakistan, the United Arab Emirates, and farther afield. In Britain, many Afghans, including Pashtuns, work as taxi, minicab, and Uber drivers. Taxi-driving is viewed in terms of professionalization, requiring regular police and license checks as well as permit renewals. It appeals to many migrants with its perceived secure earnings, independence, and freedom to be one's own boss.

Certainly, while trafficking in Afghan mobility has received attention in regard to people smugglers, mujahideen and fighter networks, passengers, and traders, there is little or no research on Afghan taxi-driving. In other contexts, taxi-driving as a form of mobile capital or labor has led anthropologists of urban mobility studies to ask more about people's embodied, temporal, and spatial experiences of mobility (Notar 2012, 283). Taxi-driving thus brings mobility to the fore as a way to learn more about distance and place-making in terrains both specified and extra to the routes, roads, networks, and national borders through which people move, stay, or remain behind. As a form of mobility capital, migrant taxi-driving is apposite for revealing reversed directions, circuits, and links to other forms of cultural, political, economic, and class capital (Jayaram 2016).

Thereby, this study of Afghan transnational migration links to some rich anthropological studies on taxis (Bedi 2016; Hansen 2006, 2012; Leonard 2006; Kalra 2000; Mathew 2008; Mitra 2012; Monroe 2011; Notar 2012; Sopranzetti 2017).[44] Taxi-driving and movement are developed in these pages to certain ways of knowing the English city, driving in the city, and to a certain cartography that involves meetings of bounded locality with some less-bounded spatial and imagined elements of transnationalism.

Central to the "traffic" of taxi-drivers' earnings are the routes and by-ways traveled by their remittances. Afghan remittances here combine with neoliberal and informal money-transfer systems *(hawala)* between sites of migration and (not always) countries of origin. While remittance inflows to Afghanistan are impossible to accurately measure, figures, processes, and operation networks have received attention. The "Migration and Remittances Factbook" (Knoema 2015) approximated US$350 million entering Afghanistan in 2015. In 2017 the World Bank estimated personal remittances to Afghanistan making up 1.94 percent of the country's GDP.[45] The International Organization for Migration estimated that Afghanistan received US$2.6 billion in 2006 in remittances from the global diaspora, and Pakistan over US$6.2 billion—with inward flows to Afghanistan declining thereafter possibly due to an increase in refugee migration during the years of crisis that followed (Vanore et al. 2014, 27). Thompson (2011, 5) suggests that around US$5 billion per year enters Pakistan via informal *hawala* transfer systems, in which Peshawar is a major conduit for Afghan money. Studies of Afghan remittances have emphasized the embeddedness of Afghan *hawaladars* in kinship, friendship, and community ties of trust and reputation that extend transnationally (Monsutti 2005); their role as key brokers for humanitarian assistance, development aid, NGOs, commercial and business relationships, and family remittances (Maimbo 2003); the diaspora's role in Afghanistan's reconstruction (Oeppen 2010); the impact of remittances on development on Pakistan's Afghan border (Rashid and Arif 2014); the economic contributions of overseas professionals (Hanifi 2006); and the ways young men's remittances build social relations of solidarity and mutual aid abroad, but for receiving families serve as a precarious lifeline (Monsutti 2012, 242).

There is much comparative scholarship on remittances from migrant communities from South and Central Asia (Kalra 2000; Maira 2002). Relevant to the local contexts of Afghan migrant drivers in Britain are studies that analyze the importance and the limits of ethnic capital, social organization, ties of trust and co-kinship in remittances involving taxi-drivers in large Western cities (Mitra 2012; Mathew 2008), and the social contexts of migrants' remittances from the southeastern UK (Batnitzky,

McDowell and Dyer 2012; Hassan 2014). If Afghan taxi-driving sets the tone for one English city's patterns of movement, this study emphasizes the ways the local circuit also connects very definitely to wider globally networked economic and familial efforts to combat the effects of war and insecurity in Afghanistan. These are all key forces shaping mobility. If Afghans differ from other migrant drivers in my field site, it is arguably because their families' fates and survival are so dependent on what they, often alone, can earn and send home. Their efforts to shore up money against an uncertain future, to manage hostile immigration polices and the very particular ruins of war and empire they live with, permeate every shift in gear, tariff, and change of direction.

In short, this book contributes to a hitherto little explored transnational genealogy of Anglo-Afghan relations in England. It is also a study of history-in-the-making, literally on the move, by way of the labor created through the traffic of struggle, taxi-fares, remittances and money, and obligations and strains associated with social and kinship relations experiencing change. It highlights ways that mobility in the economic and exploitative realm coexists with other kinds of containment. If the words and stories in these pages evoke the spirit of transformation, they do so with less consequence as ways that relations, ties, and attachments are actually changed—sometimes for the good, but often not—by migrants moving through life and across the world. Given there are as yet no full-scale ethnographies of Afghans in Britain, this book represents a modest starting point. It develops possibilities in the figure of the Afghan journeyman taxi-driver for rethinking a political body and ontology that can transcend many divisions between movement and immobility, romanticism and racism, colonialism and postcolonialism, and war and peace. The hope is that it may also contribute to debates about the mobile, temporal, and existential configurations of contemporary human societies in anthropology more widely.

Chapter Outlines

Without assuming the reader will track a linear or forward path through this book, a route at hand may nonetheless prove useful.

Having by now uncovered and disrupted representations of ways Afghan migrants are incorporated into the structures of the racially, gendered, and classed segmented labor market of taxi-driving, chapter 1 turns to Sussex, the historical location of Brighton's pastiche Royal Pavilion, the inspiration for Prince Nasr Allah Khan's "Koti Londoni" folly, and a key field site for this ethnography. It takes mobility as a continuing element that becomes literally and symbolically clear through the everyday lives of remitting Afghan taxi-drivers. Movement is important symbolically as it connects, extends, and recycles important traditions, valued Pashtun and Muslim ways of life, and community formations for men living outside Afghanistan. Uncovering details about the cyclicality of taxi-work reveals different types of movement. Involving cultural, familial, and economic labors, these are presented as ways of traveling-through-life through which mobile assemblages of local and delocalized labor production, and real and fictive kinship relations between friends and fellow drivers, are continually reaffirmed and reconstituted. They reveal ways Afghan taxi-drivers in England cope with an existence largely justified around movement and capital, and create forms of difference between themselves, non-Pashtun Afghans, and other migrant and Muslim communities.

Chapter 2 is situated in Peshawar. It accompanies migrants on a return visit to their families in North-West Pakistan. Combining theorizations of mobility, liminality, and commensality, it takes the picnic trip *(chakar)*—the pleasurable activity of transporting one's "home" outdoors—as a little-explored cultural lens through which to analyze symbolic formations of "anti-structure" and freedom, the shaping of Pashtun transnational labor, and social hierarchies constituted through migration, rest, and return. It explores the motif of hospitality shaping experiences of contemporary migration, relations between host states and immigrant guests from Afghanistan, and relations between Afghan refugees with different trajectories in Pakistan. As potent, imaginary sites of remembering and forgetting, *chakar* map destinations left, dreams of the future not-yet arrived at, and the burden of multileveled constellations of political and economic insecurity on migrants living between England and Pakistan. They sustain participants in a tension between desires to preserve the hierarchies they conceal, and desires for more freedom. I analyze these contradictory experiences through the emblematic arc of the "round trip."

Chapter 3 returns to Sussex, where Rudyard Kipling's residence in the coastal village of Rottingdean still remains—and, in fact, the chapter takes its subtitle from Kipling's short story "The Man Who Would Be King" ([1888] 2013). It examines forms of immobility in the single case of one man's deep depression in order to question what, in a field of multiple interrelated mobilities, appears not to move. First, immobility points saliently to individual attempts to re-pace, stop, and reshape oppressive realities overwhelmed with "too much movement." Next, it explores some ontological stakes of immobility which emerge through the movement and tempo of sleep, and in dreams as a form of sleep travel. I analyze five dreams of this single interlocutor, and show how oneiric imaginings intimate the way the force of past events characterizes a historical problematic that is not fully grasped in the experiences of exile, but permeates continuity into the future, in ambivalences and tensions between holding on and moving forward. In this case, they involve desires to be king, desires for the company of men, for the fires of deep passion, the beauty of youth, to find a green resting place, and to simply stop moving.

Chapter 4 builds on the analytic themes of disruption, fragmentation, and crossing to explore ways the migration experience might be captured in the mode of fragments—not only the fragmentation of place but also time, as well as of past and present (Caron 2019, 449). Drawing connections with examples including Rosaldo's (2014) ethnographic poetry of grief, Berlant and Stewart's (2019) short writing experiments, and the apothegm that border situations imply a radical break from the known (Jackson 2009, xiii), it presents a "fragmentography" of storied fragments from everyday life. These are linked by ideas of movement and migration, food and water, and terrestrial and aquatic crossings. They encompass three interrelated crossings. First are those from war in Afghanistan to Pakistan, which transformed Afghans into refugees. Second are those circuitous crossings across land and sea, which made British asylum seekers of Pakistani refugees. Third, since the 2010s particularly, are Afghan repatriations from Pakistan, which raise the bizarre specter of Afghans returning in the reverse direction like refugees to their own land.

Chapter 5 focuses on collective immobility, engaged primarily through a conversation with the seminal work of Fredrik Barth (1959a, 1959b, 1969a, 1969b) on lineage organizations, group solidarity, and Pashtun power strategies in an English diasporic context. It analyzes examples of local community organization in formal and informal spheres, and community conflicts surrounding the "hot coals" of the annual Eid-ul-Fitr celebration feast. The mobilization of the city's Pashtuns reveals the formation of a two-bloc system of competition and conflict that, by expressly *not* engaging with local government programs for integrating Muslim migrants, maintained—in Barth's terms—a "puzzling" balance. In other words, they refuse to move. Yet, in the informal sphere, lively forms of collective organization serve to establish competitive social hierarchies and to cohere Afghans closely around shifting formations of superiority, power, difference, and the status of "community." These describe some emergent forms of migrant class consciousness, strategies for gaining local power, and the transnational mobility of immobility as a political adaptation with its origins in Afghanistan. While the dynamics of political organization illustrate many continuities with Barth's argument, they also give pause for rethinking Pashtun collectivity and political organization, the relevance of Barth's model for migrant communities, and the vulnerability of arrangements to continuing change.

The closing reflections revisit what it is to be Afghan, Pashtun, Muslim, and a migrant in the contemporary world. They reprise the book's undertaking to capture some changes that affected its interlocutors over almost two decades, and its interpretive movement of incompleteness and fragmentation. Thinking of the Afghan migrant as confronted with the memory traces of contemporary war, the imperial ruins of England in Afghanistan, and a postimperial England that is trying, likewise, to reassert itself on a world stage raises questions about the use of tropes such as suffering and freedom to understand imperial and other legacies of war and violence in migrant life. Last, the book's unique perspective on mobility reveals how Afghan journeymen in England are restricted by governing regimes of state, remittance, and taxi-driving mobility, but also highly adept at negotiating their opportunities and fissures.

So, with directions in hand, which the reader may follow or discard, we might set off.

1. LIFELINES

Transnational Labor Mobility on the Road

Da chinaroh landay mangayā, saba Koch dey Lalaiyah—
O water urn under the poplar trees, tomorrow is traveling
time for my beloved.

Musafer ma-wazna khawanda, chaerta ba-yay khwainday
de deedan arman kaweena—O God, don't kill a traveler,
somewhere his sisters will be longing to see him.

Picture the glorious view of a wide, open vista from atop a hill on the Sussex Downs.[1] To the north the view overlooks an expanse of green farmland and countryside stretching luxuriously and uninterrupted to the sky. In the distance can be spotted the tiny silhouettes of cars speeding along the narrow winding line of the motorway to London. To the south in the distance glimmers the white-flecked sea—and between the two stands a wind-battered, brave cluster of green trees providing shelter, shade from the sun, and a perfect spot to barbecue. This city's Pashtun taxi-drivers frequently visit this spot and other local green settings in order to eat and on occasion to dance the *attan*, the Afghan national dance, at celebratory *(zwandai)* or congratulatory events *(mubaraki)*, to music played from their taxis which, parked closely together, gently nudge into the dance's curl.

In the spring of 2016 I attended a picnic here that the local taxi-driver Mukhtar hosted to celebrate his first son's birth. He invited some fifty guests, mostly other Afghan Pashtun drivers, to a picnic on the rolling green hills overlooking the city. He brought two sheep to cook with rice and also barbecue, forty local fish that he marinated in spices, bread, salad, black tea, jaggery *(gora)*, and two cases of water and Coca-Cola. He and his friends cooked on a charcoal stove. His guests dressed in traditional *salwār–kameez*. Replete and basking in the sun, afterward Mukhtar started the music on speakers from his taxi, and encouraged the picnickers to form a circle. While some were shy, among those who rose up the *attan* slowly assumed form. Proudly, laughingly, and with concentration, the dancers decided their routine and helped one another keep the line moving in time as "English" passersby gathered around, clapped, and took photos. Aman approached me where I sat watching at a small distance. He had begun dancing, he wanted me to know, with "no idea" of how to proceed. He had been a child refugee and fostered by a British family. He joked that he was "learning" to be Afghan.

Aman's words provoked me to think about the lines in this dance, and the *attan* as a kind of circular line dance and analogy for the drivers learning and wanting to maintain certain Pashtun traditions and values in a foreign country. The circular movement is important symbolically as it connects, extends, and recycles important traditions, valued Pashtun and Muslim ways of life, and community formations for men living outside Afghanistan. The analogy also provokes questions about lines as an organizing structure: of taxi lines; bureaucratic queues for permits, visas, and licenses; back-and-forth lines of migration and return, remittances, cellphone communications; dancing lines; as well as transnational kinship and lineage. Likewise, the *attan* serves as a metaphor for evoking images of mobility, and mobility as a continuing element in the lives of Pashtun migrants that becomes figuratively and literally clear through the experiences of taxi-drivers. It is thus an apt entry point into thinking about ways cultural forms "move" in transnational contexts.

As a rotating line dance involving few or plentiful performers, the *attan* involves repetitions of five to ten steps, ritualized hand and head movements, claps, turns, jumps, half spins, and full spins that may be reversed as the dance's speed increases—and dancers trace lines of the dance through ritualized space. Gender-segregated, varying in style and music between tribes and regions, the *attan* is commonly performed at festivals, weddings, and celebrations, accompanied by the traditional *dohl* (drum) and *surnai* (or *shawm*),[2] or popular modern music. In Logar province, my interlocutors describe how the *attan* involves rhythmic stops and full double twists as arms draw a high arc and meet with a low clap in the center. As performers abruptly switch to the local Logarai dance form, then back, the circle disappears and re-forms. The lines and circles of the *attan* metaphorically capture these Afghans' situation. Their combined expertise and ineptitude succinctly illustrate ways that people learn, follow, shortcut, and totally miss prescribed lines of production and culture, creating new lines in the process.

Pashtun nationalists might argue that lines of a more modern form were imposed on the *attan,* which has historical roots in Pashtun tribal areas straddling the Durand Line, when it was introduced as the national dance *(meli attan)* by the Persianate government in the forties. Moving the body through political space, the *attan's* stylized lines of movements thus inflect political controversies, including around the occupation and development of modern Afghanistan, feelings regarding the marginalization of ethnic Pashtuns by the Persianized structure of centralized power, corresponding conflicts around Western modernity, external interference, moderates and fundamentalists, and four decades of continuous war and displacement.

Thus, if dance can be a metaphor for understanding how lines of mobility are shaped by political movements (Wulff 2008), as a moving line that ideally produces a circle in full synchronicity, the *attan* can reveal everyday micro-level movements invisibilized in political readings of Afghan history and migration. Might then it serve as a window onto some critical theorizations of events in Afghanistan as forms of fixed historical abstraction, or move us to consider ways its bucolic, shadowy lines of war, death, and exile inhabit the taxi-drivers' lives?

This chapter draws some insights from anthropological writing on mobility, and to a lesser extent maps and lines. I bring these together to unsettle popular and historical interpretations of local and global forms of Afghan migration, and the productive cartography of an image or unbroken line between work, earnings, and remittance. According to this perspective, it is the movement that is important, not the destination.

Initially germane, for example, to a study of taxi-drivers is Tim Ingold's (2011, 14) distinction between wayfaring and transport, regarding ways that movement is intrinsic to production, knowledge, and being alive—and the fact that life is composed of the lines of its own movement in time.[3] Moving us to further consider ways that lines in motion may transform knowledge, Martin Holbraad's (2012, 99) concept of motile logic describes an "ontological reversal": one wherein motion is primordial and stable entities are the derivative outcomes of the raw material of motion, not the other way around.[4] As a continuous trajectory with internal momentum, a *line* represents the extrapolation of analytic abstraction from any "meaningful data that can register (and can interact) in motion and as motion" (101).

With these ideas in mind, the chapter analyzes some interconnected movements of transnational migration, everyday relations around "coming and going" *(rāsha aw darsha),*[5] mobile labor (taxi-driving), and customary obligations around crisis and celebratory events *(murrai-zwandai,* lit. "dead–alive"). Following these questions ethnographically also suggests several lines of inquiry regarding ways that transnational forms of Afghan labor, cultural practice, and kinship relations have been transformed and rerouted by taxi-drivers. How, for example, do mobile constitutions or lines of migrant labor and exchange shape ways that people cope with an existence largely justified around capital, and manage tensions between movement and immobility to make that existence livable? How might immobility operate in moments of change, envision lines of possibility, and recalibrate hackneyed timelines or temporal scripts with new life? How can such a perspective unsettle the colonial ethnographer's gaze falling on these Afghan picnickers dancing, post–the "Fourth Anglo-Afghan War"? How, so to speak, "can water also flow over dry earth" *(Pe wochou khwarou ham ouba razi)?*

Opening Lines

Many of these city's taxi-drivers claimed asylum as young men during the 1990s and 2000s. Investing in sons, the proverbial *shudow ghwa* (milk cow), to build and disperse family capital through remittances—in a situation in Afghanistan and Pakistan where wealth disparities among Afghans are increasing—the father typically pays his son's passage, which may cost anywhere between £8,000 and £25,000, depending on whether he takes a flight or a risky overland journey that may last months and be fraught with risks to liberty and life.

The period of the early millennium was one of consolidation when many former asylum seekers visibly "arrived"—that is, acquired taxi licenses, a symbolic gateway to financial security, earning power, freedom of movement, and being one's own boss. In 2017, Afghans estimate that they comprise around 150 men either driving the field-site city council's distinctive hackney carriage taxis, working for local taxi firms, independently, for Uber, or otherwise for private hire companies. This figure approximates the council's ethnicity monitoring statistics (in 2009, the last available full survey), which recorded that out of a total 1,573 drivers, over 40 percent were aged between thirty-five and forty-nine, and 93 percent were male; white British drivers constitute 70 percent, Afghans 10–15 percent, and Sudanese drivers an equivalent number; other drivers originate from Iran, Turkey, eastern Europe, North Africa, and the Middle East.

Most Afghan drivers have British passports and citizenship, which requires five years' residence in the UK. Others have visas granting them indefinite leave to remain, full employment rights, national health insurance, and tax-paying responsibilities.[6] The long journey into this professional field spans the social classes from illegal to low-paid worker, to citizen and hackney-carriage license-holder. Most, though not all, Afghan taxi-drivers are Pashtuns. Hence taxi-driving here also demarcates ethnic lines of productive labor. It is not an inherited trade, like taxi-driver *chillia* families in Mumbai (Bedi 2016, 1014), but rather an ethnicized mode of production that reflects these Afghan Pashtuns' limited education and English, and the acumen of Pashtuns in transport economies elsewhere (e.g., those involving trucks, lorries, cars, buses, and taxis). The drivers mostly hope their children will become educated and professionalized in other ways. Other Afghans in the city from the full range of ethnic and regional backgrounds, including Pashtuns, run shops and businesses; all Afghans have worked in low-skilled jobs (i.e., in shops, kitchens, car washes, and barbershops). Afghans reside in all the city's areas, as public housing tenants, private renters, or in fewer cases as tenant homeowners.

Taxi numbers are regulated, but driver numbers not; driver–owners can command high rents, between £300 and £450 per week (at the time of fieldwork; rents subsequently dropped after Uber and other app-based companies entered the market), depending on whether a radio and contract with a local taxi company, or a train station pass, is included; the car's condition; or if the driver has a low insurance premium. Others pay weekly rents for night or day shifts only. Driver–owners advertise their cars at the train stations, taxi-company offices, or via word of mouth. Drivers have no "contract," per se, but pay a fixed weekly rent until one party gives notice to terminate. If a driver is visiting "home," a friend might take over his taxi (and owner) for that period. Often the same number plates circulate among different Afghan drivers. The car owner's nationality plays little part. White English owners are perceived as less flexible regarding rents, punctuality, and notice periods, although less likely to "cheat" than are foreign owners, or falsely claim to have fixed a mechanical problem. Taxi-driving is a cash economy. Rents, fares, repairs, fees, food stops, loans, and debts mostly involve cash transactions. Although "professionalized" drivers positively distinguish themselves from Uber drivers, and are not subjected to the incentives and disincentives imposed by Uber's rules of work, both licensed taxi-driving and Uber work characterize a culture of insecure work in precarious times, which is unprotected by labor rights and employment law, and which contradicts the "fool's gold" of lucrative, independent entrepreneurship promised by taxi-driving rhetoric (Rosenblat 2019).

A successful asylum claim opens the door to acquire a British driving license. Working as a food-outlet delivery driver affords opportunities to learn the city's geography, and to apply for the requisite tests. The wait list is long. The licensing process involves memorizing ten local areas and over 2,300 road names; passing medical, health, safety, and disability knowledge tests; and clearing criminal record checks. This is a difficult task for those whose English is basic, and for whom the historical–cultural associations of the city's road names are alien. Marwan, a kitchen laborer when we met in 2000, crossly complained about a neighborhood comprising streets named after English Romantic poets: "If you know Byron is a famous poet, Byron Street is easy to remember, but not for us." Marwan repeatedly failed the knowledge test over two years. Yet, once qualified, a driver can earn handsomely, perhaps £1,400 or more per week, or so the more optimistic or boastful drivers claimed. The license also signifies greater responsibility to remit larger amounts, save for one's marriage, or take over full support from one's father for one's growing children's needs and education.

This process of upward mobility from arrival as refugee to asylum seeker, to becoming a taxi-driver, to settling a family can take ten years.

Along the way Afghan taxi-driving encompasses significant inequalities in income and experience. All drivers complain that taxis overpopulate the roads, and that companies such as Uber are stealing their jobs and lowering professional standards. English drivers complain that taxi-driving is an immigrant business. Driving mobility involving delivery and taxi-driving is similarly stratified elsewhere, producing uneven forms of citizenship, ethnic difference, class consciousness, and social divisions, as in Beirut (Monroe 2011). Unlike the motorbike in Truitt's (2008) study in Vietnam, taxi-driving in England does not signal the emergence of a new middle class. Rather, as Notar (2012) found in China, driving mobility may describe a type of self-made upward class mobility, as well as a punitive mobility regime, and a means to avoid marginalization. In Sussex, Afghan taxi-drivers of the council's fleet aspire to conventional forms of upward mobility and bourgeois respectability. Unlike the showy drivers of the gaudy "swanking taxi" whom Hansen (2006) studies in a South African township, they turn their music off, not up, for customers. Afghan driver–owners who have been settled for longer have regular jobs (e.g., school runs, company jobs, airport bookings), take holidays, and can afford to work less during Ramadan. Others, newer arrivals particularly, struggle to remit and to service high rents, and therefore they "fight" to secure the future.

In New York, Mathew (2008) analyzes multilevel forms of political organization and unionization among immigrant taxi-drivers from South Asia. Also drawing from his viewpoint as founder of the New York Taxi Workers Alliance, he analyzes the unrelenting exploitation of immigrant taxi-drivers who face racism, harassment, overwork, and corruption in their daily struggles to make a living—and he offers a poignant analysis of the plight facing drivers from South Asia and other countries (not refugees) who are separated from their families. These Afghans in England, by contrast, mostly avoid relations with local government, which they conflate with the national government, and the city council that licenses the fleet. As former refugees in Britain with families who are still refugees in Pakistan, they have experienced stressful encounters with state bureaucracies, and prefer to not draw official attention to themselves. They eschew the English-run Taxi Forum and the infrequent meetings of the Muslim Taxi Forum, which are attended mostly by Bangladeshi, Pakistani, Egyptian, and Turkish drivers. In 2013 a few drivers formed an Afghan Taxi Forum, but disputes over leadership, reflecting a strong resistance to allow power to accumulate in any one individual, meant it remained inactive.

The Afghan drivers' main migrant "rivals" in this city are the Sudanese drivers, who make up part of the UK's largest Coptic community outside London (numbering over seven thousand). The Afghans neither fraternize nor seek conflict with them. Publicly, their differences are subtly marked. Sudanese drivers decorate their taxis with crucifixes or images of the Coptic pope; Afghans might hang a *tasbee* (prayer beads) or small insignia bearing the national flag on their rearview mirror. Privately the Sudanese drivers invite ignominy, typified in Zia's scornful explanation: "They eat quickly, always alone, and in their cars. They hardly see their families, they chase every penny, they're shameless, they have no culture." He leveled similar criticisms against Hazara, Uzbek, or Tajik "Persianate" Afghans ("Farsibans"). By contrast, "strong Pashtun" drivers like himself pray, rest, and eat together, their queues of taxis parked outside halal food outlets signaling a (fairly) open invitation for passing Afghan Pashtun company.[7] For those of them who fail to settle families, or to achieve the dream of upward mobility, the appeal to "strong" traditional and Muslim identities is used to create superiority and difference, complicating the refugee–citizen divide in Britain and Pakistan, and creating nuances within British Afghan and British migrant difference.

Belonging to this small ethnic community of "strong Pashtuns" means eschewing stereotypical English values and behaviors—pointedly, consuming alcohol, promiscuity, divorce, and disloyalty to one's family. Thus, as did Ajmal while we were driving along one day, they disdain their drunken customers who visit lap-dancing clubs, refuse to take customers to brothels, or lecture nightclub dancers about being "bad mothers."

Ajmal, trying to co-opt my agreement via an attack on sex work, also denigrated Persian Afghans who drink alcohol, are sexually "free," live with their girlfriends while their wives at home remain ignorant, and even father children ("In my tribe we would kill such a child")—even though we both knew Pashtun drivers who behaved in this manner as well.

These kinds of oscillations and tensions between, for example, being "too Afghan" or "too British" is also discussed as symptomatic of the diasporic condition by Maira (2002) in relation to second-generation Indian

American *desis* in New York. Ajmal's vociferousness about "lost" cultural values also reflected some envy of the financial independence, decisional autonomy, and freedom he imagined the "English" enjoyed—at the same time, he and other Pashtun "traditionalists" embedded in oppressive remittance regimes asserted their ethnic superiority by scorning "modern" Afghans while without any irony deploying expensive smartphone technology to tune into Pashto pop, Arman Radio, Voice of America Pashto, Shamshad TV, or Taliban *tarānas,* featuring lines such as *Sharāb aw kebabuna rakam rakam chamoona akhair ba arman darshee chey nazilshee arzarbuna* (Alcohol and kebabs, such an array of pursuits, you'll regret it when punishments finally befall you).

In such kinds of relational valuation they cherished their precepts of cultural and religious conservatism, imagining lines of security and continuity after four decades of war in Afghanistan, which resulted in an estimated two million civilians dead, and the replacement of all permanency with the urgent imperative to make money. Their assumed cultural authority is not, I argue, the genealogical imposition of a preexisting conservatism on the English landscape, but rather negotiated as drivers move around, drawing on ideas about history, culture, and politics as they map out of new forms of life.

Lifelines

I turn next to ways the language of the line comes back into play in remittances, and in the pressures remittances bring to bear on those who send and receive. The men do not receive tangible goods in exchange for their remittances, making these a question of pure obligation to elder kinsmen. The transnational familial and intergenerational relationships generated through migration thus illustrate how remittances are key to ways that Afghan families cope with war and the structures of global capitalism within a kinship-ordered transnational mode of production. Remittances have material and nonmaterial value as forms of economic, familial, and cultural labor. They signify forms of production through the immersion of drivers in myriad real and imaginary currents of involved activity (Ingold 2011, 10).

Relevant studies of remittance networks centered on Afghanistan include Edwina Thompson's book *Trust Is the Coin of the Realm* (2011).

Thompson analyzes how the principle of trust works through a palimpsest of historically layered, global, and local substate practices to enable Afghanistan's "money men" *(hawaladars)* to gain a foothold in international financial markets, around a deterritorialized convergence of licit and illicit flows between drug trafficking profits, war economy actors, offshore spaces, and international banks (207). Alessandro Monsutti (2005) also examines Hazara remittances from Pakistan and Iran. He describes how informal money transfers *(hawala)* involve a dealer and lender *(hawaladar)*, an intermediary *(dallal)*, and notes of credit and trust (183). Customers route their money through *hawaladars,* and neither save, take loans, nor earn interest (189). Monsutti identifies four types of *hawaladar*: small shopkeepers who travel around to collect migrants' savings, purchase goods for their shops, and repay en route; settled shopkeepers; large international businessmen holding import–export licenses that allow them to transfer money legally in addition to their other activities; and "pure *hawaladar*," who solely lend and transfer money (181–82). Trust and reputation derive from kinship, friendship, or community ties; economic cooperation occurs between relatives and households, ranging from mutual support, to the pooling of capital, to distributing family labor among brothers to lessen risks (198).

These tactics also apply widely among Afghan migrants. My interlocutors prefer using the informal economy, and to not accumulate official records of the sums they remit.[8] Their remittances are typically small. They travel along diverse channels—by *hawala*, Western Union, occasionally as cash with returning friends, or perhaps by daily ATM bank withdrawal if they are visiting Kabul, Peshawar, or Karachi. Typically, a driver can hand his cash to a trader *(hawaladar)* who, working from home, an office, or shop, sets a favorable exchange rate and either charges no fee or a small one (typically £10 per £300, or £12 for £600). London-based Afghans with export trading licenses can "hide" *hawala* transfers within legitimate businesses, and more easily transfer money to any major city in Afghanistan, Pakistan, Iran, United Arab Emirates, or Russia using middlemen if necessary *(dallals)*—and also to "smaller" centers (in Jalalabad, Mehtar Lam, or Maidan Shar, for example). In Peshawar, smaller amounts (£200–£300) are routed through smaller shops and trading offices in *kar khanou* (workshops, industries) markets; larger amounts (over £600) usually involve the money-changers in Chowk Yadgar bazaar.

My core interlocutors now mostly remit by bank transfer using businesses with export licenses owned by or introduced to them by relatives in London. Keeping remittances within broader kinship networks ensures trust; a transgression would bring shame (and the debt) to families back home, perhaps leading to violence and stubborn disputes. They now deposit sums locally into a bank account without the need to travel to London. While there is a local Afghan *hawaladar*, they are loath to allow him to become too powerful in the community. They neither want unrelated Pashtuns to profit from their remittances, nor know the amounts they send home. While the city's local Sudanese also use established *hawala* systems, their brokers cover separate geographical territories, and the two communities do not share business.

Relationships with *hawaladars* are built around trust, and strengthened through use and over time. On his first time, a user typically gives the *hawaladar* a copy of his passport, and takes a pin code by which his contact can collect it. After trust is established, pin codes may be dispatched with, and the London dealer may even send money on faith, or perhaps his counterpart in Peshawar passes over a sum before he has received it. Money rarely goes missing: these migrants usually remit relatively small sums.

The following example illustrates the importance of trust and a *hawaladar's* reputation. Some years ago the taxi-driver Zahir used a London *hawaladar* (my core interlocutors' contact) to send £50,000 to Dubai, and the sum went "missing." The London connection swore he sent it; the Dubai end swore they received nothing. Because the sum was large, contacts from the Sussex site dispatched first to London and then Dubai to check and confer. It eventually transpired that a link in London had spent the money gambling. The *hawaladar* repaid Zahir the sum in full, absorbing the loss himself. Thereby he redeemed his honor, trust, and credibility—and thereby his business—and presumably made arrangements for the errant gambler to repay the debt.

These taxi-drivers' remittances service living costs in Pakistan or Afghanistan, children's education, and purchases of gold or household goods (ranging from cell phones to vacuum cleaners), which they transport home on return visits. After all, *stirgey pe khpelou banzhou na drandeegi* (your own lashes do not weigh heavily on your eyes). In the immaterial value of remittances thus also lies the affective transport of control, familial and filial loyalty, guilt, frustration and despair. More enviable drivers purchase private cars, or undertake expensive Haj and Umrah pilgrimages. Since the millennium, several taxi-drivers have also invested in properties and businesses in Afghanistan. Examples include Gul Fazl, who bought three new-build houses in Kabul's suburbs; Hayatullah and his brothers, who purchased fifteen *jereebs*[9] of ancestral land in Jalalabad province; Malik, who built a house in Logar; Marwan, who built a house with a swimming pool (for male relatives only) in Wardak; and Khalid, who bought a supermarket in Kabul to let commercially. These investments also reflect the rise and decline in foreign and returnee investment, aid, reconstruction finance, property prices, and violence and security: that is, the "ebbs and flows of political tension which regulate movement" (Monroe 2011, 97), here of money, risky investments in the future, and the homeland.[10]

Other drivers initiate transnational ventures in mobility and productive capital, transporting secondhand trucks overland to Afghanistan, symbolically and practically reversing the routes they traveled to claim asylum. I first met the brothers Zia and Najeeb when they were shop-workers in 1998. Since then they became taxi-drivers and driver–owners. Stopping in the taxi rank to chat with Najeeb one day, he explained he was using his waiting time to search auto-trade websites in order to export used Hino or Mercedes Actros lorries, tractors, tractor-trailers, or lorry-trailers from Europe through Turkey and Iran, to the customs near Herat in Afghanistan. Najeeb seeks the leisure and autonomy afforded by lucrative deals in the global Afghan mercantile classes, such as his wealthier relatives enjoy in Dubai and Moscow. His cousin now receives the lorries in Herat, transformed from deportee to powerful broker who can dispense contracts as he pleases. All the goods are insured and protected.

"Of course, they are!" Najeeb explained impatiently, becoming suspicious that my interest in the detail was leading to an inquiry into his tax affairs.

Over time, amounts lessen, especially after migrants settle families. Hamid described how "most send like crazy for a few years" then become "normal like the English," drawing on the idea of cultural pollution as an explanation for why a "good Pashtun" might slack off. His accusatory tone expressed the pressures he felt to keep remitting, in his case for a wife he had not chosen, children he had not wanted, and his relative lack of autonomy compared with other drivers, and me (he imagined). Hamid's friend Razi refused to remit anything once he arrived, a decision that infuriated his father. He financed his university education instead, eventually acquiring a job at an international NGO, whereupon he did help his family. In regard to amounts, whereas Matiullah sends £1,000 monthly for his wife and four children; Saeef sends "small" amounts (£100 per month); and his brothers in Europe remit the same. Bibiana's husband has separated, a shift likely to increasingly pertain as migrants' families become more embedded in the UK. After fifteen years, he no longer sends remittances, only small monies if requested, for hospital bills or weddings. He services two private taxis of his own, a mortgage, a Mercedes for private use, and his UK household costs. To give some idea of the scale of these remittances, while no official figures exist, a rude average estimate of £300 per month per taxi-driver (which in 2017 a number of drivers concurred with) would suggest £45,000 in monthly remittances from this small subgroup within the city alone (adding up to £540,000 per year).

Remittances thus optimistically shape the taxi circuit as a globally networked economic force existing within a small locale (Monroe 2011, 95). However, for many the motile knowledge acquired driving a taxi means adjusting ideals, and recognizing that the reality of migration means "arrival" is an illusion. As Nabi described when I saw him after one weekend of low earnings and little sleep, "There *is* no money. There is *just driving*"—for the money one spends, which is earmarked for others, is never enough. Driving rich, driving broke, what point is there in shedding tears? *Teyrou obou pesey cha bael na da warai* (No one has baled water that has flowed by).

Fractures

Drivers are unmarried and married. Both single and married men remit, to families in Pakistan or Afghanistan. Most send remittances to their father, whose authority over his sons traditionally should endure through his lifetime. A migrant's father may neglect his children if they fail to remit, or if they treat a wife badly. Those who cannot afford to settle families, whose children are not British by birth, visit every year or so (if to Pakistan, they visit for a ninety-day visa period). British immigration requirements for family settlement applications have become much stricter since 2012, amid public and political concerns about immigration.[11] Nonetheless, for those who make it, taxi-driving expands and transforms generational lineages, for example through British-born children whose parents, now occasionally grandparents, received asylum. While he may send remittances, the UK householder's *(kooranaiy)* finances are separate from his natal household where kin live as "bone," constituting one flesh, and resources are shared among as many as one hundred members. The migrant son must remit until his sons support him, or he can "separate" financially and establish his own household line.

Anyone may become a householder *(kooranaiy)*: if the *qaum* is too large; if a wealthy or powerful member wants his own segment *(khel)*, and therefore a strand named after him; or if his wife and children live in Britain. Sons may additionally choose a name *(takhalus)* to reflect political or personal aspirations, or fraternal affinities if their father has more than one wife. This often becomes their "surname" on official documentation (substituting earlier naming styles comprising the three names of grandfather, father, and son together). A son's *takhalus* may not necessarily be the same as his brothers' or father's *takhalus*. Other reasons for a split may be because the segment has simply become so big it is difficult to identify members—for example, there may be seven sons named "Hashmat Gul" in one generation alone, and the father wishes to distinguish his strand. Or perhaps young people in the wider *qaum* are indulging in immoral behavior, and a father wants to separate from this association. For example, Hashmat's son could start a *qaum* called Hashmatzai, the suffix "zai" meaning son. While he would still be part of his segment, Yaad *khel* for example, and the larger Ghilzai[12] tribe, after time people will accept the growing *qaum* and its name. Thereby Hashmat's son would also honor his father by naming a descent group after him.

Arguably the burden and heartbreak of uncertain family relations and attachments falls most heavily on those men who support families who have lived as refugees in Pakistan for many years, without imminent prospects of uniting. They may mollify their children's longing for their absent father with money or gifts, and harshly encourage them to withstand their pain. To illustrate, one rainy day this summer Mirwais dropped me into town. I asked after his three sons in Peshawar. As we talked, he relayed that his eldest son, aged seventeen, had confided to his paternal uncle (perhaps hoping for him to intervene) that he hardly knew his father. To dispel his discomfort, and demonstrate the necessity for sons to endure hardship, Mirwais deployed the following proverb: *Nmaray da sroo warkawa, kho nazar pe da zmarai sata* (Feed them mouthfuls of gold, gaze at them like a lion). He also described how his youngest son had telephoned to plead his father to come, and he had joked, "Never!" leaving the boy in tears. "I miss him," he continued.

Over time, many work and remit less. Hamid worked hard in shops when he arrived in Britain in 1998. A bright future beckoned when he leased a fishmonger's shop with his brothers, which is where I initially met him. He sent his entire earnings minus his living expenses home to Pakistan. Some years later, they all qualified as taxi-drivers. The pressure Hamid felt to keep remitting nurtured a merciless depression, not unusual among former refugees. He slowly capitulated, becoming financially dependent on his brothers. He borrowed his taxi rent from them, accumulated debts rather than wealth, with his lifeline, his taxi license, worryingly adrift. This situation has continued for well over five years. His father initially asked him to remit £1,000 per month; he now despairs of receiving the minimum to cover basic costs. Hamid speaks often and obsessively of his insuperable inability to accumulate money "like all other Afghans"—his anguished failure to simply "be normal" variegating what Wool (2015, 25) describes as the agonizing undoing of selfhood in failed aspirations to ordinariness, or "aspirational normativity," around notions of honor, home, and family for veterans affected by war.

Occasionally on weekend nights Hamid, too depressed to work, dropped into my family home for tea. We often had the same conversation. It involved a joke about a starving man who asked his wife what he should bring her from the market. In response, Hamid laughed bitterly, she asked him for hand-embroidered dresses. How could he provide luxuries if he could barely survive? Was he worthless without money? I sensed an element of hopelessness and also anger. He borrowed money to make increasingly frequent, long visits "home" so his family could care for him, although neither Britain nor Pakistan felt like home. By forcibly reversing the expected direction of family care he sought to appear to keep pace with migrants who could afford expensive return visits. Still, "family" seemed more an evanescent and ethereal idea than a viable reality, and he was always chasing money that was not enough.

"My son called today. His mother wants money for a goat for the Loy Akhtar festival,"[13] he offered sardonically. "I have nothing to send them."

At other times, fearful in listening to him wish for death that he might end his life, I pressed, "You don't care that many people care about you?" He replied, "I don't care about my mother, father, children, wife, my friends, even if *you* care. I don't care about myself." In such exchanges he warned, rejected, and showed (perhaps inflicted on) me, not "even" a friend, the never-ending de-mooring of certainty in the life he inhabited, this prolonged exposure to dying. Yet by suspending the rules governing social categories and relations, he also indicated the terms of his invitation to be understood—that is, as living abjectly outside of any "normal," conventional (certainly any codified Pashtun) way a life may be understood or made bearable. His struggles were reflected in his appearance, which had inexorably altered. No longer a young man open to the possibilities of life, as when I first met him, he looked tougher, hunkered inward, the sharp contours of his physical form highlighting the biopolitical in the ways that people endure the harsh, edge-like conditions of chronic economic and associated moral failure (e.g., a bad father, bad son, a "weak Pashtun").

Contour Lines

To what extent are the labor lines of taxi-driving choreographed or improvisational, in step or out of time? This city's limits stretch approximately ten miles along the Sussex coastline and a similar distance inland. City circuit jobs yield between £5 and £15. While lucrative fares into London are rarer for drivers who do not drive for radio companies, delivering Saturday night revelers home to satellite towns and villages can yield high returns. Weekends are the longest, busiest shifts. Drivers congregate for Friday prayers at the mosque, work through with little sleep until Sunday evening, and may break at Sunday lunchtime for football or cricket. They compete to earn the most, and encourage one another to work long hours. As a mobile home away from home, the taxi contains everything a driver needs for living[14]—everything, Ghazi complained, except the ability or freedom to sleep.

The city tempo changes gear as the weekend approaches and the city's main taxi rank becomes full. Taxis make serpentine progress, bumper to tail, around a wide concourse. On public show amid the Saturday shopping crowds, Afghan drivers stand about, exaggeratedly shake hands and hug in greeting. These drivers of the council's fleet constitute a driving elite.[15] The council taxi is a valuable object of monetized motorized power that re-territorializes public space and establishes "new hierarchies over who has right-of-way" (Truitt 2008, 14). The newly qualified driver juxtaposes the economic progress and mobility the taxi promises against his erstwhile immobility in the migrant economy. Comparably, Hansen (2006, 186–87) presents the *kombi-taxi* in a South African township as a metonym for proliferating desires, and the racialized imagining of masculinized black economic empowerment on the way to freedom. In Bangkok, Sopranzetti (2017) analyzes motorcycle taxi-drivers as operators of mobility and central political actors in contemporary Thailand. He elegantly charts the shift of Bangkok's motorcycle taxi-drivers over a decade, from individual entrepreneurs who competed with one another, to becoming a powerful collective force for political mobilization in the city that could filter, block, evade, and channel flows of information and people during the army's crackdown on a public protest to the Thai government in 2010.

Afghan taxi-driving in this English field site is likewise political, and a cruel theater in the fight for survival, security, and prosperity. Yet many feel that politics is futile. After so much war, money is the only reliable raison d'être or political protection.

The biopolitics of taxi-driving that regulate migrant bodies as "bodies that matter"—insofar as they are producers of remittances in the context of asylum (Zylinska 2004)—shapes the body as a stiff-shouldered, tired, round-bellied conduit for local and global monetary flows, a mechanized mobile form of migrant labor and a "accumulation strategy" (Harvey 2000, 174) that creates social and moral hierarchies. Drivers mostly work at night and therefore sleep little. A failure to organize bodily rhythms to the city's temporal rhythms results in lower income, loss of reputation, physical and mental stress. The city's rhythms of progress and circulation, its limits and landmarks, bind drivers into a collective enterprise with unpredictable conditions—like the English weather, which lashes them with financial precipitation.

Dissolving and reconstituting as drivers enter and leave, the circuit produces instant information about traffic, Afghan politics, and community news. Key nodal points of congregation are the taxi ranks, Afghan-run food outlets, mosques, and snooker halls. By contrast is the solitary labor of seeking hidden opportunities in the city's interstices and backstreets. The prize, the newly qualified driver Noor wanted me to know, is the "hunting job," the out-of-town night fare where prices may be negotiated up.

Encircling the city, on weekend nights columns of taxis trailing through the main arterial thoroughfares resemble, drivers joke, *de megai-yānou katār* (a queue of ants). They set the tone for the city's patterns of movement (Monroe 2011). If motility is the capacity to move, taxi-driving describes the law of filling space, opening space, disappearing space—space standing for money, stalled and blocked potential produced through weaving mellifluous lines across the cityscape. It leads to managing queues, delays, gridlock, and frustrating times not earning to become a skill, and patience a virtue. These frustrations are captured in the saying *De sabar de wani mewa khawgeha wi* (The fruit of the patient tree is sweet). Finding my way into and around drivers' lives, working around their timetables of trust and availability, also instituted patience as a requirement for fieldwork.

Taxi-driving also shapes agonistic relationships with customers and strangers who view Afghans with hostility, pity, or compassion. Alternately, drivers' desires may become sexualized in the "the experience of being a hunter, and the promise of flirting with nameless women" (Hansen 2006, 188). The taxi's close interior forces boundaries around intimacy and conventional gender segregation to be momentarily suspended, on literal seats of desire, with confusing or even judicial consequences. Perceptions of "easy sex" are viewed with opportunism, offense, or a challenging test of moral fiber. Taxi-driving mobility requires different modes of social negotiation or "user competence" (Monroe 2011, 96), including around violence, risk, intimidation, and sexual norms.

For example, one evening Omar picked up three young women, ebullient en route to a party. The girl sitting in front raised her bare feet onto the dashboard. Affronted, Omar requested she refrain. She refused. Stopping outside the police station, he requested an officer to assist him in stopping the girl's immoral behavior. Expecting male sympathy was futile: no crime had been committed. Ajmal, who told me the story, ended it laughing, saying in a superior tone, "Poor bastard, he has no idea." By contrast, taxi-drivers' wives, sisters, and daughters, Ajmal emphasized, irritating me with his attitude, are sexually clean, dutiful, properly behaved, and uncorrupted by English culture. Ajmal often advised me to pray, fast, stay home more, and avoid alcohol. I usually bristled that I was happy enough to try to be a good person. *Our* women here, he continued, socialize only with other Pashtun families and relatives, "never" with unrelated men, and they "prefer" to sit in the backseat.

Aside from the *attan,* many Afghans learn English dance forms in nightclubs, and with English girlfriends they kept hidden to avoid their friends' bawdy jokes with their censorious undertone. Since some of my informants had two and sometimes three "mothers," the discourse also circulated that it was quite acceptable to have a wife abroad and girlfriend "on the side."[16] Even so, relations with English women could be fraught. Less the elegant formal partnering of a pas de deux than a bloody fracas, one Saturday night Mukhtar telephoned me, as he sometimes did, sounding distressed. Wali, he explained, had just had a fractious interchange with a drunken couple; the woman had accused him of being sexist and hit his head repeatedly with her keys, drawing blood. Exiting the care, Wali had smashed her cell phone on the road, whereupon her partner had punched him. Shaken, he had called Mukhtar. Should he call the police? Mukhtar had disagreed, advising they would not help. Wali should make money instead and not lose valuable earning time.

Among friends, drivers' stories characterize much loud and jocular fraternizing. A particular impromptu meeting one evening at an Arab restaurant typifies the informal way I mostly conducted fieldwork. I had dropped into this cramped, dimly lit, and busy outlet and saw the new driver Sabawoon and two friends, all in their twenties, finishing a break. They invited me over, and I ordered a tea.

"What news, how's work, anything new for my book?" I asked.

Sabawoon began expansively, "Well, just last night one French woman asked, 'Where are you from?' You know we hate this question. She said, 'I'm so happy I wasn't born in your country.' I talked for *fifteen* minutes:

'Do I look bad? Did I hurt you? I support the Taliban, they're like me, human.'" Perhaps, I provoked, a French man would not have elicited such a lengthy lecture.

Ghaffar laughingly agreed. He interjected.

"Black guys think they're so tough. I took three guys late last week, drunk. On the motorway one said he had a gun and would shoot me. I replied, 'I'm Afghan, I'll kill you. Finally, they called me 'brother'!"

Making his contribution, Qasim offered, "I was attacked once, standing in the taxi rank. One Sudanese, he usually behaves like a gangster, walked over and punched me down while his friends held me down. *From the floor,* I punched him back, there was such power in my fist! Another Sudanese thanked me!'

Their talk, here as elsewhere, instantiates tough, masculinized power relations in public space (Monroe 2011, 93)[17] and depictions of masculinity which, by telling me, they wanted favorably noted about them. Violence, drunken customers, drug dealers, fare dodgers, abuse, racism, perceptions that they are terrorists or rapists, an unhelpful police, and long waiting times are all common issues for taxi-drivers—similarly identified by Mathew (2008, 122–23) among South Asian drivers in New York, and by Leonard (2006) among nighttime taxi-drivers in Albuquerque.

In short drivers' narratives show how Afghan taxi-driving in England is not simply a matter of transporting a fare or traveling from A to B, or following a pre-mapped journey from migration to remittance to security. It is a local activity that relates to global concerns, and one that emerges, interacts, and is inter-animated through migrant labors of social, economic, and locomotory connection. The drivers' stories problematize schematic mappings of Afghan migration, revealing lines that do not necessarily follow prescribed directions, and circles that do not return people to the place they started.

Lineages

I turn next to examine the ways mobility, friendship, and kinship relations converge around practices of "coming and going" (*rāsha aw darsha*) and *murrai–zwandai* (lit. dead–alive). The enfolding of mobility forms into practices surrounding life (*zwand*) and death (*marg*) involves permanency and transience in friendship relations. I heard many times explained that a friend *(mulgureee)* is ideally of equal social status, from one's *qaum*. Friendships may be temporary though deep between transient migrants; and "permanent" kinship relations fracture irrevocably in the long-term difficulties faced by separated families and individual migrants.

Rāsha aw darsha is a term commonly used to describe everyday comings and goings between friends, such as visiting, playing sports, eating, or shopping. It means cooking a meal and driving a friend to the airport when he visits his family in Pakistan or Afghanistan, a transnational adaptation of the practice in Afghanistan where friends, neighbors, and relatives visit a departing traveler with sugared breads *(musraghey)*. When he returns friends again gather to welcome him and share food. Return visits facilitate flows in material, comestible, and affective traffic. Before Saifullah's last visit to his family in Peshawar he telephoned me one morning to ask if we could we shop for his gifts together. His friends would be sleeping, so I could read the labels and help him finish quickly.

We spent the day driving around, shopping for electronic goods, medicines, vitamins, hair dyes, infant formula, toiletries, household goods, colognes, and sportswear. On his return from Peshawar, foodstuffs including fresh *gora* (jaggery), *jalghoza* (pine nuts), *charmaghz* (walnuts), *badām* (almonds), *nakhud* (chickpea snacks), and *tootān* (mulberries) traveled back. The taste of home is important in other ways, namely protecting migrants from acquiring foreign habits and attitudes; although Saifullah often praised England as a good country ("I love England, it's peaceful; this country gave me a passport") it also links to his disparaging description of England as "a country of *taste,*" by which he implied, perhaps bitterly, people's preference for immoral or sexual enjoyment over family obligation.

Beyond the contours of the city, *rāsha aw darsha* creates routes and ties connecting Afghans to communities and relatives in the capital. Fazl boasts of having over one thousand kinsmen living in London. He regularly drives to Southall every Monday night to visit friends (who are also relatives, and minicab- or taxi-drivers) and cook, relax, play cards, or watch cricket, and at dawn perhaps sleep eight or ten in a room. They congregate in Habibullah's small flat above an Afghan minimarket in an area densely populated by South Asians, Somalis, and Afghans. These gatherings between "equal" friends do not involve formal relations of hospitality *(melmastia)* in Pashto (Canfield 1988). None is "rich," all contribute: perhaps lamb, pomegranates, mangoes, watermelons, raisins, or biscuits *(kulchey)*. Last time, Fazl took a twenty-kilo bag of rice, "to last" over future visits. Agha contributed some tasty lamb and spinach dishes cooked by his wife. Because these friends routinely travel to eat and spend nights together, their trips also constitute a mode of communal living ("free" of rules) to which each variously contributes sundries, electricity payments, and supplies including onions, tomatoes, and tea. Over shared experiences and food, rough jokes create strong ties and competitive social hierarchies, challenging the normative sociality of family rules. These shared, quiet nights during the week after the busy weekend allow friends to support one another to endure life's hardships, and create easier relations of kinship than those with family back home. Agha described the import of such relationships using the following proverb: *Ghār pe ghre na warzi, insān pe insān warzi*, which translates literally as "Mountains do not move toward mountains, humans move toward humans," meaning that humans (or friends) are amenable, they help one another—perhaps pointing bitterly on this occasion to the intractable demands of remittances he bore. *Rāsha aw darsha* links thereby to the ways freedom in the productive life of taxi-drivers is practically elusive, fleeting, subject, for example, to licensing controls and timetables, but always imaginatively present (Sopranzetti 2017).

Between unrelated taxi-drivers at work ("road friends"), the first invitation home is extended formally to a guest. The host serves his friend. Haji Aziz wanted me to know that when he first invited Wali for food, he ceremoniously washed Wali's hands, even paid for his cigarettes, in a performance of Pashto commensurate with his family's higher standing. Later on, formalities are dropped. For example, Haji Aziz asked Wali to lend him money. He thought Wali would probably agree, for the sake of a useful friendship. Indeed, Haji Aziz later confirmed the loan. Thus some friendships between taxi-drivers also map new social relations within a kinship idiom, exceeding the labor designed to produce capital ends. These relations also extend transnationally. For example, Wali's mother stayed with Haji Aziz's family in Peshawar when she traveled there for medical reasons. To reciprocate, Haji Aziz allowed Wali to drive his wife and children to Jalalabad, according him brotherly respect through a favor usually reserved for male kin. In such ways, fictive kinship and friendship form and dissolve as drivers move in and out of each other's lives, and reciprocal exchanges also travel back "home."

Rāsha aw darsha also reveals the ways that production, culture, and money as energy are hindered and retracked locally and transnationally, and movement is a vital currency in the city's culture of circulation. Invoking ideas of immaterial labor in motion, the practice approximates what Elyachar (2010) describes in Cairo as forms of "phatic labor." Combining Marxist political economy with Malinowski's ideas of "phatic communion," phatic labor shapes communicative channels, collective "locomotory practices" like the "laying of cables or fibre-optic lines" along which deals are made, disputes settled, and goods, values, reputation, information, and finance flow (Elyachar 2010, 457–59). While "just being sociable" may have *no* economic interest in addition to being invisible and unreproducible, it can also realize economic value (459). These taxi-drivers' phatic labor involves commensality, sociality, and reciprocal interest-free lending (for businesses, remittances, debts, emergencies, or special occasions). It describes the ways that taxi-drivers *feel* the road and create channels and spaces of attunement to forge friendship, trust, indebtedness, affects, unspoken communications, and useful invisible connections. As a mobile form of social capital, it allows drivers to borrow enough from friends to purchase a license plate that, costing around £20,000 through private sale in 2000, rose to almost triple that, and then dropped after Uber's entrance onto the market. These connections between taxi-drivers bear on how extended kinship networks describe an alternative to formal welfare provision among British Pakistani textile workers and taxi-drivers (Kalra 2000, 189),[18] and Punjabi taxi-drivers who mobilize ethnic networks to improve their working conditions in New York (Mitra 2012).

Murrai–Zwandai

The roads traveled for *rāsha aw darsha* also keep *murrai–zwandai*. *Murrai* refers to sadness, a death, or great loss; *zwandai* to happiness. The term *murrai–zwandai* pertains primarily to funerals and weddings. It is a relationship involving friends and kin. It is not a ritual such as a *jenaza*, the term for the funeral and associated rituals surrounding the cultural processing of the dead body.[19] I prioritize mobility and contingency in *murrai–zwandai* relations, emphasizing visits and support between migrants, not specific rituals.

Regarding funerals, in Peshawar families may organize a procession of male relatives to transport a corpse to their ancestral burial sites in Afghanistan (women travel separately to offer condolences). Poorer families may bury the body inside Peshawar's refugee camps or a private Afghan plot. British migrants cannot usually travel overseas for funerals, which in Islam must occur promptly. When Sher Agha's grandmother died, as the closest relative in England, Sher Agha organized funeral prayers in a Southall mosque. He called on his closest relatives and friends who kept *murrai–zwandai* by assisting with preparations and cooking. His *qaum* is large; funeral prayers occur regularly, usually on Sundays to ensure taxi-drivers do not lose earnings. Despite the sadness of the occasion, these are moments to rest from work, meet relatives, eat and pray together, reaffirm ties and ideas about continuity and tradition—they are opportunities, that is, for "life," for maintaining cultural, religious, and family obligations in all-male environments. If a parent dies, migrants might return home for a mourning period, or offer prayers locally. As Afghans have become more settled, prayers in the local mosques have become more common, as have prayers at the deceased relative's home involving all the women from local households. In some cases, they would not be told of the death of a parent until they next returned home, with secrecy here reflecting a form of protection or love while the relative is away. While not attending a wedding *(wāhde)* may incur disapproval, male relatives (or representatives) perilously neglect a close relative's funeral.

My informants celebrate weddings less commonly together. Taxi-drivers' marriages are mostly endogamous, arranged within extended kinship networks. Mobility around weddings is evident insofar as a groom—from among these taxi-drivers—likely travels to marry a "traditional" bride from his descent group. However, weddings in England are increasing as communities become more settled, and London-based musicians and singers are drumming up steady trade. A British Afghan groom is valued for the mobility and security he offers, while an Afghan bride is valued for her sexual purity, illiteracy, and obedience, although notably the introduction in 2018 of English-language tests after two years for migrants on spousal visas (i.e., not citizens) is likely to most severely affect these women. Occasionally a father may give his child in marriage to a relative or business partner to cement that relationship.

In Afghanistan, the *ourā* refers to the procession of the groom's relatives who journey to the bride's house to display the wedding gifts (the *jora*, lit. couple), such as dresses, perfumes, jewelry, and gold. The serious point of this occasion of merrymaking is to show one's status, wealth, generosity to both families, and success as a British Afghan working abroad. While historically a bride journeyed to her husband's house atop a camel in a highly decorated, enclosed chair *(dohlaiy)*, now wealthier or returning Afghans can arrange a convoy of expensive cars decorated with flowers to collect her. Paying for guests' international airfare may also form part of the display. Take Ghaffar's parents, who flew to Afghanistan to bring his bride "home" to England. I first met Ghaffar's father, Waleed, when he worked in an Asian supermarket ten years ago. Waleed has since settled his wife and five children, and, as the city's first taxi-driver to assist his son to acquire a spousal settlement visa for his daughter-in-law, he made a respectable and enviable show of it.

Among Pashtun taxi-drivers, divorce is rare—marriage a one-way journey. The bride proverbially leaves her husband's household only in her coffin. Yet for many wives abroad, the reality of married life remains distant, in the future, and always painfully elsewhere—one determined by the taxi-driver's ability to conquer the temperamental road, and to meet the government's financial conditions.

A close relative's wedding may require traveling to Pakistan or Afghanistan, which presents opportunities for globally dispersed families to reunite. When I visited Zahid to convey my good wishes before he left for his brother's wedding in Kabul, he elaborated that he is the youngest of twenty-eight siblings (by two mothers) and has sisters who left Afghanistan before he can remember. Some he would hardly recognize, he admitted with embarrassment, especially since their return visits did not coincide with his. Kabul's Hotel Intercontinental is no longer the exclusive wedding venue of choice. The past two decades have seen luxurious wedding halls proliferating in the well-heeled Taimany and Shahr-e-Naw districts. Weddings provide opportunities for plentiful, opulent displays. His bride was from a wealthy segment of the family. Zahid's father shared the costs of a lavish wedding. Zahid described to me later how a thousand-plus guests attended. They enjoyed folkloric songs played on the *rubab, daira*, harmonium, and *tabla* by peripatetic musicians who travel the wedding circuit. As his family is conservative, the women celebrated at home. Or perhaps conservatism on this occasion was determined by affordability. Otherwise, separate halls may be hired for men and women. Zahid's guests were offered innumerable pilau, lamb, barbecue, chicken, *kofta,* and meat dishes; waiters nicknamed "golden hands" *(tilayee lāsuna)* circulated at dazzling speed, serving soft drinks from gilded trays held aloft. While the groom would return to England to work, and his bride remain in Kabul, Zahid reminded me, quoting an unattributed song lyric, that *Meena pe tloau aw ratloau ziateegi, ariyouw mayān pe dey poheegi—that is,* love grows by coming and going, every lover knows that.

Lines of Reprise

What story do we attribute those who appear immobilized, without life? How do taxi-drivers complicate the metaphor and tendency in mobility studies to juxtapose forms of movement-as-life (e.g., migration, economic progress) with immobility-as death (e.g., depression, or staying or being left behind)?

Let us consider two examples below. One Saturday evening my friend Hamid phoned me. After exchanging pleasantries, I asked him if he would work all night now, earnings could be good. "Everyone is *pulling* me to work," he complained. "I *can't* work. Everyone is working, I have nothing. My family want money, my friends push me, too. I just need time for *myself.* I'm pulled from every side, I borrow my taxi rent, I'm *really* mental. I'm panicking."

Desperately restless and anxious, he raced around, inscribing attempts to "escape" into lines of flight, stopping here and everywhere—the food shop, pool hall, Afghan takeouts, his married sister's home, mine. Trapped between exhausting and inexhaustible energies, he felt stretched to snapping. "I want to die," he continued. "My heart is painful." And he insisted about himself, *Koug bar manzil ta na raseegi* (a lopsided load will not reach its destination). In such tensions between work and prosperity, mobility and immobility, such as engulf Hamid, taxi-drivers may be less immobile than trapped (Mathew 2008).

Whether trapped or immobile, the absence of forward momentum and the experience of being "overtaken" in the race toward prosperity is an experience of reversal, of traveling or falling backwards into debt and irredeemability. It reminds us that theoretical sequelae are not reducible to ontological ones, and of the danger that theories of movement and (counter-)linearity will remain indifferent to life outside theory. If anthropology's endeavor is in thinking through theory ethnographically: through transactions of movement and inaction (Massumi 2002, 178)— might we consider instead what immobile spaces enable or offer individuals in terms of synthesizing experiences of movement and inaction that are held, or imagined to be held, in tension? Might we not envision a break, for example, from Freudian temporal flows that repetitively insinuate the traumatic past into the future in a deterministic repeating grid of psychic traces? Or keep lines "open," say, by returning to Derrida's (1987) notion of aporia, which describes a state of perplexity and impassability whose logic is paradoxical insofar as its conditions of impossibility are also conditions of possibility?

To consider these ideas, I turn finally to a story recounted by Ihsanullah, Zmarai's cousin, whom I first met in 1999 in Brighton. Ihsanullah since moved to Southall where he works as a taxi-driver. He has friends and relatives among my informants, and they keep *rāsha aw darsha* by regularly visiting each other. On this day we were driving through the Sussex Downs and had stopped to enjoy the view.

Ihsanullah's story is situated in the bloody street fighting between political factions in Kabul during early 1994. After Najibullah's government collapsed in 1992, Kabul came under siege. Around twenty-five thousand deaths occurred in early 1994 alone. Neighborhoods in Naqlia, Karte-Naw, Mukoriyan, Shah Shahid, and around Bibi Mahru hill suffered murders, rapes, and systematic looting. At the time, Ihsanullah was a young man living in Kart-e-Naw. He fought the Northern commanders and their *gilam jam* (lit. carpet snatchers), for the forces of Hekmatyar's Hizb-i-Islami party. As his story unfolded, he set the scene one day at dusk, when people were coming out to pray. Ihsanullah saw a commotion outside his home; a number of people gathered near the end of his gully around a sheet of corrugated tin that seemed to be covering a dead body and blocking an open gutter. They were discussing what to do. He pushed forward and decided to act. Slowly he managed to lift the tin, which revealed the dead man's face upturned in the cold water. Bending forward, he placed one hand under the head, another under its bottom.[20] As he lifted, the flesh melted and the decomposing head and face dropped into the gutter. Close to the body, he inhaled what he described as an overpowering stench into his mouth and brain. Soon after, because of the intensifying violence in Kabul, his entire family fled to Peshawar.

Ihsanullah's story begs connections of body to the psychic and somatic in the specific social and cultural environment of Pashtun refugees in England. Interesting is his story's emergence as a sensorial memory.[21] Intertwined with the ending of a subsequent romantic relationship is the smell and the taste of death, its connection with loss and rupture—the flight from home to Pakistan, the symbolic or perhaps real journey from love to madness, of becoming exiled to himself.

Twenty years later in London, now in his mid-forties, Ihsanullah only drove his taxi occasionally. He had troubles sleeping, ruminated about death, and battled a deadening depression. He rarely contacted his wife and children. He found transient happiness in a relationship, but his girlfriend left him for another man when she discovered he was married. He missed her. The last time they met she had offered him a strange, "foreign"-tasting sweet. Had she put some kind of black magic on him?

For months Ihsanullah had heard a constant *tak tak* sound in his head and continually tasted "poison." He consulted his doctor about the noise and the taste, and demanded an MRI scan. The results were normal. A realization crystallized. His girlfriend's new partner had "obviously" given her the sweet to poison him. The poison was lodged in his brain. If he could kill her partner, he would recover. His friends, alarmed, dissuaded him. Finally he conceded. Maybe, he said, it was that corpse: the taste of disintegrating flesh, Kabul disintegrating, life disintegrating. London is full of killers and suicides, he complained. All the warlords' men are here, big commanders driving taxis. His cousin had leaped from a bridge after his asylum application was refused. As Ihsanullah became locked down into his terrors, his living situation became deracinated. Following an intractable dispute with his landlord he was evicted. The unbidden return of death, flight, and displacement in the telling of this story contrasts with dreams many Afghans hold of returning to an idyllic existence. Ihsanullah often expressed his desire to acquire farmland in his natal Nangarhar province and, like Zmarai, to buy cows and produce milk (a re-signification of the *shudow ghwa*, the migrant "milk cow"), build a house in lush green surroundings, and forget his troubles—his longing for home captured in the famous lyrics by Ahmad Zahir he sang to me: *Lārsha Nangarharta kameez tor mata rawrla, taza taza guluna, dre tsalor mata rawrla* (Go to Nangarhar and bring me a black shirt, bring me three, four fresh flowers). Yet if aporias are paradoxical, tentatively, we might upon scrutinizing Ihsanullah's "loss of direction" find an enduring attachment, sense of responsibility, and respect for all he has apparently abandoned.

Conclusion

Ihsanullah's story is extreme, but not surprising. In the day-to-day labor of taxi-driving many drivers face difficulties driving for long shifts, financial fears, and depression; many view their cars as "iron cages" of financial obligation (Notar 2012, 282). These taxi-drivers differ from Afghan migrants to Britain in the eighties who more typically came from the educated elite, and adapted well, although below their trained level. Nonetheless, given that the licensed driver has in many senses "arrived," it is perhaps striking, and a route for investigation, that several drivers had contemplated suicide. This points to particular pressures enfolded into Afghan taxi-driving mobility: that is to the effects of living through forty years of war, displacement, uncertainty surrounding return and Afghanistan's future, to the sacrifices migrant sons make for older and younger generations, to the harsh consequences of their failures, the necessary monetization of close kinship ties—and to ways that a sense of claustrophobia and exhaustion remain constant to drivers' interior landscape, all while their exterior window-view changes.

This chapter extends what we know about diverse transformations being produced by global and transnational flows of Afghan people and capital. It shows how political transformations, regime changes, shifting ideas about social class, political life, the international state system, Pashtun identity, lifetimes of war, and the management of unpredictability and insecurity by transnational migrants and their families are all enfolded practically and imaginatively into taxi-driving. The taxi-drivers' narratives provoke some useful starting points. They map new histories of movement between Britain, the subcontinent, and Afghanistan. Far from the barbarians of popular discourse, these taxi-drivers are rather conventional. They desire family values, to make money and lead easier lives, and to form close, valuable ties. The new mobilities of capital, human resources, and autonomy that they create also unfix ideas of a permanent return to Afghanistan as the ideal "ending."

Such experiences apply to first-generation migrant communities everywhere. Revealing a human condition as a dynamic–processual balancing of loyalties, their experiences contribute to the study of material and social remittances involving Afghans; and to what we know about the social contexts of remittances from Britain. They also problematize two contested male archetypes: the stoic Pashtun who fulfills the provider role through obligation, self-sacrifice, and guilt; and the carefree young man's existence driven by individual desires. Many migrants' families have now consolidated forms of capital and investment; remittances are not always essential for their economic survival. For others, kinship ties are painfully snapped or contorted through lines of remittance that fail to materialize, and stable futures that do not arrive.

Wayfaring (Ingold 2011) provides one useful starting point for discussions that also moves us beyond Ingold's "beyond." While Ingold is decisive in his incision, cutting through where theory has bifurcated, and lost the dream to classification, wayfaring as a kind of anti-genealogical mover beyond all referent seems over-romantic. Further, the notion of freedom implicated in much writing on immobility often seems to imply a model of reality, or ontological position, where movement (as freedom) or its opposite are seen as either foreground or background in different contexts (N. Khan 2016). To capture the pleasures and pains in the lines created by remitting taxi-drivers, might we instead hold both together and prioritize a reality condition over a liberationist reading, and develop ideas of motile logic to analyze ways life's meanings are transformed contingently through independent trajectories (Holbraad 2012, 97). This can allow two positions to be experienced at the same time, if ambivalently, and therein contribute to alternative readings of immobility both anthropologically and ethnographically.

These drivers also reveal the ways that lines of remittance and other lines take shape in relation to and against the line formation of the dance—and the ways that bodily comportments and relations to work and pleasure differ with these varying lines. Of note are ways the demands of remittances, and the social relations these demands create, facilitate a very different type of dance that is detrimental to social and personal health, as in the case of Hamid. The language of the circle that forms through an initial line of the dance also leads to questions raised by the return visit. These are explored in chapter 2.

But let us return, at the chapter's end, to the dance. In 2014, I received an invitation to celebrate the Eid-ul-Fitr festival, following the fasting month of Ramadan. Some taxi-drivers had arranged a picnic in a local park, as they had in previous years. They hired the local sports pavilion, which provided facilities for ritual washing for prayer *(wuzu),* and shelter should it rain. They bought rice and lamb for *pulao,* chickens, local fish, bread, sweets, vegetables for salad; invited children, special guests (myself included), a few women; and erected a net for volleyball. I contributed two boxes of mangoes.

After dark, Zmarai suggested they move their taxis closer together, switch on the lights, and play music. They would dance the *attan.* For the next hour they stopped, started, and practiced their moves. A small fleet of cars ferrying Fazl's relatives arrived from London.

Over seventy attendees paid a fee to cover costs and participate in the largest annual gathering of Afghans, mostly Pashtuns, yet organized by the city's taxi-drivers. The dance metaphorically captures these Afghans' situation in Britain. Continuing beyond the journey's end, or the dance's choreography, outdoor gatherings and picnics reveal Afghans' firmer hold on the English landscape. Yet equally, for many migrants, forms of life, death, and living death are alarmingly at stake in these lines of motion. These lines have revealed how accumulation can be more incoherent than strategic, formations of tribe and kinship relation more fragile and contingent than atavistic or predictable—and how the shattering of personhood through war and migration is permeated with ongoing violence.

2. THE TASTE OF FREEDOM AND RETURN

Give excitement to the world from me
Paint the earth and sky anew
Create another Adam from my clay
Kill this slave of profit and loss.

—Rehman Baba

It was dawn and branches of narcissus sopping
Trickle from its eyes they were dropping
I said beauty what, why you crying
It said my life is but one big smile

—Nazo Tokhi

This chapter takes the *chakar* (pleasure or picnic trip) as an analytic lens for exploring mobilities and everyday inflections of larger journeys, movements, and transformations of Afghans involving war, transnational labor, migration, and return. It turns to the Pakistan side of the transnational context of Pashtun migrants who were refugees in Peshawar before coming to Britain. Specifically, to a small group of taxi-drivers who, between April and July 2010, returned home to visit their families in Peshawar, where I visited them. These were my core interlocutors, whom I have known since the millennium, with whom I developed deeper relationships in my fieldwork, and whose lives I was able to observe and follow more closely in different contexts.[1] In Peshawar they made numerous picnics *(mela)* and pleasure trips *(chakar)* with friends from their *qaum*

89

(descent group) also visiting from Britain and Europe. I accompanied them on several *chakar,* which were also occasions for storytelling about other *chakar.*

These *chakar* are typically all-male phenomena between friends who take several cars for a day or longer to picnic in rural locations involving idyllic mountain landscapes, glacial water, greenery, and flower-filled meadows. These friends travel the breadth of Pakistan's North-West Frontier and the borderlands *(soba sarhad)* with Afghanistan in search of freedom—driving into the mountains, across the plains between Kabul River and Budni Nal, or along the historic Grand Trunk Road, following the Adezai River alongside Charsadda district to Adezou and Attock. Farther afield, they explore the valleys of Swat, the glaciers, forests, and meadows of Kalam, Kohistan, and Kaghan. Or, taking the Khyber Pass, they traverse their ancestral lands in eastern Afghanistan. They undertake few or no such trips with their families (i.e., their wives and children).

Chakar (lit. pleasure trip) is a noun, verb, practice, and event. Comprising the cooking and sharing of food, these impromptu affairs differ from a *melmani* (a meal hosted expressly to mark social, family, or business occasions), a *sail* (or large organized event such as a wedding or music performance), a *mela* (or large picnic not involving significant travel), or annual pilgrimages such as to Mazar-e-Sharif to celebrate New Year. Picnics and feasting outdoors were enjoyed by Afghan kings; these migrants' *chakar* gesture in contemporary form to older traditions.

Their pleasures of nature, food, and commensality in motion also have comparative significance in and outside Afghanistan (see Baily 1988b, 136–39; Doubleday 1985; Dupree 1973; Roden 1984). The *Oxford English Dictionary* locates the first reference to an English picnic in 1748 to describe a fashionable social assembly in which each person contributed a share of provisions. Battiscombe (1949) locates the first picnic in English literature in Goldsmith's *The Vicar of Wakefield* (1766), and refers to the elite *London Picnic Society* (1802), to Charles Dickens's anthology *The Pic-Nic Papers* (1841), and to "picnickery" as a censorious reference to frivolous behavior. Manet's painting *Dejeuner sur l'herbe* (1862) criticized Parisian morals in the impressionist style. After the Romantics, the picnic became a "supreme pleasure of outdoor life" involving the requirement to travel (Beard 1965). Roden (1984, 4) describes how "the pleasures of outdoor food . . . serve, as Jean-Jacques Rousseau said, to 'liberate the soul.'" Non-English traditions include *colazione sull'erba* in Italy, *comida campestre* in Spain, *so pong* in China, *pikunikku* in Japan, *Shem en Nessem* in Egypt where thousands gather for the arrival of spring (ibid., 167–68), *Sizdabh-be-dar* in Iran, and *hidirellez* in Turkey. In northern Afghanistan large *melehs* (Dari) during the spring festival Now Ruz inflect pre-Islamic Iranian traditions of eating and enjoying outdoors (Doubleday 1985, 67–69). Recalling Hemingway's ([1964] 2000) musing, *chakar* are also inflected with nostalgia for the sumptuous freedom and "taste" of youth: as inscribed in this chapter's title, "If you are lucky enough to have lived in Paris as a young man, wherever you go for the rest of your life it stays with you, for Paris is a moveable feast."

As a ritual practice occurring outside normal time, space, and place, in opposition to strict everyday moral conventions, *chakar* additionally constitute a space of liminality (Turner 1967) and the "spontaneous generation of *communitas* in situations of radical structural change" (Turner 1974, 248). They are situations for participants to forge new social relations of equality and symbolic moments of freedom. The participants' liberating evaluations of food, taste, and commensality also express relations of deep inequality, despite the strongly egalitarian Islamic and tribal ideologies to which these Pashtun friends fervently subscribe (Tapper and Tapper 1986, 68). *Chakar* circumscribe an interplay between anti-structure and emerging structure that re-inscribes participants into hierarchies of inequality and obligation, illustrating the "trick" in liminal situations that apparently dissolve structure while structures are established (Szakolczai 2009). Exploring this paradox can generate insights into contradictory manifestations of liminality in the fragile conditions of productive life at stake in particular and larger conjunctions of transnational migrant labor. *Chakar* also highlight migrants' search for relief and alternatives to their emotional, cultural, and economic labor in these spheres—illustrated in my informant Zalmai's words while traveling with friends in Kaghan Valley. He had lost his voice through an excess of laughing and cigarettes but croaked, "It's *freedom* here, not like in Peshawar."

Correspondingly, this chapter queries: How is a Pashtun ethic of equality deployed in *chakar* to conceal, reproduce, and stratify dominant social hierarchies of power? How do *chakar* shape possibilities for transformation, and foreclose others? What facets of eating, preparing, and sharing food render *chakar* a potent site for expressing losses, and for constructing diasporic identity and male collectivity? What role does being on the move play in shaping spaces of alterity, of return to a just and untroubled past, and in recalibrating oppressive migrant realities as a historical sense of liberation—not just from the burden of remittances, but from the Afghan migrant's experience of always being away from home?

Friends, *Qaum*

In the liminal, oppositional space constituted on *chakar,* friend connotes a particular kinship relation. Ideally a friend is from one's *qaum. Qaum* may also apply to unrelated acquaintances, such as trusted friends, implying, through the kinship idiom, ties of solidarity, loyalty, and strong obligation (Canfield 1988, 186). This chapter thus contributes more broadly to the anthropology of friendship (Bell and Coleman 1999). Friends should be trustworthy, and of equal wealth and social status. Most important, friends must, my informant Zahir stressed, "keep each other's secrets"—namely, allow each other the freedom to deviate from the strict cultural or family conventions of Pashtunwali. While brothers, whose relation is hierarchical, must behave properly or do Pashto before each other, friends understand each other's predilections for cigarettes, girls, hashish *(chars),* or religion and may behave "freely as equals." Brothers are not ideal friends. Among South Asian youth in London, Gerd Baumann (1995) argues similarly that the interstitial figure of the cousin, trusted kin but not implicated by potential disgrace as a brother would be, is important in allowing for transgressive fun. Kinship in the context of friendship may also "coerce" trustworthy behavior. As my informant Fazl explained, if a relative behaves dishonorably (steals, insults you, is violent), one's shared male kin can intervene to punish him. Moreover, "outside the family, confrontations can become violent." Friendship here thus connotes a context for escaping the bonds of kinship within the boundaries of kinship—for coping with, without renouncing, the contradictory load of cultural control and economic responsibilities formed by ideas of who Afghan Pashtuns are and should be in transnational contexts in the modern world.

These friends-cum-relatives belong to a descent group of the Ghilzai Pashtun tribe. Like the majority Ghilzi, they originate from around

Jalalabad, Khogyani, Kaga, Nangarhar, and Laghman in southeastern Afghanistan. Ghilzi Pashtuns are known for their extensive wealth and global business interests, strict adherence to the Pashtunwali, and political "neutrality." Many have built powerful businesses through kinship networks dispersed across the global diaspora—trade being dependent on buying neutrality from political groups and successive Afghan governments. Unlike their wealthier relatives, however, these British taxi-driver friends' investments are smaller, or they may live primarily hand to mouth, and they conduct neither business nor politics together.

Chakar, Liminality, Freedom

Let us return now to Peshawar and to *chakar*'s configuration as a "round trip." This reveals various ritual and symbolic manifestations of liminality in a dynamic of transformation, power, and freedom that, nevertheless, returns participants to the place they started.

According to Turner (1967, 97), "Liminality may perhaps be regarded as the Nay to all positive structural assertions, but as in some sense the source of them all, and, more than that, as a realm of pure possibility whence novel configurations of ideas and relations may arise." This study of *chakar* examines how liminality can assist cultural understandings of events involving the dissolution and formation of order, and conditions of uncertainty, fluidity, and malleability (Thomassen 2009). In addition, it explores how liminality is enfolded into more enduring spaces, structures, and experiences of arrested time-consciousness, transition, in-betweenness, and isolation produced by war, neoliberal globalization, uneven geographical development, postcolonialism, and transnationalism.

First, in northern Cyprus, Yael Navaro-Yashin (2003) likens being a subject of a state outside international recognition as akin to inhabiting an abjected space between life and death wherein the symbolic presences and absences of the state circumscribe everyday experience as political liminality. Her metaphor of "no man's land" to describe existence in peripheral, non-recognized, or illegal administrations captures the ways Afghan Pashtuns negotiate being refugees on land annexed in 1947 when Pakistan's borders were created along the Durand Line, by which the British demarcated the Raj from Afghanistan in 1893. Far from a liminal space of curtailed action or an "in-between" space or "buffer zone," as is often argued of the borderlands, Marsden and Hopkins (2011, 4) argue that they are intrinsic to a geography that "binds, connects and thus helps to forge powerful forms of solidarity, community and collective identity that endure across time and space." I suggest that, in order to understand how this region is fully connected trans-regionally and trans-nationally, yet for Afghan Pashtuns and Pashtun nationalists redolent with the melancholic sense of historical loss and dispossession, we might more fruitfully hold both positions together.

Liminality additionally enfolds temporal figurations associated with the specific transnational political context these men experience as members of refugee families in Pakistan, and as asylum seekers in the UK. These are figurations associated with the spatiotemporality that shapes Afghanistan in terms of arrested development or underdevelopment, deficiency, deprivation, premodernity, cultural primitivism, and the incapacity to *move* fast enough toward civilizational progress and modernity. These discourses are reinforced through studies of trauma, pathology, incapacity, and war-related rupture, invoking liminality as a biomedical metaphor of Afghan immobility, blocked progress, and arrested development. Afghans, as asylum seekers and refugees, are positioned in what Nguyen (2012) terms a condition of permanent transition, wherein political discourses are collapsed into conceptions of the viable human. "Not yet" fully capable of self-governance, consequential to history, or human, the refugee figure is subjugated to neoliberal empire, first in relation to war, second in relation to the gifts of freedom and refuge, *stuck* between war's remains and the rehabilitations of peace (52).

Second, Turner (1974) describes liminality's dialectical relation to societal marginality and inferiority, in spatial terms of being positioned in-between (liminality), on the edges (marginality), and beneath (inferiority). This bears on ways the ritual liminality of the *chakar* is inflected with the broader political–economic condition of "never arriving" that these migrants experience in relation to their dream of capital accumulation ("coming up"). Their perennial obligations of remittance mean they cannot dedicate themselves fully to building lives "here," or enjoy the fruits of their labor "there," instituting in-betweenness and marginality (or here *and* there) as permanent features of everyday life. This vision of upward mobility that results in perpetual labor and self-sacrifice implicates freedom as a fantasy or "technology of patience" that suspends questions about the cruelty of now (Berlant 2011, 19)—and ensures that kin relations primarily organized around the material reproduction of existence can continue.

Third, *chakar* invoke a historical problematic wherein travel and commensality converge in ways people contest, subvert, and imagine the freedom of an idealized time before the devastation of the country by war, before the hegemony of Pakistan, and before the oppressive forms of (colonial, state, family, and cultural) authority they now face. Liminality here enfolds a sense of grief, of loyal waiting for the country to recover, in which desires for freedom and progress cannot "yet" be fully embraced. It bears on Hansen's (2012) elaboration of a "melancholia of freedom" characterizing life in post-apartheid South Africa. The "call of history" as a framework for cultural self-making is, Hansen argues, profoundly rooted in a sense of loss and displacement: because of contradictory attachments to the oppressive past, which cannot fully be grieved for or acknowledged, subjectivities "fail to fully embrace what they are supposed to be or become" (4). As British citizens, these Afghans are also new contradictory "subjects of freedom": their imaginary freedom similarly equivocal insofar as it enfolds desires to block the work of separation, to loyally preserve their love for the lost homeland, what it means to be Afghan and part of a "traditional" family, while they retain the ambivalence of these attachments.

Our returnees hungrily reimagine an epoch when all the lands they travel belonged to Afghanistan—their imaginings of freedom the more poignant in the intensification of forced returns since 2014. The mythic return of Pashtun lands to Afghanistan, encapsulated in the apothegm *lar aw bar yao Afghan* (up-down, all Afghan), expresses nationalist demands for an independent Pashtunistan that will unite separated Pashtun tribes "from Kabul to Gwadar"; in the poetry of Ahmad Shah, Khushal Khan Khattak, Rehman Baba, and Ghani Khan; in the Taliban's blend of radical Islam and Pashtun nationalism; and in Pashtun music and films produced in the region through which they deride and berate Pakistan's so-called hospitality toward Afghans.

Looking back to an era when Pashtun heroes vanquished the colonizers is well rehearsed in the oral traditions of the Ghilzai tribe, who were prominent supporters of Ahmed Shah and preeminent in destroying British forces in 1842 in Jalalabad (Ahmed 1980). Yet in the romanticization of the period in British history, rather than document the East as the opposite, the enemy, the West documented itself. It built an immutable Indian landscape effaced of conflicts in which the wanderer could meander freely, and ponder the predicament of the unsuccessful dream underpinning late nineteenth-century travel writing: "What you wish for is exactly what you cannot have" (Said 1987, 39). *Chakar* invert these themes. They are a dynamic space for imagining and enacting autonomy and freedom for Afghans wandering about the Frontier, as visitors from England.

The Slavery of Profit and Loss: Migration and Return

Many migrants with wives and children in Pakistan visit "home" and stay with their families for a few months every year or two. The return visit establishes spatiotemporal and gendered codifications of power, status, and economic difference. In the UK the migrant must be thrifty—*Lug oukhwra tel oukhwara, der oukhwra gundair oukhwra* (Eat a little, eat always; eat a lot, eat waste). In Peshawar he must display his wealth, elevated British ("Londoni") status, and generosity: *Wugata laka de muzi, oukhwra laka da qazi* (Make money like a spendthrift, spend like a judge). These expectations bear on studies of masculinity and migration outside Afghanistan. Karen Fog Olwig (2012) identifies material success, generosity, and reputation as characteristics of a distinctly masculine return narrative that protects Caribbean migrants' respect in the family, de-emphasizes less socially acceptable reasons for migrating—such as desires to separate from an unhappy marriage—and hides ambivalent feelings toward kinship ties and obligations.

UK Afghans like Nawroz, who works long shifts in a carwash to send small monthly remittances, must borrow to visit home.

"Can you stop sending for a while?" I ventured.

"No," he replied. "My father, brothers, would shame me. They'd say, 'Are you in nightclubs, drinking alcohol? *Send* money. *Chey na kar, alta tse kar?* Without work, what is there?'"

Such Damoclean pressures illustrate a criticism of Turner's overly romantic, apolitical take on liminality and its destabilizing potential: "[Liminality] transgresses or dissolves the norms that govern structured and institutionalized relationships and is accompanied by experiences of unprecedented potency" ([1969], 128). They highlight the social fragility of many Afghans in Britain, and some difficult subjective and political dimensions of liminality in contexts of transnational migration. This is far from an actualization of the prevailing narrative of free flows of money and people associated with global capitalism. Liminality here captures a sense of permanent uncertainty in lives, goals, and places experienced as not (not yet, maybe never) one's own, arising from the burden of multiple configurations of political and economic insecurity, marginality, everyday racism, war, and the loss of homeland that these men carry as subordinate sons on behalf of their families.

The returnee should distribute gifts, costly in large extended households. If he cannot afford gifts for all, to preserve harmony and "equality" he may indulge the women this time, children the next. While his children receive new mobile phones, the visiting father can assert his authority and punish an errant child or guilty mother. While he is honored for his "sacrifices" abroad, if he fails to remit sufficiently, his father may neglect his children, or summon him home permanently. Although things will change when his sons "work" for *him,* perhaps, Ghaffar reflected, he will "work his whole life and *others* enjoy the world on his money: *Cha chey oukhwra duniya dahaghoda* [He who eats the world, enjoys it]. Or, *Wugee khaiyta ba marasee kho wugee stirgey ba marey na see* [A hungry belly can fill, but hungry eyes are never full]."

Not all returnees desire or can afford to *chakar. Chakar* may be budget or extravagant affairs, involving the cost of renting cars, hotel rooms, and catering. Following Bourdieu (1984), *chakar* comprise a prerogative of symbolic struggles (for distinction) in which cultural aesthetics of taste (luxury, freedom, or necessity) are intrinsic acts of social positioning. As Mujibur elaborated, "*Chey zar larey, tse gham larey.* If you have gold, what sadness do you have. If you can afford to picnic, there'll be no trouble in your heart."

As "special occasions" (Bourdieu 1984, 79) involving the region's finest natural furniture and the production of excellent dishes, they establish hierarchies between friends primarily determined monetarily and by a willingness to spend. There is no official host or organizer, nor are there official guests. These affairs ideally occur on impulse. All should share equally in the cost, planning, and labor. Occasionally, one returnee might foot the entire bill, "so all friends can enjoy." His generosity *(sakha-wat)* comprises neither hospitality *(melmastia)* nor a desire to play host.

As not all can afford to be equally generous, these shared aesthetics of taste create less liberating, pleasurable forms of equality, as the inverse, invoking the "contradictory" ways—in a Gramscian sense—that agency, identity, status, and difference are renegotiated in everyday practices. Consider Baryalai's words: "At Adezou near Charsadda, we sometimes picnic up to eighty people. We take Landcruisers, stay until night, swim, eat fish, joke. Once a policeman stopped us at the checkpost, he saw we were Afghans, Mohajirs [i.e., refugees]. Agha was smoking *chars* [hashish]. 'You're smoking,' he said. Fingers held high, Agha retorted, 'Look! What will you do?' We drove off, laughing at the policeman with his look of officious disgust."

Returnees are required to assist with domestic duties, and submit to their father's authority. Gul Nabi, in his fifties and himself a father of five sons, must smoke cigarettes secretly on the roof terrace lest his father find out. *Chakar,* like migration, legitimately create distance, autonomy, and freedom from these obligations. Still many do not go on *chakar* with friends, preferring the pleasures of tasty familial or uxorial excursions. On Friday nights husbands may drive their wives, and children too, to eateries on the Kabul River. One night, Hamid, observing his mother's playful mood, loaded the car with family members and drove to visit his maternal uncle, buying kebabs en route. The women in the roused household cried with delight, "What shall we cook?" "Nothing, we have kebabs! If you are very kind, bring plates."

Food, Commensality, Equality

While Afghan food practices in diasporic locations have received some attention (Monsutti 2010b), studies of Pashtun cultural life, food, and commensality are little researched. Tapper and Tapper's (1986) study among Durrani Pashtuns in Afghanistan provides the most detailed elaboration. The Tappers reveal rich symbolic meanings in the evaluation of food in four domains: religious belief and action, political and economic competition, personal health, and misfortunes caused by occult powers.

Durannis switch between frames of reference according to context in order to preserve the dominance of Islam, which conceals hierarchies and intense competition over political and economic power in an ideally egalitarian society (Tapper and Tapper 1986, 63–64). Hospitality and eating are ways that success or failure in such competitions is judged, and how conflicts are resolved (68).

Eating *(khwaral)* and commensality *(yaozai)*—eating as one—are important Pashtun cultural values. Food is intrinsic to hospitality. A delegation proposing marriage or business may divine their answer in the number and quality of dishes served. Food defines the symbolic boundaries of gender, sublimating Afghan women as excellent household cooks ("better than Pakistani women or Persian Afghans who go outside") and husbands as providers. Men and women eat apart in public, and often at home as well. Ghaffar cannot see his younger sisters-in-law unveiled. His father jokes that on the occasions that he takes his daughters-in-law out, to hospital or for Eid shopping, he fears he will lose them, because of their full *chador* (head and body covering). Food signals piety and difference, the privations of Ramadan distinguishing Pashtuns from other UK Muslims who may not "fast seriously, or take their religion strongly." The food industry sustains many new migrants who provide cheap labor in kitchens or small restaurants.

The forms of commensality these friendships involve mostly occur in all-male contexts. If a man visits a married friend at home, he should not see his friend's wife, though she will prepare the dishes he eats, nor should he see any evidence of her. She should maintain total *purdah*, keep her *namus* (sexual honor), and sit in another room, perhaps watching television with her children. During Ramadan, Eid festivals, and on other informal occasions, Afghan homes receive many visitors, and wives prepare meals for their husband and his friends (or for women visitors, when husbands in turn must be scarce). Certainly girlfriends should be kept "hidden." If not, the relationship is an open target. Hasan, in his early twenties, lived with his Polish girlfriend. One evening she offered to cook for his friends, a large fish dish with cream sauce, although absented herself from the all-male party. The friends universally complained the food was "disgusting." Khalid washed and baked it again; it was "hopeless," irrecoverable. They cruelly threw it in the garbage and ordered takeout. Hasan was duly chastened by this symbolic attack on his open romantic liaison.

Commensality is thus an important symbolic means whereby Pashtun taxi-drivers assert identity and build friendships in the UK. After quiet weekday nightshifts, they relax in each other's homes. They play cards, the boardgame *carom,* and may cook, infusing the dawn with redolent smells of traditional dishes such as *sherwa, shola, borani, Kabuli pulao,* or spicy biryani and *karahi* influenced by Pakistani cuisine—lamb dishes, particularly when cooked in ghee, having the best "taste" *(khwand)* and most prestige. Or they compete to display their cosmopolitanism, experimenting with "Afghan macaroni" or "Mexican chicken"—untroubled by the obvious paradox of the "traditional innovator," as Monsutti (2010b, 224–25) observes among Afghan Hazaras in Iran. Unlike migrants who have installed gas-fired *tanur* in their homes, on which their wives prepare Afghan bread *(dôdey)* and delicious variations such as *pastai, dustakai, nigharai, peerakai,* or *pateerai,* these men rarely eat fresh bread, a staple Afghan food. Even after many years, their lives are less rooted, more marginal, in-between. Rather than spend on expensive household items, they send all spare money home, or spend on food, a more transitory satisfaction. Food practices thus enfold tensions between tradition and innovation, nourishment and lack, boundary maintenance and loss of autonomy, purity and pollution (Douglas 1972).

England demands that migrants "make it" (money, food, community) for themselves. "English food," like "English culture," with its licentious attitude to alcohol, nightclubs, and sex, signals a moral lacuna, a boundary of Pashtun and Muslim identity-articulation, and symbolic distaste for "foreign" incursion.

Notwithstanding, over time culinary adaptations belie the narrative of a steadfast Pashtun culture that is resistant to change. The taxi-driver Razi described as much, while taking an opportunity to detail his innovative cooking skills: "In Afghanistan people never cook chicken or any bird with potato," he instructed. "Potato only goes with lamb, goat, or beef. But I discovered in England that potato is *very* tasty with chicken, too. It's the same with *mooli* [Asian radish]—we only use it for salad, but Bengalis cook it in fish curry. It's delicious. What's more, in curries you *should* really cook the onions first, then the garlic and meat. But now people fry the meat first, to make it crispy. So you see, things change." Other examples belie the strict oppositions narrated between the sumptuous pleasures of "home" and England's deprivation. On special occasions, or simply if the weather is fine, large groups picnic in the English countryside. These are opportunities to laugh, tease one's friends, hide the salt, and complain, "There's no salt in this food!"

When Ajmal acquired his taxi license in 2011, he hosted a picnic in a local beauty spot. Around thirty drivers attended. He bought two sheep and some chickens, and brought along a barbecue, plates, salad, bread, and lemons for the meat. His roommates brought blankets, flasks, and green tea. The occasion affirmed the hegemony of work and their collective endeavor.

"Next year I'll get married," Ajmal asserted. "Afghans want education nowadays. My priority is money. I'll do taxi, then maybe open a shop. I'm British, but don't feel totally British. When I visit Peshawar I miss England's police, law, peace, roads, polite people; then I feel more English." Pondering this predicament, he reiterated the aphorism, "Afghans must work, catch up with the world." Indeed, Ajmal followed his plan, and six years after qualifying as a driver, he opened an Afghan barbecue shop in the city center.

The festival of Eid-ul-Fitr marking the end of Ramadan provides a grand opportunity to eat well with friends and relatives.

"*Rāza!* Come!" Sher Agha enthused to me. "We're making a party in the park. Should we ask the city council for permission?"

He reflected.

"Nah, Afghans don't like rules. We weren't conquered. If officials come, we'll offer them lamb, they'll be happy."

He and a friend cooked three sheep; each guest paid a fee to cover costs. More proud than plaintive, they grumbled.

"We're like workers!"

Aside from needing to admonish some young men drinking beer ("Which Pashtuns are you? Alcohol is not welcome here"), no mishaps occurred. Most wore *salwār–kameez* dress; they danced *attan*, played football, and recorded the "fantastic" occasion on their mobiles.

Occasionally friends make ambitious trips across Europe, driving through countries they crossed to claim asylum, reminded of their condition of perpetual Otherness shaped by contemporary racisms surrounding asylum seekers, Muslim immigrants, and war in Afghanistan. They communicate their hurt through jokes.

"The girls in the nightclubs looked at us very badly, they hate foreigners. We laughed. How much they hated us!"

Transports of Delight

Chakar create liminal moments of freedom, intimacy, and equality. The "trick" (Szakolczai 2009) in this situation has relevance for Bourdieu's (1977) concept of "misrecognition" and Žižek's (1999) notion of fantasy as an ideological category that capitalizes on the enjoyment of secret, behind-the-scenes transgression, but supports the status quo. Laughs here assume importance in creating moments of freedom from life's "tears." One afternoon in Peshawar I accompanied a party to Charsadda district to eat fish. Among this group were old friends visiting from Moscow, Dubai, and London. Relaxing by the Adezai River at Saredheri, all enjoyed an uninterrupted view of the water, where pleasure boats waited lazily for restaurant patrons reclining on charpoy cots in tented rooms on the opposite bank. The conversation turned to one of the company, Toryalai, who scraped a meager living in Peshawar driving both his small Suzuki taxi around town as well as trucks to Afghanistan. One brother lived in London, another was a wealthy "agent" smuggling migrants to Europe. The three brothers had argued, and separated their finances. Toryalai explained, "*Zmka haghra swazi chey woor pey baleygi* [The land burns where the fire is]. I'm poor, my younger brother doesn't care. He's so rich, he carries two brands of cigarettes, Marlboros and locals. He was born in Kacha Garai [a refugee camp], his tastes are poor. He smokes locals but gives his friends Marlboros!"

Hamidullah interrupted, "Toryalai's story is hilarious. He was lucky, he bore children fast after marriage. Then three sons died, *powpowpow*, one after another! A *very funny* joke!" The group laughed uproariously. Seeing my consternation, Mujibur elaborated: "He's brave, it's no great loss. Younger ones can't help the family." Toryalai laughed along. "Toryalai's my soldier," Hamid continued, "he'll drive me anywhere." Joking, they encouraged one another to stoically, manfully bear life's trials. Toryalai asserted he could trumpet an array of horn blasts: imitate an ambulance's siren for the city traffic; small repeats for a village, showing he respects local ways; a long blast for the Khyber Pass, showing the truck-drivers his manliness despite his little car—his inferior status among this group of visiting relatives from "London" reflected in self-deprecating buffoonery.

The "spontaneous generation" (Turner 1974, 248) of thrills and risks to reputation in the group's stories exemplifies *communitas* in the skillful creation of new status hierarchies. Good oratorical skills are highly respected in Pashtunwali, essential to negotiating power, patronage, and personal prestige in a predominantly oral tradition (Barfield 2003). Although on *chakar* relations of hospitality are not enacted, and monetary equality is fixed at the outset, reputation by contrast rests precariously in ribaldry, acuity, and a cut-and-thrust verbal jousting style—in rhetorical forms of fun that establish social reputation, masculine identity, and power (Gilsenan 1996). Jokes like "You can sleep with my wife!" outrageously reverse the imperative to protect one's wife's sexual honor *(namus)*.

By transforming potentially serious transgressions into jokes, friends create intimacies and trust, and they interrupt the formal demands of culture. *Chakar* thus address ways that practices of gender and liminality are incorporated into new social and cultural contexts created through transnational migration—specifically, ways that segregated forms of male–male emotional and physical intimacy may be expressed on the return picnic outside the dominant boundaries of manliness, without threatening the individual or group (Walle 2007). Though Toryalai envied his friends, none of them enjoyed the privileges of Peshawar's wealthiest Afghans. Their *chakar* are formal occasions where guests are fed in return for recognition, allegiance, and support, or to cement economic or political ties, illustrating the ways Ghilzi convert wealth into social relations of reputation, honor, patronage, indebtedness, and gifts through hospitality (Canfield 1988). Such parties might employ a chef, carry guns for protection, invite businessmen or officials, and stay in the plushest hotels. The host's high status is most lavishly communicated when he does not eat with his guests, and through the quantity and quality of the dishes he serves. It is his privilege, Mujibur explained enviously of his wealthy younger cousin, to take his guests to the forest, cook them excessive amounts of lamb, and, in a conspicuous show of waste, leave the uneaten surplus behind.

Affronts to ideals of equality are unwelcome. Later the friends were playing cards, sitting in a circle, an egalitarian arrangement that also applies to shared meals. Simakai, visiting from London, reclined backward and intoned imperiously.

"Toryalai, you don't eat *karahi* [meat dishes] at home, here you eat free!"

To take him down, Mujibur began joking about Simakai's wife.

The momentary risks to reputation on the picnic are also reflected in the card games played. On this occasion they played Ghal aw Bādcha (Robber and King) to determine who would assume the roles of king, minister *(wazir)*, commander, soldier, and robber—a childish game that gestured to a time of freedom before adult responsibilities. By the game's end, all is clear. The soldier catches the robber and parades him in turn past the commander and the *wazir*, who insult him. Finally, the robber reaches the king, who can forgive him or (more fun) choose his punishment. When played in the family, girls may typically be pulled hard by the nose and ordered to "Ouba wachka!" (Drink water!), clean the room, or cook food. Boys may be slapped.

Zalmai sat back and recalled how, as a boy, this uncle had ordered him to stand outside in the snow for an hour, as a punishment for his errant behavior at school. Another time, he found himself king and his uncle the robber. "Give me money for the cinema!" he ordered. His uncle obliged.

Demonstrating how the game's thrill, like the picnic, lies in its potential to momentarily reorder established hierarchies without threatening them, on this occasion Toryalai hilariously found himself king and he commanded Mujibur, the unfortunate robber, to pack up and wash the dishes on behalf of all.

A Hunger for Freedom

Chakar enable men to cope with the serious projects of work and remittance, but also take distance from a persistent difficulty, allowing it de facto to continue, or surface in moments of bitterness, resignation, or jokes. *Chakar* also underscore their wanderlust, desires not to work, to joyfully pursue impulsivity, contingency, and the unexpected as ends in themselves; therefore, their anti-structure disposition should not be overstated. Berlant (2011, 138–39) reflects on eating precisely as a way to feel out alternative routes for living *without* requiring an express agenda for living. Eating interrupts the "crisis ordinariness" of the endless present and the precarity of contemporary capitalism with "the opportunity to identify with *pursuit,* the raw energy of desire."

These travelers, pursuing interruption, push hard toward the freedom of alterity and an unknown destiny. The immediacy in the corporeal satisfaction of appetites allows them to forget the present, and create moments outside everyday paces and places—exemplified in this impromptu trip they took to the high Ushu Valley in Swat.

Stifled by Peshawar's oppressive heat and the seemingly endless days of the return visit spent indoors, Mirwais marshaled a group of friends. Why not drive to see Ushu, rumored for its remoteness and beauty? All would share the costs. Mirwais and Zmarai borrowed their family cars; Hamid contributed in kind by negotiating good rents for a third, and a guesthouse in Ushu. I had been visiting friends en route in Dir, and joined them.

Exhausted after driving in three cars for two days without sleep, they installed themselves by the Ushu River. In the mountainous terrain, there was no lamb to be bought anywhere. The butcher had deceived them by selling them goat! But all shared the preparations for a sumptuous feast of *karahi, pulao,* and kebabs cooked on charcoal. The icy river was barely supportable for *wuzu* (ritual ablution), though ideal for cooling fresh mangoes. A large rock at the water's edge, with two seat-like indentations, allowed a thrilling experience of the rushing waters. As the food cooked gently, they competed, hurling rocks, teasing each other: "Your wife is stronger than you! Your son doesn't listen to you!" Zmarai experimented with a chicken *kolokhak* (a regional dish from Maidan). He put rocks *(lutta)* on the coals and stuffed the chickens, "English style"— with raisins, nuts, and rice. But the heated shards began breaking, endangering the meal. How precarious, how delicious! At dusk, they put on the car headlights, music, and danced the *attan,* attempting increasingly ambitious jumps and turns, laughing at their ineptitude. The night ended in a guesthouse, drinking tea and playing cards. They all shared two rooms. Wazir jumped onto the garden swing at midnight: "Look, it's the swing scene in *Sholay!*"[2] Everybody laughed. For Mohabbat, it was idyllic: "With your family you must be respectful, you feel pressure because you love them. With friends you're free, strong, you can laugh, smoke, what matter if you don't sleep? Picnic is picnic!"

A Flavor of the Past

"When I remember the mountaintops of Pakhtunkhwa (my Afghan land), I forget the throne of Delhi." Before he left England, Mirwais recited to me, in English, these verses by the founder of modern Afghanistan, Ahmad Shah Durrani, intending to convey the bittersweet flavor of returning to one's beloved home. Indeed, Mirwais's exuberance was heightened by his imminent departure home to Peshawar for the duration of a ninety-day visit visa and, he hoped, some precious respite and relaxation with his family.

While the return visit is important in creating alternatives, the everyday structural assaults on Afghan people and personhood in Peshawar are hardly restful. So these travelers depart, speeding away from the predictability of their obligations, the hot Peshawar plain, air and noise pollution, poor water quality, and shrinking green spaces—into an embrace of transience, impulsivity, adventurism, exhilaration, idealism, mobility, and change. They race along the Peshawar–Islamabad motorway, emblem of modernity, or haltingly proceed along the cacophonous ring road past truck stops and NATO supply convoys leaving for Afghanistan, or take the Grand Trunk Road, originating in the sixteenth century under the Pashtun emperor Sher Shah Suri, a historic artery of the Silk Road.

Their freedom is neither boundless nor boundaryless but shaped by the roads they travel, the structure of the *chakar,* and the physical and symbolic boundaries of province and ethnicity. The ancient Afghan fortress town of Attock, bordering Khyber Pakhtunkhwa and Punjab provinces, is the farthest east they travel the Grand Trunk Road.[3] They remain on the "Pashtun" side, their favorite spot opposite the fort. Only three hours outside Peshawar, they frequently swim here, relax, play football and cards *(tayka, piskot, stop),* watch birds dive, and order fried fish. At dusk they pack up and drive home, stopping at the Afghan settlement Now Kar (Nowshera) to drink fresh date juice—a last taste of freedom before the sobering Peshawar skyline.

In imprinting the landscape with raucous experiences of freedom, *chakar* express important attachments to a time before the swallowing up of Pashtun nationalism and Afghan land within "Pakistan." They illuminate the ways that Frontier Muslims challenge, subvert, and identify with the ongoing persistence not merely of colonially derived geographical boundaries and conceptions of acceptable behavior, but also a range of cultural, religious, and social dynamics that exist alongside these (Marsden and Hopkins 2011, 17). These include the worsening relations between Pakistan and Afghanistan in the GWOT, and the forms of bordering and restricted or policed mobility Afghan refugees experience in everyday life in Pakistan (Alimia 2019). At a time when Pakistan perpetuates racialized tropes about the undifferentiated Pathan, Pashtun, and Afghan into discourses around crime and terror—and about the need to secure the unruly borderlands—they also link to forced and coerced forms of physical expulsion and return.

Hence our returnees' nostalgic imaginings do *not* reflect desires to return to, or be free from, the past, but to create a practical sense of future through representing the past as the place to find respite and resistance (Battaglia 1995, 77). This became evident when Surgul and I, leaving Peshawar on the Grand Trunk Road, were stopped by police. "Stop, Mohajir [refugee], we need you [to fill our pockets]!" Shamed, startled, Surgul retorted, "*You're* the refugees. All this land is Afghanistan. Beware, your home is rented!"

The nexus of history, identity-formation, and travel entailed on *chakar* bears on Marsden's analysis of the movements of Tajik and Afghan refugees moving around northern Pakistan. He highlights the "invisible" imprint of Soviet and British imperial expansion, preexisting memories of trans-regional trade, and people's older experiences of mobility on imaginings and understandings of shared selfhood, and different political, religious, and moral indexes, as they move about in everyday life (Marsden 2008, 241). Although *chakar* also involve ways of being Muslim—for example, the pleasure of prayer in rural mosques or beautiful settings—the temporal signatures etched into the landscapes traversed appear, for these participants, more self-consciously related to citizenship status, exile, and belonging, ways they understand themselves as returnee migrants, refugees in a homeland annexed by Pakistan and the site of foreign imperial wars.

The routes they travel return us to the theme of water, here as a regional factor in Pashtun identity (Leake 2017; Malik 2016), and to ways water resonates ideas about shortage, blockage, the Punjabi appropriation of the state through Pakistan's waters (Akhter 2015), overflow, and flooding for twenty-first-century refugees who have outstayed their welcome. The situation was exacerbated in the 2010 floods, Pakistan's worst natural disaster, when thousands of people in Khyber Pakhtunkhwa were displaced; thousands of roads, link bridges, telecom networks, livelihoods, homes, small businesses, schools, and clinics destroyed; and the Jalozai refugee camp in Nowshera—housing many Afghans—badly affected, as Toryalai explained as we drove past, with the smell of dead bodies lingering for weeks.

The themes of hospitality and commensality also return us to the specter of historical border disputes between Pakistan and Afghanistan; Afghan struggles for land, entitlement, rights, and resources; and Pakistan's shifting policy toward Afghan refugees—from the hospitality extended by General Zia-ul-Haq to "Afghan brothers" in the Soviet war, to the "hostis" (Derrida 2000) of the hospitality of current times. To explain his view on Pakistan–Afghanistan relations, while driving back from Attock, Hayatullah recounted this story about Abdul Ghaffar Khan (1890–1988), leader of the Khudai Khidmatgar "Red Shirts" movement for peaceful independence from India (Banerjee 2000), in order to favorably compare Afghan Pashtun to Pakistani hospitality:

> When the Pakistanis have no place to cry, they come to Afghanistan; when they become strong, they run back to Pakistan. They treat Afghans as Mohajirs but when they're in trouble, they say, "We're Afghan."
>
> In Najeebullah's time when I lived in Kabul, many tribesmen and followers of Abdul Ghaffar Khan came from Pakistan to bury him in Jalalabad. Even Najeebullah attended his funeral.[4] They cried, "We're Afghan, our fathers' blood is Afghan, we speak Pashto, please support us." We hosted them well, gave them food, a big hotel, and organized a large music concert. I remember watching it on television. The song "Ma gul wurta warerai kho Gulpām ne razi" ("I Bring a Flower but Gulpām Does Not Come") became a big hit. I remember the singer wore a *lungi* turban, not a modern style. We gave them so much that everyone said, "Their visit even made *niswar* [chewing tobacco] expensive, all the shops were empty." I remember it vividly.
>
> Bādcha Khan is a hero in Pakistan, the "Baba-i-Qaum," but he played both sides. His *qaffin* [burial cloth] was red, but Muslims should be buried in white. He's buried in Jalalabad, my city. There was fighting around his funeral. Gulbuddin threatened to destroy his grave. But Bādcha Khan's daughter-in-law threatened Hekmatyar and the funeral was peaceful. She was brave—or had support

from India. Ghaffar Khan worked for India and took money from Afghanistan. For most Afghans he's a hero. For some he's a devil.

Mukhtar, with strong agreement from others, offered the common narrative that all Afghans' problems were due to Pakistan, whose governments had made deals with foreign countries against Afghanistan for its benefit. He, too, cited a song, "Ay sarbaza yāra" ("Oh Beloved Army") by Bakht Zamina, a Pashtun singer with an unrivaled beauty and voice, who was killed in Kabul in 1980.

The song was a hit during the Pakistan–Afghan hostilities in Babrak Karmal's presidency (1979–86) that resulted from the Soviet invasion and the exodus of millions of Afghans to Pakistan. The song is enjoyed by both Pakistanis and Afghans. Mukhtar, who had stored the song on his mobile phone, remembered, "The very *same day* she died we bought our first television and watched the broadcast of her funeral at Shah Shahid *ziarat.*" As we sipped our date juice in the car at Now Kar, they sang the song (unsure of the words):

Ay sarbaza yāra, ay sarbaza yāra, khayza pe marchal bandey, biyar ba
    dey weda kuma, soori de woorbul landey
Ma mla tareleyda, zema de watan pe nang, gora chey pe sha ne shai, ze
    pe jug tatar bandey
Da Pakistaney dukhman me preyda pe dey khaura key
Stirgi ye worubasa tash pe youw deydan bandey

Oh beloved army, oh beloved army, climb up upon the front line, then
    I'll give you sleep, in the shadow of my hair
I tied my waist-belt tight, (to fight for) the honor of my homeland, be
    careful not to fall behind, go ahead with your chests forward
Don't let this Pakistani enemy on this land
Take her eyes out with just one look

Hospitality, Asylum, Transnational Belonging

How do these themes play out for former refugees living transnational lives between Britain and Pakistan? Anthropological themes in hospitality have been extensively applied to contemporary migration, relations between host states and immigrant guests, and people from Afghanistan (Candea and da Col 2012; Canfield 1988; Derrida 2000; Elphinstone [1815] 1992; Herzfeld 1987; Lindholm 1982; Marsden 2012; Ortner 1978; Shyrock 2012; Tapper and Tapper 1986). While *chakar* may involve formal Pashtun relations of hospitality *(melmastia)* (Barth 1969b), these do not. Occurring within transnational contexts of refugee migration in both Pakistan and Britain, they are nonetheless suffused with manifold ideas that link hospitality, asylum, and international politics to the picnickers' search for freedom. They invoke central anthropological problematics of hospitality involving "identity, alterity, belonging; sovereignty, politics, and inequality; the relation between the individual and the collective; commensality, consubstantiality, and kinship," as well as "connections between families, homes, nations and homelands; guests and hosts who stand for collective entities, immigrant communities, corporations, and states"; and citizenship status and borders (Candea and da Col 2012).

Pitt-Rivers (1968) saw hospitality as anything but benign. In rural Andalusia where villagers suspected him of being a spy, he uncovers an intense interplay between trust and suspicion in the ways the guest is at the absolute mercy of the host in an ambivalent situation, and his social and political rights are suspended (24–25). For Wagner (1981) hospitality is intrinsic to the condition of ethnography; it marks the limits of what knowledge may be revealed. Intrinsic to the "gift" of hospitality thus resides the element of power. Derrida (2000) criticizes the language of an "open house" in which "we" (the French) should unconditionally welcome foreigners (Muslim immigrants) while retaining exclusionary sovereignty, and the power to accept or reject them. For Derrida, the paradox in hospitality is that the guest cannot join the household, but must always remain an outsider, and subject to the host's protection or ambivalence. The refugee's time, Agamben (1994) argues, is curtailed; he should eventually either become a citizen or repatriate. As a "guest," the refugee likewise should assimilate to the host society's customs, without fully becoming equal, and always remaining marginal to state ideology and discourse. In this way the host state's hospitality serves as a border mechanism "for holding a dangerous stranger in abeyance," and "stabilising the relationship between stranger and host community" (Pitt-Rivers 1968, 20). This analogy of the outsider guest is salient for the picnicker's return (as a former asylum seeker in England) to the site of contested Afghan land where Afghans are excluded from citizenship. Notwithstanding the exclusions faced by Afghans in Pakistan since the eighties, Afghans, in Karachi particularly, are key players in lucrative illegal and semi-legal land developments that have themselves displaced communities from thousands of slums, informal settlements, and pastoralist lands.

Shyrock (2012, S28) links hospitality as a quality of people, households, ethnic groups, and nations, and a concept that defines the limits of European citizenship and refuge. In hospitality rhetoric he locates many contemporary problems of human mobility regarding ways the exile, the stranger, the migrant, are all assimilated to the category of "guest." Despite hospitality's intrinsic link to mobility, the guest is not free to move: either around the host's house, or within or across the borders of the host nation. In Britain, the refugee guest, Zarjan mused, wants to save his life, find peace, security, and new opportunities, and he chooses a worthy host country. The host should therefore honor its obligations. Because asylum may (or in many cases not) be granted, applicants are, Zarjan described, "guests at risk": "If the law or government changes, they can deport you. Britain gives food and shelter. Maybe a better word than refugee is *musafer,* a visitor or passing traveler who eats where he stops but doesn't belong there."

Connecting families, villages, and places of refugee settlement, hospitality thus configures the "migropolis" across which refugee Others may variously move, but not freely. Asylum implies a particular hospitality relation for Afghan arrivals in Britain. As my interlocutors describe, *mung pana akhistey pe England key* (we come to claim a safe place), *chey sur aw mal ta moh khairwee* (to save life/head and possessions), *chey pakarar ouso* (to live in peace), *chey khe zwand wuko* (make a good life), or *mung Englandta rana nanawatai you* (we come for refuge). They are wary of the host whose food offerings humiliate them.

Humiliation here refers to British government food vouchers, introduced in April 2000 for asylum seekers only as a replacement for cash benefits, and to deter economic migrants. They were scrapped in 2002, reinstated in 2005, and rescrapped in 2009. Asylum seekers received a maximum of ten pounds a week in cash, plus vouchers they could exchange for food and other necessities in British supermarkets only. The vouchers amounted to 70 percent of the minimum income support offered to British citizens. Furthermore, supermarkets operated a no-change policy. If an individual handed a ten-pound voucher for a smaller charge, no change was issued.

Food vouchers deeply stigmatized asylum seekers. The vouchers also impelled them toward the "tastes" of British food, as vouchers did not cover purchases in halal meat shops or Asian supermarkets. Asylum in the refugee context, Zarjan reflected bitterly, implies a "deal": subjugation and humiliation in exchange for uncertain citizenship. Unlike the Pashtun ideal-concept of *nanawatai* (refuge), which dictates that an asylum claim should be accepted, the English are more equivocal.[5]

Hospitality *(melmastia)* has been prioritized in Orientalist readings as intrinsic to a Pashtun's honor and the code of Pashtunwali (Elphinstone [1815] 1992, 1:226).[6] Hospitality to strangers, regardless of background, was an obligation offered without expectation of reciprocity. In ideal form hospitality to one's tribesmen obliges the recipient to reciprocate adequately when the occasion demands. Between Pashtuns hospitality is highly variegated and may involve informal occasions between friends, business partners, and kin, and formal occasions where the host *(koorba)* feeds his guests in return for allegiance, recognition, and support, or to cement economic, business, or political ties (Barth 1959a; Canfield 1988).

Hospitality differs from generosity *(sakhawat)*, which may be extended without expectation of return (i.e., charitably). Hospitality involves the obligation to offer tea, food, or a bed to a guest *(melma)*. Extemporizing on hospitality's meanings in Pashto, Najeeb described how a stranger *(nabalada)* passing through your village should be guaranteed a meal and blanket for the night. If he is a brave, a *kochi* (nomad) perhaps, he might sleep in the mosque; or someone will offer his *hujra* (guest quarters) for the night, and send him off the next day with food.

Akin to the context of refugee migration, the Pashtun householder's guest is not permitted to freely cross domestic thresholds. Male guests are typically received in the householder's *hujra*, a building away from the main domestic dwelling. The *hujra* comprises a stage for displaying the host's wealth and largesse, and *not* for displaying women, internal domestic tensions, financial struggles, and social and political conflicts that may lurk beneath—what Bourdieu (1990, 274) calls "the world of intimacy, that is, the place of all that pertains to sexuality and procreation." In this sense the *hujra* implicates Shyrock's (2012, S24) notion of hospitality as "stagecraft," as do the border regimes of the "host" societies who receive Afghan refugees.

For Afghan Pashtuns in Europe, hospitality creates relations of indebtedness, belonging, and resistance to ideal forms. These range from those who avoid reciprocity in extending hospitality to kin in need, to hosting guests for advantage, to an unbounded generosity such as Najeeb experienced when, arriving in the Netherlands without means, he lived with his cousin gratis for several months.

Studies of hospitality in Afghanistan have highlighted ways that politicians and people negotiate power, patronage, and personal prestige in a predominantly oral tradition (Barfield 2003). Among Afghan traders in Kabul, Marsden (2012) deploys the pressure cooker to symbolize the potential of host–guest relations to explode business negotiations, partnerships, and commercial relations. Shyrock (2012, S23) describes feasts in Jordan as agonistic events, "a kind of war" wherein guests may make or break their host's reputation, and relations collapse into enmity, indebtedness, and subjugation.

Hospitality is thus potentially dangerous and also a double-edged sword. This is literally demonstrated in this example concerning Gul Agha Sherzai that Najeeb related, angry at Sherzai's alliance with the northern Hazara political Alimi Balkhi in the 2014 vice presidential elections.[7] Sherzai was an infamous former Pashtun governor of Kandahar (2004) and then Nangarhar province (2004–13), a wealthy businessman and ex-warlord from Kandahar who amassed enormous wealth from the opium trade, was implicated in human rights abuses, and accorded the sobriquet "Bulldozer" by President Hamid Karzai. In March 2008, Sherzai appeared on Afghanistan's Tolo TV program *Mehman-e-Yār* (*Guest of Friends*; Dari). The irreverent interviewer provoked the expansive Sherzai, who was seated at home while the camera panned over his vast table covered with sumptuous dishes.

"You famously eat very well? Will you be called to account on Judgement Day?"

Sherzai responded with a story (paraphrased here): "Food is God-given. God *likes* me; therefore I eat good food. Let me tell you a story. In King Abdur Rehman Khan's time of old, one mullah complained that the king was too fat to understand poor people. The king, hearing this, invited the mullah to a feast in his palace. An enormous chicken sat at the table's centerpiece, above which a sword hung suspended by a thin thread. Anyone who served himself chicken risked his life. The mullah was too afraid to serve himself, so the king served them both. This was his answer to the mullah."

Thereby Sherzai illustrated the dangerous sword edge of the lavish hospitality expected of chiefs, the power plays and risks involved for a host who protects his guests in exchange for their acceptance of subordinate status (Dietler 2001, 87), and he asserted the power of the warlord over the ulema. He suspended above the televised view of his own table an ominous question concerning the fate of those who might refuse his or a warlord's patronage—just like a king of old Afghanistan.

The Refreshment of Memory

Returning to Peshawar, food and memory form a potent confluence in constructing private remembrance, shared memory, and intense experiences of an epochal shift (Holtzman 2006). Through the peripatetic, shared gustatory pleasures of actual physical return, friends both "refresh" and create new memories of Afghanistan. The picnic, as a pleasant tradition of transporting one's "home" outdoors, creates sites of collective escapism to which they habitually return. While food and memory are famously linked in European literature in Proust's recall of the taste of a *petite madeleine,* the sensuality of food may revivify less pleasant associations pertaining to spatiotemporal displacement or migration (Sutton 2001): for example, longings for a time *before* the losses of homeland, and intimacy and care in the family, through war and exile. Below I present three different examples in which *chakar* serve to refresh and create memories that are enfolded into narratives, themselves becoming rituals of remembrance which friends, wherever they are, can revisit.

First, one afternoon Baryalai and I were drinking tea in Peshawar's sprawling *kar khanou* market from which his uncles traded across the world. Their offices overlooked busy exchanges in car parts, trucks, cigarettes, textiles, electronics, electrical goods, building materials, carpets, rice, teas, sports goods, leather jackets, almonds, tires, and radios. The occasion reminded Baryalai of a similar afternoon when, sitting in the same offices, he and his friends impulsively decided to visit Afghanistan.

This *chakar* served as a joyful "refreshment" of memory following a decade of exile:

I was joking with friends in *kar khanou*. Someone said, "Let's go to Jalalabad!" Another said, "But I've no sandals [*chappals*]!" so we bought some! We called other friends to join. What a plan, I hadn't seen Afghanistan for ten years! We bought charcoal, gas canisters, blankets, firewood, food, toothpaste, glasses, every provision, and gifts for old friends in Jalalabad: shawls [*patoo*], watches, clothes. We finally departed at dusk, nine friends. We rented a minibus and reached Torkham late. No matter, we were going to Afghanistan! Across the border we drank *kāwa* tea. Daringly, I hugged a guard, exclaiming, "I feel I'm home!" Everyone laughed. We rented another car and set off, joking. The driver said, I feel I'm with friends, I've never laughed so much at work.

Near nightfall we approached Raziabad, it started raining. Laughing, we alighted to enjoy the beautiful smell of the mud and olive trees of Afghanistan. Reaching Jalalabad at night, we tasted kebabs and fresh juice, then went to our friend, laden with fruits, grapes, apricots, walnuts, almonds. Over seven days we visited Beysud Pul, Khogyani, Kaga, Nangarhar, and the historic Mimlai Bagh gardens. We received many invitations, but preferred the informality of the picnic. Friends joined us, we cooked together, *equally.* We were so happy, *and* refreshing our memory of Afghanistan. Then onto Laghman, joining friends already picnicking, a formidable force. One villager shouted, "Go home, the Taliban will catch you." "No!" we laughed, "We'll catch the Taliban!"

In the second example I had accompanied some friends to the Afghan border at Torkham. To reach the border, travelers must take the Khyber Pass, a favorite site for *chakar*. The Pass has a long history of invasion and occupation, dating to the Indo-Aryans' passage to India in 1,500 BCE and Alexander the Great's passage in 327 BCE (Caroe [1958] 2006, 45). Since the 1980s it has witnessed combat between Pashtuns, Afghans, Russians, and Americans, enabled trade between Central Asia and Afghanistan, been the site for UNHCR repatriation schemes, a conduit for NATO supplies to Afghanistan, and seen a flourishing trade in hashish and weapons in the summit town of Landi Kotal. It has enabled Afghans in Peshawar to travel to Afghanistan to deal with the common problem of land disputes. When Ghaffar heard that family land in Jalalabad had been appropriated by poorer relatives, a fight seemed unavoidable. Responding immediately, he collected "fighters" (Afghan National Army soldiers) en route and reached Jalalabad in five hours to find the bird flown. In Peshawar his father received a contrite phone call saying, "Relatives needn't fight, forgive us."

Travel on the Pass by foreigners requires a permit. The "agencies" operating at Torkham posed a significant danger. Still, traveling in Toryalai's Suzuki, I could pass as Afghan, see my companions' favorite picnic spots, and we could enjoy kebabs on the way: *Razey chakarta larsoo!* (Let's go on a *chakar!*). The farther we traveled from "Pakistan" into tribal country governed by a stricter Pashto, the more infused with liberation my consorts became. "The closer I get to Afghanistan," Mujibur exhorted, "the more relaxed, brave, able to talk sweet words I feel. Put me in Punjab, I feel very down."

Since Pakistan's reinforcements of the porous Torkham border with a wall erected in 2016 and 2017, this shared fieldwork story has itself also become infused with a bittersweet sense of times past, and change, and no return. The trip was a jolly of boisterousness and excellent tales of *chakar* that they had enjoyed preceding us. We set off, driving through the *patak* (checkpoint) at *kar khanou*, past shops selling guns and hashish. Here Mujibur leapt out to take photographs, thinking to impress me with his knowledge of the illicit. Then onward we drove, toward the fields at Beygari ("Here we play cricket with Afridi teams!" he exclaimed), through Jam bazaar where is issued a warning ("This is dangerous place for weapons, hashish, and sex films"), past Khyber gate, Jam, Jamrud, and Khyber rifles garrison, toward Landi Kotal, where I was regaled with hilarious, thrilling tales ("Here many friends came one night with guns, were we brave or stupid?!"), onto Shāgai, with its perfect hilltop view of Peshawar ("A beautiful place to pray after picnics"), then Ali Masjid fort ("What a spot for barbecues!"). On we drove through Khyber, and finally we reached Lwargai, where we stopped to enjoy kebabs. We were honored when a local businessman vacated his office so we could eat there undisturbed, and bought a box of tissues from the neighboring store so that I, the foreigner, could presumably wipe my hands as I ate. Once replete, we set off again. After we rounded the sharp incline at

Michni post, we passed a plume of queuing trucks, and so descended into Torkham.

We disembarked in the rain. "Don't talk!" they ordered. "It's dangerous, although very strong humanity is here, especially for women." Silently, anxiously, we approached the border crossing. Entering Pakistan were drivers, traders, families in their finery. Crisscrossing the eerie landscape like elegant veiled birds, women were being ferried in cart-like wheelbarrows by porters or gallant male relatives. Though I was reminded of the deceptive chivalries of symbolic gender violence (Bourdieu 2001), I envied them, serene in their wheelbarrows, protected from the mud that had splattered me.

The last, imaginary *chakar* serves both as a mnemonic for recalling intense personal losses relating to homeland, and as a site of biographical self-narration. It was recounted by my friend Zmarai in Sussex. We were discussing his feelings about returning to Kabul, his natal city, where he grew up during Soviet occupation and fled during the civil war in 1992. A melancholic, liminal state of ambivalent attachments and loyalties to the past is expressed obliquely. Zmarai's story augurs another transcontinental overland passage ahead, to the UK: a personal journey *without* return, of becoming more foreign, strange, and "Other" to himself:

The sun rises in Jalalabad and sets in Herat. If Afghanistan were safe, we'd make a big *chakar* from Kabul to Mazar-e-Sharif in the north. Our first stop is Charikar, a shady green city. We'll buy succulent grapes. The road climbs alongside the water, icy in winter. I heard it's lovely nowadays; Friday nights during summer are busy with Kabulis picnicking on the grass. At the mountaintop, we'll see the Salang tunnels. We'll drive through Woolang. Here was a checkpoint and Soviet base, nestled in the mountain's curve. Many trucks fell from the bridge. Sometimes lorries carried beautiful grapes; the Russians would steal them, or stop you, ask for cigarettes, or say, "I'm Muslim. I know about Allah, nothing else. My parents prayed secretly."

Onward to Salang. Once I was driving with my uncle. The road was icy. When we entered the tunnel, the lights went out. A Russian tank entered, then swerved, smashing us into the mountain. It was terrifying. One climbed out, bleeding, drew his gun, but didn't shoot. At the mountaintop is a lake; the Russians made electricity here. We can't picnic; it's a government area.

Downward to Bachey Haji hotel, a pit stop for travelers from Mazar-e-Sharif. The food isn't good but fine if you're cold. Then onto Khinjan, where they grow delicious mulberries. The *seekh kebabs, qurut,* and *pulao* dishes are delicious here, the water fast, good for throwing rocks and praying; fish jump. Onward, down the mountain, over the bridge to Dowshi. Here it's warmer, the landscape widens; there's a short season for melons *(khattaki),* the sweetest in the world! The locals guard them fiercely; they don't even send them to Kabul. Next is a shop making fresh iced milk *(sheeryakh).* They pour whole milk into a huge table with a hole, surrounded with salt and ice. They mix it for hours and serve it with frozen rice-grain biscuits. A beautiful handmade ice cream. A tiny old shop in Dowshi's backstreets making magic, who'd believe it? Next, the desert. In Soviet times, the entire road from Kabul to Mazar-e-Sharif was under government control; tanks were on the road. Sometimes mujahideen robbed containers here. They'd send a ransom to Kabul or sell the goods.

Follow the fast-flowing river, and we'll reach Pul-e-Khumri city between Kabul and Mazar-e- Sharif. In Russian times, Afghans called it "Moscowkochak," "small Moscow"; there were dancing girls there. We should relax, buy petrol, pray. It's safe; there are still Soviet buildings there, a big cement factory, and a mountain spring, Chushmey Sher (Tiger's Eyes). Next we're at Dasht-e-Alwan, four hours from Mazar. The road slices the desert here. In spring it's an enormous carpet of red tulips—a symbol of blood shed during the anti-Soviet revolution with longer historical resonance dating to the Mughal invasions—and a beautiful picnic area. People stop at the roadside, take rugs, food, dried fruit, charcoal, crockery, and stay several hours; at night it's dangerous. We'll leave before dark over small hills covered with poppies and pistachio trees. This is Rabatak, freezing in winter, dangerous during Russian times because of hijackings. So let's speed on to Samangan, for the sweetest water, yoghurt, and girls in Afghanistan!

After at Tashqurghan are the juiciest peaches in Afghanistan. We're almost at Mazar-e-Sharif now. We could turn right to

Hairatan and Uzbekistan, but we'll continue to one of the four gates of Mazar-e-Sharif, city of the tomb of Ali. Once, I was at that bus station with my little brother. We saw one Uzbek shoot one Hazara dead. Blood flowed *everywhere*; a fight started. We hid behind a tin signboard, I thought I had protected us, but I realized the bullets could pierce through and kill us. It was terrifying. I was more scared for my brother than myself.

These examples provide insights into how reprised memories of *chakar* serve first-generation migrants in the ritual evocation of feelings of loss, longing, and love toward the homeland. Their memories are overlaid with experiences of freedom that, likewise, are neither permanent nor total, but contained momentarily in the picnic. They involve imaginings of escape from contemporary obligations of love and labor, and from their status as refugees on Afghan land—undermining conventional forms of security, while simultaneously highlighting the insecurity of their situation and its undermining.

Conclusion

This chapter has examined picnics in a society frequently associated with oppression, fanaticism, obscurantism, and war. Here Afghans are enjoying themselves. Who could have guessed? *Chakar*, I have argued, serve to evaluate and manage displacements following war, the shaping of male Pashtun labor within transnational contexts of migration, returning, and never arriving—wherein "return" enfolds a nostalgic imaginary for the freedom before the massive transformations that produced the dilemmas of homeland and belonging for Afghans—and desires to create and protect memories and shared histories of untroubled times. These imaginings of identity and connections to Afghanistan do not reflect desires to return to or be free from the past, but rather create alternative perspectives on the future.

This study of picnics thus makes a small contribution to calls to study freedom ethnographically, and the ethics that the exercise of freedom furnishes in different cultural traditions and social and historical contexts (Laidlaw 2002). *Chakar* create contradictory experiences that sustain participants in a tension between desires to preserve the hierarchies

they conceal, and desires for more freedom. They illustrate tensions between individual yearnings for freedom under economic and ideological relations which, having to be preserved for the subject's own sake,
shape the search for enjoyment. "Freedom" thus fits neatly into a human
condition defined by economic necessity and moral continuity without
actually challenging it.

Chakar enfold several meanings of freedom. The personal experience
of freedom *(azādi)* connotes freedom from rules—in other words, independence and autonomy in a Pashtun family value system that restricts
behavior—and represents an inversion of everyday rules and restrictions.
Occurring on the return visit, the *chakar* also connotes freedom from
everyday obligations and work, including from domestic duties on the
return visit.

In contrast to licensing regulations and market conditions that "control" taxi-drivers' work, the work on *chakar* (cooking, shopping, driving, organizing) is of the picnickers' own choice and making. It relates
specifically to *sartayree* (good times, fun), comprising an activity with
"taste" *(chakar key khwand da),* of sensory experiences of joy, love, voice,
respect, and recognition—hence the "taste of freedom."

Related to *azadi* is the concept of *khpel waqi* (one's own power, autonomy), which suffuses the *chakar* with historical ideas of liberation
from the occupation of Afghan lands and oppression of Afghan people
in Pakistan—as well as with larger political imaginings of freedom from
imperialism, war, and the interference of foreign powers in Afghan affairs
and lives. *Khpel waqi* also refers to the intimate, personal capacity to act,
and to the limits of freedom highlighted in what is possible or impossible
in any situation (Jackson 2013, 215). Jackson highlights the dynamic interchange between how we are constituted in the world and how we constitute ourselves: that defines freedom, in Sartrean terms, as "the small
movement which makes a totally conditioned social being someone who
does not render back completely what his conditioning has given him"
(9). Rather than seek to substantivize terms such as culture, freedom,
and autonomy, these terms capture the struggle in people's lives to reach a
compromise between living meaningful, viable lives on their own terms,
and accepting the different terms of others: "This is the meaning of being
at home in the world" (248).

For Afghan refugees and returning migrants, it is a balance and struggle they both do and do not reach or maintain, but play out repeatedly in the circular motion of the round trip. To draw an analogy from Borges's "Circular Ruins" ([1944] 1998), the *chakar* may additionally be seen in terms of infinite recursion or endless return to the dream, which by being repeatedly dreamt becomes the creative work of shaping a new reality. Borges's story interrogates the border between wakefulness and sleep, dreams and reality. Thereby he usefully critiques the idea of liminality in the sense of meaningful borders between related concepts. When the unwelcome intrusion of reality occurs, and reveals reality as the product of the dreamer, and the dreamer in turn as the product of a dream, the only solution to the problem of circularity is to return to the dream—in this case the respite that interrupts work.

What accounts for the double bind in which these friends participating in *chakar* are caught, lies at the intersection between two enjoined sets of social relations through which power is exerted and surplus labor exacted—and more precisely, in a level of political economy wherein the trips are therapeutic, while also sustaining deceptive realities impelled by exploitation and hierarchy. What distinguishes these travels from, say, Western middle-class travels around Asia—which are also modes of constructing identity that people undertake without dreaming of not returning to work afterward—is the societal structures within which they occur, and the uncertainties in which Afghanistan's future remains shrouded.

Chakar involve shifting and insecure hospitalities. They involve Afghans' status in Pakistan and Britain, and ways families bear or indulge the long return visits of remitting sons. These men often visit friends around the UK—these travels are akin to a "classic rite of youthful male exuberance and freedom" that maintains multi-local notions of diasporic identity and return among British Punjabis (Qureshi 2014). However, *chakar* on the return visit relate more directly to their complex identities as transnational migrants, refugees, and exiles. Occurring only every few years, these visits have heightened significance in replenishing and creating memories of the homeland—compared to the travels of young men who never left Afghanistan or Pakistan (e.g., Marsden 2008).

The return visit is important in creating new transnational identities. These perpetuate global power asymmetries, emphasizing returnees' British identity compared with an underdeveloped Pakistan (Bolognani

2014), where Afghans must remain refugees—if they are lucky. In the UK these migrants stress that they are "more Afghan" than other groups—highlighting the importance of differentiating their aspirations in the transnational global economy, both from the values they associate with Western-style modernity, and from the conservative ideals central to their identities as Ghilzi Pashtuns, "strong" Muslims, to political tensions in Afghanistan tied to Pashtun anxieties about the dominance of a Persian-speaking minority political elite in Kabul, and to Afghans' status as refugees in Pakistan. By underscoring their strict adherence to Pashtunwali (even if in practice they transgress it), the men position themselves and their *qaum* as culturally superior to other segmentary lineages, subgroups, tribal factions, and large families related to the Ghilzai and other Pashtun tribes. Their *chakar* define important ways that economic, social, and cultural capital is generated through food and friendship, and food signals variegated subtleties of inclusion–exclusion, inequality, difference, refinement, and taste.

Finally, the motifs and inflections of hospitality on *chakar* invoke relations between states and refugees, border limits of belonging to either Pakistan (as permanent refugees) or Britain (migrant–citizens), the transformation of relations between Pashtuns on the move, and between migrant kin in diasporic settings. *Chakar* are dually bound and unbound to identity. They preserve ideals and power relations in Pashto, shape formations of alterity and consciousness, and critique and mitigate the pressures of family obligations and culture in migrants' realities. Participants do not desire actual transformation, but rather to interrupt, re-pace, and re-emplace lives conceived of in terms of movement, on their own terms. Perhaps the further uncertainties the actual satisfaction of emotional appetites would risk is one reason *chakar* occur outside the structures and spaces of the everyday. While the taste of freedom is good in the moment, so is the hunger for it that is sustained.

3. IMMOBILITY DREAMS

The Man Who Would Be King

"We are not little men, and there is nothing we are afraid
of except Drink, and we have signed a Contrack on that.
Therefore, we are going away to be Kings." "Kings in our own
right," muttered Dravot.

—Rudyard Kipling, *The Man Who Would Be King*

Kipling's novella *The Man Who Would Be King* dissects the hubris of British imperialism through the story of two opportunistic would-be rulers
who overreach themselves and fall into moral and mental deterioration.
Kipling narrates the story while traveling in the Intermediate carriage
of a train in India. Intermediate, an "awful" carriage for Eurasians, loaf-
ers, and drunkards, encompasses a narrative that is neither wholly imperial nor native, neither fantasy nor reality. There he meets two English
chancers, Daniel Dravot and Peachey Carnehan, who, "going away to be
Kings" (Kipling [1888] 2013, 6), join a caravan traveling from Peshawar
to Kabul, and eventually carve out a kingdom for themselves in Kafiristan, a valley in remote northeastern Afghanistan where a priesthood
worships a cult of Alexander the Great. Dravot tricks the locals into accepting him as the son of Alexander. He becomes crowned as king and
god, and Carnehan accepted as his son. Against the wishes of the priests
and his own "Contrack" which prohibits women, liquor, and undignified
behavior, Dravot marries a local girl. The terrified girl bites Dravot at the
marriage ceremony, forcing the two deceivers to flee. Dravot descends

FIGURE 1. The man who would be king. Photograph by the author.

into madness, is apprehended, and beheaded. Carnehan laments, "You behold now . . . the Emperor in his habit as he lived—the King of Kafiristan with his crown upon his head. Poor old Daniel that was a monarch once!' (24). Carnehan thereafter is transferred to an asylum and dies the next day.

The allegory unfolds along two key narrative positions. Concerning "real kings," first there is Kipling's initial bemusement at the idiocy of corrupt power, which turns to disapprobation. Peachey, the second inner narrator, tells the story of the "pretend king," in which the image of Alexander the world conqueror drives the adventurers' hubris with tragic consequences. We might bring this narrative to another kind of fantasy that also tricks hopeful young men, as similar would-be kings and conquerors, to enter the "world stage" as asylum seekers propelled by war, political instability, and a utopian vision of transnational mobility, security, getting rich, and "moving up." Their failures to achieve this vision implicate the painful undoing of selfhood in the boundary regions between life and death, sanity and madness, waking and dreams. The relevance of the story's interplay between mobility and immobility, beggar and king, political authority and mad oracle, is literally and figuratively epitomized in the picture of Zmarai's taxi shown in Figure 1. Beset by an overwhelming depressive desire to sleep, and to not move, he hardly worked but still displayed a toy crown in his front window for several weeks. Gifted to him by a drunken customer, he was reluctant to discard it. "It suits me," he insisted.

Immobility

This chapter returns from Peshawar to the English county of Sussex, home to two of Rudyard Kipling's residences.[1] Its focus is on immobility, querying how immobility speaks in particular ways to reality and imagination, inclusions and exclusions, and marginal qualities of migrants' lives in one man's struggles to survive deep suffering. This involves exploring ways that "not moving" might shape, coerce, or forbid possibilities for action and transformation; ways immobile aspects of everyday living create a painful mode of self-protection within the heavy conditions of family exchange that sanction sons' migration in return for remittances; and ways experiences of aporias and interruptions to the dream of success and upward mobility might produce forms of living death (wishing for death, a way out, suicidal ideation). It also questions how we can relate to lives experienced as stuck, immobilized by their losses, or an inability to transcend their confines; how exactly a person is stopped; and what politics of recognition position the immobile as a form of death-in-life in the first place?

Additionally, it questions how much pain, grief, or hopelessness of a continual falling short can be tolerated before symptoms cannot reasonably be regarded as normal. Immobility here also draws particular attention to the subjective "difference between ordinary madness—those myriad mysteries and mystifications of existence that vex but do not destroy us—and those experiences that so overwhelm us that we completely lose our hold upon life" (Jackson 2013, 157).

The chapter returns to the relationship I formed with my interlocutor Zmarai,[2] whose story about the 1989 Battle of Jalalabad opened the book. During this research, Zmarai's deteriorating mental state assumed increasing concern, for him and also for me. Telling his story from multiple perspectives allowed him to express confusing emotions he usually suppressed. Writing his story helped to allay my growing worries. Thereby we became trusted cocreators of a peculiar public–private expression of distress comprising our combined attempts to read the unreadable. For me, the problem became a research question. If it was for him in part a means to release tensions without acting to change his situation (part of his "inability to move"), not moving in turn brought with it suffering and depression, and an inability to change his situation he found difficult to fathom.

The chapter uses three interlocutionary approaches to analyze his case. First, it draws reflections from *khapgan*—the Pashto term for depression, or "feeling down," that he most frequently used. Second, it reflects on four life-history interviews I conducted with Zmarai in 2010 and 2011. Third, it interprets fives dreams from several he shared with me between 2009 and 2017. To link an apt image from the short story "Circular Ruins" ([1944] 1998), Jorge Luis Borges describes a taciturn man who lands his canoe on the riverbank, kisses the mud, and heads to the circular ruins of an abandoned temple where he sleeps—to dream another reality. This story reminds one of the ritually induced dream of the person who is ill, possessed, or paralyzed with conflicts, who goes to a saint's tomb to dream and sleep, sometimes for years, until the dream of deliverance releases him (Pandolfo 1997, 184). The image also bears on the fantasy of stasis that arises from the migrant's nightmare of movement, and on immobility's entanglements with ideas and desires for free will and freedom. Correspondingly, the chapter explores ways that immobility, in the form of sleep and its correlate dreaming, might reconfigure or re-pace oppressive realities as spaces of hope, death, autonomy, and freedom. It aims to move beyond broad historical claims, and to speak to more subtle notions of temporality and spatiality—to a place where the time of immobility is marked by an endless present, merging aspiration, dreamworlds, sleep, and resignation.

The chapter also builds on diverse anthropological analyses of suffering that focus on single cases.[3] By ploughing the heuristic value of immobility in a single case, it offers insights into the interplay of migrant subjectivity with the body, strategies for coping with the violent past, for "going on," surviving, creating futures, and even hope. This highlights the "deep agony" of tensions between cultural ideals, moral and practical compromises, desires for cultural closure, openness and ambiguity, which constitute a "tangible tug-of-war in which the metonymic link between the person and the group ideal is stretched, fought over, perhaps broken" (Gay y Blasco 2011, 459). It also reveals the potential in the silent, uncertain meanings at the edges of cultural–psychological–political orders of explanation for misreading ways that people inhabit worlds of suffering. Hence we might also reach beyond the mythic traumatic primal scene of migration, to rebuff culturalist understandings of migrant subjectivities via a focus on post-traumatic stress disorder (PTSD) (Khan 2017b, 42), and the ways a racialized rhetoric of anachronism reenters the classification of refugees through diagnoses of abnormality and mental illness (Nguyen 2012, 53). This links to anthropological critiques of the argument that emotions are "culturally constructed," that culture precedes or is somehow separate from the body, or that imply psychological individualism or isomorphism with essential cultural forms (Hsu 2008).

Certainly Zmarai's suffering may be a case of "ironic illness" involving an embodied interplay between agency and self-deception, and the inability to move (Lambek 2003). Lambek argues that illnesses may be ironic in the sense they are embodied, intrinsic, and *not* conscious or reflective, while the sufferer is also not deceived: "The irony of the illness is precisely an expression of its evasion at being pinned down by sufferer, observer, or therapist" (52). However, let me stress: I do *not* reduce Zmarai's mental suffering to any strategy of resistance, rational choice, or need. Nor do I suggest it results from a lack *or* surfeit of culture that prohibits emotional expression, in an elaboration of the Orientalist trope of the oppressed Afghan woman in relation to men. His desires are *not* after all for any radical forms of renunciation or transformation. In his words, "I just want to feel *normal*. What does a blind man want from God? Two eyes" *(Lund le khudai chey warey? Dua stirgi).*

In the sense that immobility represents an obstacle, a psychoanalytic reading offers us the prospect that an obstacle can only be recognized, or constructed, when it can be tolerated, however painful that is (Phillips 2012, 28). Obstacles, Phillips proposes, serve to paralyze any realization or even recognition of alternative unconscious projects: they are a way of not letting something else happen. Analyzing a person's repertoire of obstacles is the clue to understanding what they desire, and their fantasies of continuity. The obstacle reveals what we desire, not vice versa.[4] For Phillips the essential work of the obstacle is to conjoin contradictory states of mind—that is, what we consciously know and live with, and what we may unconsciously desire and not necessarily know.

This implicates the terrifying prospect of Zmarai's desires to choose an alternative life to the one mapped out for him, which he endures bitterly, and all the risk of further loss and failure that might entail.

Immobility, Migration, Making It

Immobility has developed in anthropology as a cipher for political, economic, material, cultural, and affective assemblages of blocked, stuck, and transitional movement involving, although not exclusively, geographical, spatial, global, local, and human components (Salazar 2012, 2013; Salazar and Smart 2011). In the key fields of transnational migration, diaspora, and exile, anthropological takes on immobility have pertained to structures, classifications, and experiences of confinement, arrested time-consciousness, liminality and isolation produced by neoliberal globalization, war, and transnational migration (Khan 2016); to immobility's broader relation to the conditions at stake in conditions of economic and social productive life (Napolitano 2007); and to ways immobility is imposed, but also governs people's efforts to subvert, refuse, or reshape teleological narratives of freedom, progress, or integration.

Querying immobile organizations of productive migrant labor can shed light on the conditions of desire intrinsic to ways that immobility might recalibrate the losses that outweigh profit in the capitalist dream of upward mobility. This may involve the need to compromise, and strike a balance between one's desires for oneself and one's loved ones, and the losses involved in pursuing these. In this sense immobility is intrinsically relational, and inseparable from mobility (Bergson 2002, 119). It is relevant to many migrant, illegal, and low-paid workers who suffer the paradox in a vision of upward mobility that results in an endless present in which hopes of progress have stopped or become traumatic.

Far from the lateral freedoms Hardt and Negri (2004, 135–37) identify in the possibilities for upward mobility under contemporary capitalism, this implicates the deferred realization intrinsic to hope. While Harvey has described how the inequalities of global capitalism produce "spaces of hope" across the globe, he also shows how migrants' dreams of making it are often lost in the soulless "romanticism of endlessly open projects that never reach a point of closure" (2000, 174).

Berlant (2011, 19) similarly addresses the fantasies people direct toward "that moral–intimate–economic thing called the good life": a fantasy in which life is dedicated to moving forward but which is actually "stuck in survival time, the time of struggling, drowning, holding onto the ledge, treading water, the time of not stopping" (169). For Hage (2009b) the conditions of permanent crisis most of us now inhabit have led to an intensification and normalization of a sense of "stuckedness." "Imagined existential stuckedness" is the feeling that life is going nowhere (98). The more one invests in waiting to get somewhere, the harder it is to stop waiting (104).

In the sense one either cannot or will not move, immobility's passivity is ambivalent, and has received attention by anthropologists at several analytic levels. Immobility may encompass positive strategies of active resistance, a response to shame, a refusal to play the game of assimilation, of waiting, and a link to diverse epistemologies and heterologies of modernity (Hage 2009a; Crapanzano 1985; Pardy 2009). Dwyer (2009) distinguishes between existential waiting as a disposition toward life captured in the question "What next?" and situational waiting—not least because situations implicate a political economy of waiting and awaited movement, in which "time is money" and waiting a waste of time. Waiting, like boredom, is a state of detachment from desire that protects us from what we wait and hope for—which may not be happiness, as the desire for exemption, just to stop. Oustinova-Stjepanovic (2017) intertwines a sense of failure, with self-derogation and an incapacity to act among Roma Sufi Muslims, in contrast to inaction as a strategy of resistance. These temporal readings beg connections to Biao's (2014) arguments that migration is a fundamentally temporal practice instead of a spatial one, wherein a focus on temporality enables a more insightful understanding into the ways migrants experience and negotiate structural control.

I disagree that people might "choose" severe mental pain to avoid working. Zmarai's suffering is too protracted, incoherent, and despairing to describe any rational choice, active resistance, or moral failure to manage the ideological demands of neoliberalism. Rather, as Das (2015, 23) writes, it is important to recognize what kinds of grief and exhaustion are braided into moments of giving up, how difficult it is to completely abandon the family, or its demands for survival—and to develop a narrower attentiveness to the fragile, nuanced ways that people negotiate caring and defeat according to their capabilities and circumstances.

Immobility as the Inability to Move

Zmarai and I were watching the Pashto film *Kabar la zawal da (Arrogance Will Lose)* at my home. In the film, Pashtun morality and ideals were engaged through the tragic story of an overindulgent father whose son, willful and self-indulgent, ruined his family. Afterward, Zmarai uttered uncharacteristically, "It's hopeless."

Startled by his admission, wondering if the film's themes of winning and losing had disturbed him, I pressed.

"Everything's hopeless." he expanded. "I've stopped. I've worked hard. My friends are buying homes, bringing their families here. I should be going up. I've shown nothing to the world, or myself. I'm not moving. *Ze der khapa yum* [I feel very down]."

In 1998 Zmarai's father paid his overland passage to Europe, which cost around £10,000. After working for cash for two years working in Asian shops in London, Zmarai moved to Sussex, where I met him and his three brothers working in a food-shop kitchen. The brothers worked hard and eventually bought the business. They sold it in 2002 and sent the entire substantial profits to their family, who used it to buy land in Afghanistan. The large remittance raised their reputation with relatives, and justified their expensive passage and continued presence in Britain. It also left them without capital for further investment. Two of them later became taxi-drivers. Although Zmarai's father urged him to acquire British citizenship for his wife and children ("Just give them passports and security, then send them back if you don't want them"), his inaction was not initially problematic. In households like Zmarai's, comprising around eighty members (his father, two "mothers," sisters, brothers, sisters-in-law, and upwards of fifty children), grandparents care for migrants' children. Parents are charged with enforcing strict authority. Grandparents, according to the Pakhto proverb, may freely lavish love: "The child is the tree, the fruit is loved more" *(Zoyee ya loor wana da, mlasey daiwanai mewa da)*. Children with absent fathers are especially loved for the sacri-

fices they endure. The transnational, intergenerational familial relationships generated through migration are thus compelled by the obligation
of exchange while allowing remitting subjects some autonomy and freedom from the father's control.

Nonetheless, "one flower doesn't make spring" *(pe youw gul na passar-
lai keygi)*. Despite the considerable sum the brothers remitted, the result
of five years hard labor, for Zmarai feelings of depression began super-
seding those of triumph and success. His reluctance or inability to reconcile himself to what appeared a life of self-sacrifice and unrewarded labor
became reflected in a creeping inaction or immobility. This downward
shift in momentum contrasted with other former Afghan refugees, who
he enviously complained were "fast" moving up and becoming exemplars
of capitalist success. Zmarai acquired his taxi license in 2008, but for
months he had not sent money, nor visited his family for two years. He
remained ambivalent: "I don't understand. I'm not good. Nobody understands. *Molr de wugee le zre tse khabar da* [A full belly cannot understand
a hungry heart]." The subsequent tightening of financial requirements
for immigration visas additionally led to settling his family in Britain to
assume the prospect of an increasingly fearful and paralyzing ordeal.

When Zmarai addressed his feeling of being "down" or "stuck," he most
frequently referred to feeling *khapa*. He described a sense of hopelessness, worry, frustration, boredom, a desire not to think and an inability
to move or to work, but mostly a feeling of depression. *Khapgan* (noun) is
distinct from *takleef* (hurt, pain), or the Urdu words *pareeshan* (worried),
mas'alah (problem), *ghussa* (anger), or *gham* (sadness), although these
are also used. *Khapgan* typically refers to a short-term illness or distress-
ing episode, but may also be intense and protracted. It connotes internal
feelings of depression, frustration, and self-recrimination, and may be
externalized aggressively in blame, punishment, insults, and hostility.

Sometimes Zmarai also referred to feelings of *dar* (fear) and *warkhata*
(lit. lost door), meaning shock, loss of confidence, panic, feeling *jam*
("jammed," frozen with fear), *khata* (endangered), stuck *(ze nakhwalay
ehsas kaoma),*[5] a sense of falling apart *(ze sargandaan yum)* and of en-
countering a great obstacle *(museebat)*. He talked about *badyaad* (bad
memories), *khapa wacht* (sad times) *(Kala chey khapa wacht rapyachi ze
zowregum,* "When I remember sad times I feel bad"), or simply stated,

Ze naroghyum (I'm ill). *Khapgan* also links to *khapakai*, meaning to feel strangled, or as if one is drowning or choked in one's sleep, literally or by a ghost, as folklore *(peetawee khabarey)* would have it.[6]

Less commonly, *khapakai* means losing one's breath or voice through excessive grief, shock, or talking. *Khapgan* links as well to wider ideas of visible madness *(asabee)*, perhaps psychotic states or outbursts of rage, domestic fighting *(janjal)*, jealous rage *(keenäka)*, or to ways that "over-thinking" can lead to a sense of affliction *(badmarghee)*,[7] *iqrār* (unsolicited confessions), *yaozai* (feeling alone), *zharrānd* (weeping), as well as feelings of paranoia *(andikhman)*. This is paranoia arising from the hostile environment that unseats the migrant's progress, and creates a sense of not belonging, of being unreal, out of and not quite himself—an estrangement he attributes to foreign forces conspiring to keep him homeless and alien to himself. It also links to literary ideas denoting craziness *(lewanai)*, used to describe someone who is dirty, unkempt, and living outside normal social convention—*lewanai* comprising here another mode of border control and limited condition of acceptable social and cultural behavior.

Khapgan may also suggest subclinical and psychiatric symptoms and provoke an interiorized focus on immobility's historical, non-geographical, or spatial components. Zmarai's "panic," withdrawal, his sense of "not feeling anything," hopelessness, insomnia, and somatization (headaches, backache, "cold blood," "painful hands") may be consonant with long-term anxiety, panic, and avoidance symptoms of PTSD, and relevant to the nexus of culture and psychiatry in the Afghan migrant context. In a field of manifold mobilities, *khapgan* and immobility also assume particular meanings in Zmarai's efforts to stop or re-pace his everyday communications, obligations and relationships. Foremost is his priority to hide his struggles and feelings in public. Among migrant taxi-drivers, mental illness *(asabee maraz)* implies a negative condition, a highly stigmatized imputed weakness of the mind, an attitude illustrated in the proverb *Le lewanai me wara aw me warkaw* (Neither give nor ask anything of a crazy person). Old people may acceptably become physically or mentally weak, but men of working age have no leeway. Taxi-drivers rarely spoke about such problems except to close friends.[8]

By contrast, in some community workshops I gave on mental health to Afghan women where anonymity was guaranteed, women spoke openly about many somatic and unexplained symptoms (back pain, leg pain, migraines),[9] symptoms that were partly a proxy for marital ills, and which reflected their isolation, loneliness, and bearing the brunt of pressures facing men, particularly in domestic violence (see Qureshi 2016). Grima (1992, 38) also identifies physiological aspects to Pashtun women's sadness, depression, worry, anger, and harshness. Her focus, unlike mine, is the ritual performance of *gham* (sadness) at family bereavements or separations. As the carriers for sorrow, women's emotion is variously and ambivalently linked in her study of Pashtunwali, and the segregation of social and emotional life into well-defined spheres of gendered action through the dominant dichotomy of honor and shame. The priority given to correct behavior deemphasizes personal expression. "Thinking" augurs troubles, shame, and depression (35). Thinking outside prescribed modalities may also risk the personal becoming undefinable, a point that Zmarai reiterated: "Pashtun men have a *lot* of feeling, but they must *kill* it in themselves. People tell shameful stories to get asylum, but *hardly* talk among themselves. Our culture is not strong on feelings. A friend will travel one hundred miles to help you if your car has broken down, but he will never say what is in his heart. Men control, especially. Even if they do talk, they have *no idea* what to say. An Afghan is harder than a rock and softer than a flower [*Insān le teegay klak da aw le gul na nazakda*]."

Zmarai had insights into his condition, but by repeatedly stating "I don't know" he presented his inability to understand his feelings as culturally normative, not a personal refusal or limitation, and thereby charged me with making the risky interpretations that might implicate his family, for whom he only admitted highly idealized feelings. I originally viewed his inaction in terms of a need to recuperate following his risky overland journey to the UK in 1997, forced flight from Kabul to Pakistan, unwanted marriage, protracted asylum case, years working long shifts for unattainable goals, and experiences of racism. Although I tried to cheer him, to be a *ghamkhwar* (eater of sadness), he was intractable. I also wondered if "stuckedness" could be a space for mitigating the strain of his relentless obligations, the weight of the past, the work of "integration." He dreamt often of "freedom"—not to pursue an independent life, but of being "far from the world" and his heavy responsibilities, and of distant green settings. In his habit of recklessly driving long distances without sleep he visited friends across the country, but also played with a stronger desire to escape and tempt a tantalizingly more permanent freedom.

That day we watched the film I asked him afterward, "Why do you hardly call your parents, wife, children?"

"I like them," he insisted, "but the conversation is always about money. I'll call when I have money."

"And if you never have money?" I continued. "Your parents are old. When they die you'll feel guilty you hardly called. The same when your children are grown."

"I know," Zmarai agreed, before falling silent.

After some minutes, he interjected, "I feel to suicide. Very much. Don't be surprised if you hear one day I did suicide."

"But I wouldn't be surprised," I replied in frustration. "Your life looks impossible."

Immobility and the Past

Autobiographical memory is arguably a means to sense the less tangible location of the diasporic subject—for example, in experiences of "the political unreality of one's present home" juxtaposed against "the ontological unreality of one's place of origin" (Agnew 2005, 13). This juxtaposition intimates the way the force of past events characterizes a historical problematic that is not fully grasped in experiences of exile, but which permeates continuity into the future, in ambivalences and tensions between holding on and moving forward. For Zmarai, they are etched into a sense of something contradictory and chaotic, undone, and *not yet* reconstituted. They intimate a sense of internal disheveling and melancholic tension (Freud [1917] 2005) that cannot be resolved because cultural mores prohibit voicing complaints, especially for men, and therefore working through hurts and blame in the family.

Although Zmarai did not seek any psychological therapy, in Afghanistan Omidian and Lawrence (2007) counter this Western-centric emphasis on disclosure, talking, voicing, and working through, by doing therapeutic work imaginatively figuring traumatic memories as guests to whom some hospitality is due—albeit unwanted guests. Mourning for Zmarai also implicates feelings of unassuaged guilt—at abandoning the destroyed country ("we didn't stop it; it happened in our generation"), being complicit in the family's downfall, and taking one's "chance" to make a future away from them and one's children. Additionally, war levies such enormous ruptures that there is security in observing rules and protocols that hurt. Finally, hegemonic discourses of required progress, and norms of tough masculinity silence the migrant's struggles and disappointments.

Turning next to intersections of personal, national, and family history, Zmarai's life story suggests several areas through which to interpret immobility. The first area comprises his recollections of an idyllic childhood, and a time before life became subjected to the losses of too much movement. The idyll permeates the present with a sense of strangeness and impending war:

I grew up in Kart-e-Naw, the last bus-stop from Kabul center. Kids had free tickets. When I was young, I'd take the bus with my brothers into Pul-e-Bagh-e-Umumi by the river. Vendors pushed *karachey* [wooden carts] selling vegetables, or clothes; the food outlets played Hindi music. For school we wore pants, the rule was any color! We bought them from the vendors there, and thick sweaters for the winter. We spent summers in Kabul, winters in Jalalabad. Life was difficult, we drew water from the well, firewood was scarce. We cooked on a *bukharai* [wood burner]. Tea was always cooking. My mama cooked *samanak* [germinated wheat], a food for happiness, my favorite dish. She prepared it in a storeroom in the outside courtyard during winter, a kind of religious food, only she tended it. When it was ready, the family women would cook, stirring a stick in a big pot over a blazing fire. They played the *daira* [frame drum] and sang, *Samanak dar jhosh, maa kaf meyzanim, dukhtara shishta, daira meyzana* [Samanak is cooking, we are clapping, girls are sitting, playing *daira*]. Sweet, beautiful food!

This early memory of food is also one of warmth, security, and maternal love from a time spent mostly among women. The song, sung in Dari, additionally recalls a time when Kabul-based Pakhtuns, like Zmarai's family, unreservedly participated in Persianate traditions:

My father was so smart. I remember one photograph: he was on a motorbike, smiling, wearing *salwār–kameez* dress, a *karakuli* [lambswool hat], and an expensive jacket. When I was small his business grew, he bought a water pump and expensive cars, we were rich. He traveled north, near Uzbekistan. Occasionally he'd take me. I have one strong memory from when I was around four. My father took me to a big *buzkashi* match [lit. "goat grabbing," played on horseback at full gallop] at Ghazi Stadium. They played with a *khussakai* [baby calf], it was very exciting. Then something strange happened. One player was jostling, chasing the calf; he fell, crushed under his horse, and died. People ran from everywhere. I was distraught. He was a good player; it was unfair, such bad luck. My father comforted me for a long time. He insisted the man was injured, not dead. I didn't believe him.

The symbolism in the memory forewarns of ruptures, witnessing killings and deaths, and it reveals impressions, mysterious fears, and covered-up truths, which augur later memories of bombing, defeat, the Soviet occupation, civil war, and flight to Pakistan. In 1979 war came. Rumors circulated of slaughter, flight, and the invading Communist armies and their allies who would destroy Islam, Afghan culture, remove women's hijabs, make sex easy—fears that abounded in mosques and which fathers relayed to fretting women. Zmarai was very young when the Russians bombed Kabul. The situation felt terrifying and hopeless.

People's fears were nonetheless partly allayed when the occupying Russians built schools with big classrooms and expansive sports grounds, though they were little trusted. Soviet officials *(peshakakhangan)* took every child's shoe size, promising rubber shoes *(galoshey)*. They gave awards *(bourse)* to the brightest boys, as future government recruits. Zmarai enjoyed school. Later, boys would throw *nakhud* (dried chickpeas) and *simiyan* (fried snacks) at the girls. Or they bet on football matches. Sometimes their teacher joined, using his winnings from his richer pupils to buy cigarettes.

At thirteen Zmarai joined a wrestling club near Kabul Nandari theater. In the mornings he would leave home before first prayer *(da sahar munz)* and run with friends to the ground where they would lift rocks to improve their strength, race home, then drink milky chai. After school, he'd train again, then run home, in winter sometimes hanging onto a minibus to skate on the icy roads. He was the club's champion and won many competitions. This happy interlude ended with the demise of Najibullah's government in 1992, when Kabul became terrorized by *kodata* (factional fighting).[10] As Zmarai shared with me, "One evening General Dostum's soldiers, the notorious *gilam jam* who would shoot a man for one hundred *kaldars,* arrived at the club, drunk. One tried lifting a weight, unsuccessfully. Gesturing toward me, my trainer shouted, 'Even this *child* can lift it.' I was stupid, I lifted it. The shamed soldier aimed his gun, shouting 'If I move, you'll die'; My trainer shut the club. Kabul became so dangerous; fighters killed for fun, or raped girls. I saw people killed. It was terrifying. We left. Everything. And fled to Peshawar."

His new life in Pakistan was interrupted by a forced marriage and then a second refugee migration. Migration to Britain served to legitimately create distance and generate new possibilities that released him from everyday obligations to his wife and children (whom he considered his father's choice and, therefore, responsibility). Immobility here also suggests a silent punishment or protest against the tyranny of the family in his private life, and mourning for the life he might have chosen. He shed tears as he says, "What's wrong? I must be tired":

In Pakistan we were refugees. We rented an empty house. The wrestling club was too far, I couldn't go. At school I wore the best Afghan styles. I was sporty, handsome, from a good family. My parents received several marriage proposals. I refused all. They eventually agreed to an exchange marriage[11] with my uncle. My sister would marry his son, I his daughter. They *knew* I didn't want it, but everyone was celebrating, I had to agree. I had no choice. They *killed* me. I became quiet, I cried for weeks. It was too late, I couldn't shame the family, they'd hurt me deeply. I was young, I wanted to live my life. I met her beforehand, in my house. First she covered her face with her scarf. I told her I didn't love her; she, too, had no choice. The second time she offered me dried fruit from her pocket. On my wedding night she waited hours in the room. After three months she was pregnant. I requested of my father, "I got married for you, now let me leave." He agreed. I joined my cousin in Moscow. For nine months I worked in a small kiosk.

I had no idea about England, but my cousin insisted it was good for my future. We would work, make money, a new life. The journey was terrifying. It took weeks. We arrived from Belgium by lorry, exhausted. We cut the awning with a knife. The driver was shocked to see us. He threw us out. We went to London. That was during the Taliban time. Whatever your story they accepted you. Sometimes people invented stories because the truth was too shameful or painful. We became asylum seekers. They gave us food vouchers, we sold them for less. People hated us. I was a refugee again.

Immobility in the Present

Nonetheless, after every darkness there is light *(harey tiara passey ranā da)*. In linking immobility to suffering, immobility elides various organizations of hope. Hope is interesting insofar as it describes, with positive connotations, a state of fantasy or unreality, sometimes a totally unrealizable condition of clinging to, and coping with, the impossible (i.e., the immoveable)—perhaps a "technology of patience" that can suspend questions about the cruel present (Berlant 2011, 28). Zmarai used this proverb to critique any feeling of hope: *Dunya pe omaed khwaralay say* (The world has been eaten with hope). By bearing a full immersion into the senselessness of pain, immobility may also allow threatening, inchoate feelings that have never before been fully felt, symbolized, or integrated into self-organization so that richer forms of experience may emerge (Mitchell 1993, 227–28).

Adding to these perspectives a psychoanalytic view, when varied losses of hope are extreme and combine with the violent losses of home and homeland, migration may fuse with hope in borderline pathology. In a Freudian economy of traumatic suffering, Potamianou (1997) argues that hope circumvents grief. A perverse economy that sustains suffering and masochism, hope structures a "binding cathexis." It is a stubborn means of denying reality and fear of change that preserves the link with what one has lost, effectively paralyzing other functions. Hope "guarantees lack of change, lack of mourning and the least expenditure of energy," weaving into the fabric of so-called normal organizations, uncharacterized by any specific clinical configuration (3–4). Zmarai's immobility may herein elide "normal" and pathological organizations in a critique of the promises of progress and liberty wherein life has become an activity of attrition.[12] Butler (1997, 196) emphasizes the aggressive aspects of loss and the mourner's dilemma in Freudian terms of simultaneously seeking to hold on to, and also violently eliminate, all traces of the lost object. While mourning can never be complete, and survival following loss will involve the aggressive tendencies of a perpetual mourning, the process of internalizing and incorporating the terrorizing power of one's loss is one way either to dissipate its power (196), or else to become mired in an endless timeless condition of unresolved grief. Butler's reflections suggest that "becoming the patriarch" might offer one way for Zmarai to reconcile his rage and ambivalence in new possibilities of (violent) attachment to his family—and thereby "move forward."

By not calling them or keeping contact he punitively inflicted on them his own experience of despair. He floated the plan to boycott remittances and buy his own taxi. Neither taxi nor boycott materialized. Rather than working through grief, he refused to expose himself further to hope's unbearable losses. This was a boycott of hope. He would send money or bring them later. For now he slept, played football, and wrestled with an inexorable depression. "It's everything," he despaired, "not just business. There's no solution. 'Same mullah, same Ramadan prayer every year' [*Zoor mullah aw zare tarāwee*]."

Immobility and Sleep

As a transport into another form of consciousness, sleep *(weeda)* appears an obvious form of immobility. It is a threshold and a door between waking and sleep, life and death, this world and the other than happens on the limit of the mode of presence (Pandolfo 1997, 180). Sleep and desires for sleep provide a window onto different rhythms of survival between consciousness and unconsciousness, onto the materiality of what *is* and what is not, the merging of reality and imagination. In Sussex, where Zmarai lived with two of his fourteen brothers in a cramped apartment, sleep bedeviled, tempted, and transported three men away from the borders of wakefulness into hours and hours of sleep. The contagion of prolonged sleep did not originate with any one brother, but nonetheless permeated the entire home, drawing each away from consciousness to create a shared space of not-yet waking, not-yet living, but of waiting or resting, as if to be still after the trials of a long journey.

Zmarai's inability to work combined with his refusal to give up his taxi, which would represent a defeat of hope and a public sign of failure, meant that his younger brother frequently assumed the heavy burden of paying two weekly taxi rents.

Picking me as a customer one evening, his younger brother confided, "People say I'm always joking, but *understand* I'm also not happy. You can *see* my situation. *Ze bey omeed yum* [I'm hopeless]. *Ma omeed le las wakarai* [Hope is lost from my hand]."

Their elder brother worked as a delivery driver, but only intermittently. He lived on welfare benefits and handouts from the other two. A proud veteran *mujahid* for Hekmatyar and a father of eight children living in Peshawar, his poor English meant he worked little. After two years of not seeing him, I met him drinking tea outside a cafe. Stick thin and chain-smoking, he had argued with his boss over whether he should pack a food delivery in one box or two, and walked out. He was depressed; he might go to Pakistan, he mused. All he did here was watch Pashto films. Zmarai feared from the specter of his body, skin, face, and cracked voice that he might die. Whenever he returned home late at night he opened his bedroom door to check that he was still alive.

"I'm afraid," he said. "I've lost my trust he will stay alive."

And so three brothers found solace in sleep. Sleep accomplished its work to postpone awakening, administer deliverance from reality, and also became the matter of reality, and of the work of staying alive: *Lewanai pe khpl kar khe poheegi* (A crazy person understands his own work). Sleep reversed the usual norms and time clock of shared living. Now waking had become a narcosis, the interior world the exterior, and sleep itself an "intermediate carriage" and an immobile preservation of three brothers at the limits of living.

Dreams in the Sleep of Life

Zmarai's days spent in insomnia or thick sleep beg the question of what revelations sleep might offer about immobility. In a Bergsonian view of immobility as relational is the paradox that sleep is a relatively immobile state, but the dreams of sleep a means of boundless traveling—a "journey of the soul" (Kracke 2003, 214), a bodily experience of increased mobility, transportation, and possibility, or perhaps a "profound country" of mobile and immobile intensities (Deleuze and Guattari 2004).[13] For Lohmann (2003, 1), sleep is a "doorway, and dreams are roads and destinations." In Greek mythology the relation of sleep to the final immobility of death is represented by the siblings Hypnos and Thanatos. Edward Burnett Tylor ([1871] 1877, 1:203) likewise links sleep and death in his question "What then, is this soul or life which . . . goes and comes in sleep, trance and death?"[14]

Dream interpretation assumes a significant role in Islam, constituting a documented part of the Prophet's life and teachings. Istikhara is the Islamic ritual of interpreting night dreams for guidance, particularly the universality of night dreams as a potential portal to the divine (Edgar 2011). Edgar has analyzed militants' dream accounts, including those of Mullah Omar, the former Afghan Taliban leader, who claimed to receive strategic operational guidance for battle in his dreams. Dream interpretations in Islam may be attributed to a higher order of truth or divine inspiration (Qureshi 2010). In East London, Qureshi (283) identifies recurrent motifs in Pakistan Muslims' interpretations of their dreams as mystical or supernatural encounters, or divine revelations of imminent misfortune—which largely map onto Islamic dreaming cosmologies.[15] Dreams, she argues, forge connectedness between scattered family members, affirming ideas of moral selfhood and obligation, and they allow dreamers to cope with misfortune in a normative context of communicating about ill health and bad news.

Within the domestic context of family communication, three generations of Pashtun women in Sussex I met with concurred with Islamic cosmology that dreams may be *rahmani* (good, or prophetic, from God); *shaitani* (from jinns or the devil; nightmares, bad dreams); or *nafsani* (about everyday thoughts, life, or individual problems or desires). Notwithstanding, Islamic orthodoxy about dreams downplays these contrasts, holding that most dreams come from the *nafs* and that true dreams from God are characterized by particular imagery. Sharing their thoughts, the women advanced folk beliefs that images of singing and dancing in dreams are signs of sadness, imminent conflict, or misfortune; they advised me to distrust early morning dreams whose meanings are untrue in the divine sense, but reflect daytime "interference." In their family, children (including adult children) regularly share dreams with their mothers, women with women, spouses with each other. Their familial dream-sharing connotes intimacy, care, and a mode of religious–instructional and emotional support.

And so not all dreams by Muslims are accorded Islamic interpretations; nor are all Muslims religious, know a great deal about Islam, or indeed are interested to. In Syria, Borneman (2011, 238) reveals wholly impious content in Muslim men's daytime reveries—for example, imaginings of sex, domination, and humiliation. In Morocco, Crapanzano (1975, 145) analyzes the performative function of dream symbols in the resolution of personal conflict. In Pakistan, Ewing (1994, 571) uses the pious dreams of a saint to criticize the "anthropological atheism," which produces the "embarrassing possibility of belief," and calls on anthropologists to also include their own dreams from the field. Importantly, Hollan (2003) emphasizes the element of intersubjectivity in the unintentional stimuli anthropologists provide to dream reporters.

Dream states and sleep here comprise another theoretical and methodological tool for understanding migrant subjectivity and storytelling in the gap *between* verbal and nonverbal practices, immobile and mobile states. They are personal, but also spaces where life can be accessed in impersonal form (Foucault 1985). Certainly Zmarai offered no conventional or Islamic interpretations in those dreams he shared with me. Rather, he actively sought interpretations that might help him shift his suffering through *new* insights (see DelVecchio Good et al. 1994). The particularities of our research relationship, located outside the norms of his everyday life, thus determined those dreams he shared.

Dreams have otherwise been analyzed influentially in Freud's *Interpretation of Dreams* ([1953] 1975). For Freud dreams also represented a prophetic, if not divine, event—a space of the soul beyond individual singularity, where small incidentals connect to larger points about history, time, and the political. Very simplified, Freud's dream theory is one of wish fulfillment. All dreams have some relation to desires in waking life. Once interpreted they can be validated as the "fulfillment of wishes; they can be inserted into the chain of intelligible waking mental acts; they are constructed by a highly complicated activity of the mind" (200–201). These wishes may be unconscious, distorted, related to memories, and take puzzling form. Freud also thought dreams could be a form of thought communication, or telepathy.

Freud significantly influenced anthropologists' investigations of dreams.[16] These have encompassed the nexus of anthropology, psychology, ethnopsychiatry, and psychoanalysis. While Rivers's (1923) work in Britain and Melanesia took issue with the universality of Freud's theory of wish fulfillment, Tedlock (1987) argues that analyses of dream narration should ideally combine narrative creation, psychodynamic narration, and cultural interpretation. Tylor ([1871] 1877) examined dreaming as a gateway to seeing the dead living, evidence that spirits exist, and blurred distinctions between reality and illusion. In short, anthropologists have shifted, challenged, rejected, and also applied Freudian interpretations. Addressing some common criticisms of Freud, Kracke (2003) emphasizes that Freud was not as asocial as some imply, but significantly influenced by folk culture and myths as forms of knowledge.

"Dreams are never one's own," writes Pandolfo (1997, 173). Sent from regions of death and beyond, or a limbo out of which dreams flow, they are Aristotelian "alien movements" of "delayed energetic impacts, timing devices, affecting the person from without, from a without that is also a within, and producing hallucinatory visual effects," which implicate a delayed "temporal scansion of the real, and of the uncanny marriage of contingency and return" (173).

Stories shared in the space between residuary movements and sense impressions, recollecting and forgetting, dreaming and wakefulness, and the temporal ebbs and flows of memory offer a way for ethnography to become more attuned to the unexpected. Dream-sharing allows us to enter the intersubjectivity of new worlds and time zones where words are unmoored from certainty, reversed, or overturned because they cannot easily be assimilated or expressed. Borneman (2011) takes the clinical psychoanalytic concepts of reverie, transference, countertransference, the intersubjective third, and containment to analyze three episodes of daydreaming and reverie by young men in Syria.[17] He prioritizes the intersubjectivity created in open-ended fieldwork interactions, and the analytic importance of daydreaming as a mode for disclosing knowledge and creating new communicative possibilities (235). He views dream-sharing as an intermediate, intersubjective fieldwork space where knowledge and truth can be encountered and explored. The dynamics of sharing daytime fantasies and daydreaming, unlike joint narratives or dialogues, create a "third" subjectivity that can "meander across domains"; transgress normative boundaries of masculinity, nationality, and kinship; and produce better understandings of the interlocutor's wishes and anxieties (253). Correspondingly, it's possible that I likewise represented for Zmarai a countertransferential investment in the transgressability of gender, cultural, and social boundaries, which encouraged him to unconsciously symbolize these wishes in those *nafsani*-type dreams into which he invited me.

Below I present five dreams he shared. These move us into verbalized narratives, a more intersubjective condition and a joint enterprise that pointed to the possibility of understanding, but also the condition of never entirely comprehending another's pain—as perhaps the person who lives it cannot either. They also represent aspects of private, unconventional, or shameful experience that, in telling me for this research, he wanted acknowledged. Last, they contrast profound experiences of immobility in everyday life with fast-moving, chaotic, and disorienting movement experienced in dreams.

Five Dreams of One Interlocutor

On Seeing an Illusion of the King

This dream was recounted in 2011, as part of one of Zmarai's life-history accounts I recorded:

> I have a strong memory of a dream I had when I was very young.
> Winter was approaching. It was not yet snowing, but local people
> had locked up their houses and already left for Jalalabad. There
> was a house nearby, huge, empty, maybe ghosts lived there, it
> had an enormous lock. Our doors are big, old and wooden. I
> pushed, but it wouldn't open. I noticed a small hole in the door,
> big enough to peep through. I was astonished to see someone
> standing there, a beautiful man. He was dressed all in red with a
> gold crown, king's clothes, historic clothes, ready for battle, very
> tall, slim, white and handsome. I *wanted* to meet him so much,

but I couldn't reach him. My family told me it was a dream, it was impossible I had seen him. Maybe it was a jinn showing me something; you know how they come and then disappear. I *swear* I saw him.

The symbolism of the dream intimates a sense of approaching winter (imminent war, migration, flight, transition), the vast empty house (insecurity, flight), the door (to "other" worlds, another self, another time), the enormous lock (hindrances to happiness, to stability, his distant father; being denied opportunities; shut out, looking in; the end of a phase, of childhood innocence); the king (the absent father's honor and prestige; his own desires for honor and prestige), receiving messages from the spirit world (the jinn). The memory forewarns of war, and reveals mysterious realities, undercurrents, half-truths, adult concealment, being excluded from realities, and of personal truths not taken seriously. Recounted years later it was prophetic insofar as his burning desire to meet, or to be, the king was destroyed (became unreachable) by the trials of war—or perhaps, he mused, just by life.

The dream is also a representation of Zmarai's lifelong preoccupations with status and its loss (his own and his family's). It occurred in the lead-up to the Soviet invasion of 1979, a few years after the last king of Afghanistan Zahir Shah was deposed. The king's red robes may thus symbolize the death (blood) of the monarchy. The color red in the national flag also signifies in national consciousness the blood spilled in Afghanistan's quest for independence, especially during the Anglo-Afghan wars. Insofar as Zmarai's "kingdom" and sanity were also threatened by witnessing the excesses of bloodshed, red also signifies a personal history as well as a family history of patriarchy. Zmarai's father had acquired sufficient wealth and status to establish his own *khel,* or patrilineal segment. He chose for this new descent line a name featuring the color red *(lal).* Thus, red also signified the beginning of new symbolic "monarchy," Zmarai's confusing new obligations as a son to sustain it, and the possibility he might in the distant future establish his own kingdom, too. Becoming a king was thus a suitable and worthy aspiration. Hence, the toy crown he displayed on the dashboard of his taxi also represented a bitter irony or joke in the context of his present circumstances.[18]

On Striving to Reach the End of the Journey
(or Wishing to Stay in the Dream)

When migrant realities are unmoored from the certainty of home, and impel migrants into forced movement and uncomfortable levels of speed, what can we make of dreams that reflect the nightmarish inability to stop moving? Zmarai recounted this dream (paraphrased) late one night when we had stopped for coffee at a service station on the road back to Sussex after a *chakar* to London:

> I had a recurring dream whose unfolding I follow like a familiar visitor. It is night. The bus is crowded, late. It sweeps along the perimeter road around the immense city to the shiny imposing new quarter. My destination is home, but first I must reach the train station that will take me to the airport. The bus is overcrowded, old, circuitous; I dismount with the aim to arrive faster, anxious I will miss the plane. The new city is beautiful in the semi-light with its huge glass windows, historic buildings, wide boulevards. I cut through, purposeful as a blade.
>
> I believe this is Europe. I am certain of my way, until I turn through the empty library concourse, which has transformed into a parade of ornate boutiques. Slowing my progress, the buildings pull me into a corridor of gold carvings, strange immense reception halls.
>
> When I cross through, the landscape sharply changes, curving into the city's oldest quarter. I recognize the streets, the old black bridge. Now this might be Moscow, or Pakistan. I urgently push ahead searching for the old man who will help me. Stepping past wordless people, I climb tiny stone staircases that wind around interconnected buildings housing tiny one-room homes.
>
> No one speaks my language, no one helps. I see the train station in the distance. I desperately hurry to catch the train to catch my flight. So many people waiting, I can barely breathe. All push past the ticket barrier toward the ancient brick staircase descending underground. Tiny labyrinthine offshoots funnel the packed crowds to their platforms. I descend far underground, into the bowels of my voyage. I eventually find the airport train.
>
> At the airport they are calling my name; last call. I rush

through immigration but my visa is invalid. In desperation I
run onto the runway. I am on the plane. The seats are positioned
around the interior like a bus. I feel strange, I don't know where I
am going.

The dream is superficially about being overtaken, frustrated speed,
obstacles to progress (the bus to the train to the airport), the strangeness of lost direction which is part of the migrant condition—following
Benjamin (1999), for whom train stations are dream houses of the collective ("I don't know where I'm going")—new reception halls (processing
centers, political hospitalities), a maelstrom of disorientation and frustration ("I desperately hurry") perhaps related to the journey through
many countries to claim asylum, a feeling of exile and alienation or
the migrant's rush to get ahead, feeling abandoned by the father (the
old man cannot help), positioned as the outsider (by people speaking
a different language). Zmarai is propelled on a journey (through hidden, "underground" fears in his mind and imagination) whose end is
desperately elusive. He rushes to escape through the familiarity of the
city's old quarter (the past), encounters the strangeness of the empty
library (the pointlessness of education, perhaps my project specifically), and registers in passing it the shiny upmarket center (the desired
future).

For Freud ([1953] 1975, 215) strong emotions, including distress or
anxiety, may be fulfillments of wishes in special intensity.[19] Correspondingly, the intense anxieties about not arriving in time that dominate this
dream suggest Zmarai's wish may be to not arrive but rather to *stay* in
the dream—and thereby to exit the fast-paced, disorienting temporality of the progress project, and enter a temporality of something else.
The dream augurs a dispossession of the present where possibilities of
an alternative future might emerge, but *if only* he repeatedly misses his
destination. Thus things speed up, as if running on a wheel, in order for
nothing to move. The dream takes on all the disorientation of forced mobility and transformations, and "condenses," in Freud's terms,[20] manifold
historical implications of wandering around alleys and dead-ends into a
nightmare, a point of no arrival, and a rich symbolic mine of refusal that
masks itself as disorientation. These elements also elide in his waking
problem of immobility.

On Fears of Failure and Humiliation
Allayed by the Next Generation

I see a dream. I am walking through a field, the scenery is pastoral, I am enjoying the view of the grazing sheep, the grassy path and fresh earth as I walk along, with the smell of wind in my face. This could be the Sussex countryside. But as I move along my journey, the mood shifts abruptly and I become drawn against my will into a deep, dark tunnel, which descends underground, dank and wet.

My surroundings are now transformed into the city crowds of Kabul, I am overcome with terrifying fear. Approaching me in the tunnel are a group of men, frightening, with knives. I am struck by the realization they will rape me. I feel rooted but I am moving forward against my will, unable to turn back. Then, mercifully, as by some divine deliverance, as if from nowhere, my nephew appeared and led me up to daylight and safety. I suddenly wake up.

In a Freudian interpretation, the down below relates to genitals (Freud [1953] 1975, 390–94)—the tunnel here signifying a rape. Freud sees characterization as key to the way experience in dreams assumes the hue of a dramatization (114). Although not all details may be remembered, the experience may be deeply disturbing. Here it takes the nightmarish form of the desire that "I do not wish to be humiliated by the community of men, the taxi-drivers, my tribe, my family. I wish the younger generation to save me."

This dream ruptures the idyllic pastoral scene with a lethal and vitalizing confrontation with terror and reality. If dream space is interior to sleeping bodies, it draws its vital energy from reality; therefore excessive to the space of the body, it may become more real than waking (Pandolfo 2016).

This dream of Zmarai's occurred in 2016 during the week his elder brother's son had arrived in the Jungle Camp[21] at Calais. In the urgency surrounding the camp's closure in autumn 2016, he was among those unaccompanied child migrants transferred to join relatives in Britain (through another underground tunnel, the English Channel). His father, the elder brother Zmarai lived with, had borrowed more money to pay for his passage from Peshawar than he could hope to repay in a lifetime. Zmarai's dream also expresses desires that his own sons will save him, and intimates the impending crisis if they cannot. It refers to the normative expectation that when sons become men they will assume economic responsibility for the family, a "natural" life-course progression that will eventually allow a father relief and the opportunity to "return" to care within his family.

Relatedly Nushin Arbabzadeh (2013, 74) criticizes the "tyranny" of Afghanistan's conformist society, which requires a man "to father many sons and raise them as obedient foot-soldiers under his command." In pursuing this dream, Zmarai could be ruthless with his own son: "He *must* go to university and study. It's my choice. I told him, 'If you don't, I will smash your bones. Go sell dal on the street.'"[22] His nephew's imminent arrival brought Zmarai's fears and sense of personal failure around his own children into sharp focus, while he also hoped his nephew might acquire a government apartment where they could all live together.

The sexual character of humiliation is unsurprising and, in terms of wish fulfillment, first suggests that perhaps Zmarai wants to be raped, in the sense of being socially destroyed (as a respectable working man) but passively, without culpability. Next, it bears on ways that expressed sexuality among taxi-drivers is strongly heteronormative. Male rape signifies humiliation, and homosexual sex is deemed a humiliation akin to rape for the "submissive" partner. A man who exhibits characteristics not typically hypermasculine is deemed soft, unable to survive in a man's world, and subjected to endless ribbing.

While homosexuality is shameful in Afghanistan, and gay men are vulnerable, homosocial, homoerotic, and homosexual desire outside the identity prism of "gay" sex may nonetheless be culturally endorsed—as with Islamicate sexualities elsewhere (Babayan and Najmabadi 2008). Sex between men and young boys in Afghanistan may be practiced and idealized,[23] and an erotic, sexualized element also characterizes male relationships. Close friends sleep together on one floor, in close contact. They talk crudely about heterosexual sex and exchange compliments such as "Those trousers suit you, your penis looks strong in them." Endorsing physical forms of desirable masculinity, they describe other men in everyday conversation as "beautiful," having "a strong body," or being "very handsome."

An ex-wrestler, Zmarai valued physical prowess highly. He pushed his son in Peshawar to lift weights, train, and send photos of his torso, which he proudly showed me and other friends. These aspects invite a third interpretation concerning reversal: the wish that "if only it had been the other way round!" (Freud [1953] 1975, 440). For Freud, it is remarkable "how frequently reversal is employed precisely in dreams arising from repressed homosexual impulses" (440). Thus it may also be the prospect of Zmarai's homosexual desires, including the wish to be humiliated violently,[24] that causes him to suddenly awake. Or perhaps it is the wish to exchange places with his son and be cared for by a despotic father.

In Afghanistan, sex outside marriage is a crime that may be punishable by imprisonment. All sex leaves a person in an impure state requiring ritual cleansing *(wuzu)*. The taxi-drivers, as "good" Pashtuns and Muslims, publicly endorse all sex outside marriage as immoral. Those whose wives live in Pakistan attribute emotional distance from their partners as manly and honorable,[25] rationalizing their separations, and they idealize intimacy between men, not spouses. Zmarai offered an example from conservative villages where men sleep separately from their wife, for fear of becoming too "womanly." While they joke about the easy virtue of English women, some inevitably fall in love and conduct affairs of varied secrecy. Given these Pashtuns likely marry endogamously, this constituted a fecund if rather self-destructive dead end. Zmarai himself had a painful love affair with a younger English schoolteacher who ended it after she discovered he was married with children. The situation (not uncommon) was mutually painful. He offered to take her as his second wife, in "secret." Unsurprisingly, she refused.

During this period I received a tearful phone call from Zmarai, who had just awoken from sleep, wanting me to interpret his dream, which we discussed. "Put it in your book," he demanded. "Call it *sham aw patang,* it's used a lot in Pashto poetry." *Sham aw patang,* indeed used in poetry and also in music, denotes the candle and moth; *sham* is the candle, symbolizing love's fatal attraction to the moth. The virtue in being burned in the fires of passion is not a uniquely Pashtun motif, but pan-Islamic with Sufistic connotations (Doubleday 2015).

Sham aw Patang: The Transient Transports of Love

> I dreamt about her. There was a volleyball match, the location was unclear. It looked like a ground in Afghanistan, but it was here.

Some students were playing volleyball, she was in charge of the game. She was wearing a long black dress, looking *so* incredibly beautiful, sitting on the side. I was moving past in a pickup truck, sitting in the back—like people travel in Pakistan. We drove faster to catch up with her. I was *chasing* her. I shouted, in front of everyone, *Patang!* She turned toward me; I recognized her face. I was wearing beautiful Afghan clothes in gorgeous colors and a beautiful *patoo* shawl, I showed off to her. I shouted, she saw me, she loved my clothes, I was beautiful, too. She called back, *Sham!* Everybody turned to see us. She took the ball and very playfully threw it toward me, *so* fast it flew toward me. I caught it, laughing, we were both laughing, we played with the ball together, incredibly happy with our game, we forgot about time. But then the ball turned into a balloon in my hands and it flew away, the air came out. I panicked, I caught it, but couldn't get any air in.

She walked back toward the ground, the game was over, no longer with me. I entered a room at the side, a beautiful, light, clean room where I found a man.

I said, "I have *Patang's* balloon." He said, happily, "*Patang*, I know her!" I asked him, "Is she with another man?" He replied, "No, she's sad, all alone." Her balloon had no air, we couldn't play again, although I kept it with me. The dream finished, I woke up.

The symbolism of *sham's* dream is poignant—the speeding "pickup" truck (mobility, migration, the lorry that carried him to England, the speed with which he was swept off his feet), the students' volleyball game (her workplace, the school), the balloon (the game of love), the fast ball (love that caught him by surprise), love (happiness, pleasure, timelessness, escape), narcissism (I was beautiful), the sunny room (love occupies the peripheries, separate from "real" life), the sexual symbolism of the deflated balloon (their sexual relationship could not keep her with him), his keeping her dead balloon (nobody else can have her), the game being over.

I provoked him, asking "So, you're the candle, she's the moth—she chases you and burns in the flame, and you live?"

He answered, "She thinks her future will be destroyed with me because I have a wife. It's true. Other times, I think I'll be okay. But truthfully we're in love; neither can have the other. I feel sad for her, myself, my wife, my children. This is my first experience of love. What life do I have? Deep love is dangerous." Others travel far for love, literally. One day I was chatting with Wafi where he worked washing cars in a multistory carpark. Addicted to heroin since he left Afghanistan, he had intermittently stopped but was now taking heroin again. He planned to rob the cash box from his boss and escape to Amsterdam, where he had citizenship. Afterward, to lighten the mood, he told me this tale.

Before coming to Europe, one icy freezing winter, Wafi drove northward from Kabul with a friend through the treacherous, snow-covered countryside to meet a girl he had met online and been chatting with by mobile phone. The car became stuck in a blizzard; they took hours to free it. Eventually they reached her village outside Mazar-e-Sharif.

He phoned her, she ran through the snow toward the car, afraid her family would query her absence, her scarf pulled tightly over her face. "I've driven three days through the snow for you," he exaggerated. "Now show me your face".

She undid her scarf, showed her face for one minute, then apologized and ran back to her house. He laughed at the absurdity of it—and I also sensed, the fruitlessness of other long and difficult journeys (to Europe) he had taken likewise for scant gratification.

Superficially romantic, sexual, or sexually charged liaisons may break down the disconnect between imagination and the real (Borneman 2011). Here they highlight Wafi's desires for love and intimacy but which, distanced from his family, children, and local Afghans by geography and his heroin addiction, he sorely lacked. Leading me to also reflect on forms of distance in my relationship with Zmarai,[26] I mused that meeting and driving in his taxi afforded a contained form of privacy and intimacy—where we could speak freely, and where any erotic transferences on my part as researcher or on his part (Borneman 2011, 241) were put to rest by his sexualized talk of young women, which reassured me, as ten years Zmarai's elder, that we were friends.

The Sadness of a Dying Breast

"I had a dream of a young woman's breast. Her breast was so beautiful and white. The thought it would die and turn to nothing was so unbearably sad. I felt like crying. It was so sad. I had a strong thought it would be better for it to turn old and ugly and die now, rather than be buried in such beauty in the earth where the insects would eat it." While the breast may refer to Zmarai's lost love affair, the dream's mood is not sexual, and the breast appears more a symbol for maternal love and nurturance; white the color of breast milk that mothers eventually withhold from their sons to prepare them for the world of men. Zmarai's fears of the decaying breast imply fears of his mother's death, sorrow about the loss of his own beauty, innocence, and youth; the bodily assaults of age on his soft emotional feminine or maternal side, the enveloping sense of lost dreams.[27] The dream also reflected anxieties about the inexorable movement toward his inevitable, unwanted (self-disgusting) physical deterioration, aging, and social decline. It also intimates his early relationship with his mother, the unacknowledged pain of separation, and his desires to remain at the center of her world. In part it described not so much the "man who would be king" as the arrested development of the would-be king who, traumatized by the world outside, would refuse it, and remain a beloved infant (Freud [1914] 2013).[28]

A Note on Speeding (and Sex, Rage, and Death)

Zmarai's problem of immobility also implicates the paradox that a person may enact self-destructive desires to feel alive: to play with dual desires for life and death, turn aggressive instincts inward in suicidal tendencies and depression, and outward in self-destructive behavior. Where they involve hypersexuality, extreme movement, catatonic states, and excessive sleep, these states may also map the biflected symptomology of mania and depression, of the light and shadow side of life, and the analogy between dreams and madness. They also disrupt assumptions that reduce all migrants to asexual accumulators of capital and senders of remittances, and point to the intimate connection of sexual and economic spheres in Muslim labor migration to Europe, particularly masculinity and male sexual desire in the decision to migrate (Ahmad 2011).

Zmarai told me in 2000, "I am like a snake, I live by different time. In winter I sleep sixteen hours a day, but in summer three hours only, or I stay awake for three days. I'm not like other people, I have two people in me. I cannot control that other person."

Between 2010 and 2017 I charted six such worrying episodes, each lasting several months. During these times he became irritable, angry, incommunicative, more paranoid. He refused to listen—he insisted the news was "lies" and saw double meanings to every action. Speeding up in speech, thinking, and behavior, in addition to exceeding legal driving limits, he reported feeling nothing, sleeping less, buying new clothes, and flirting more with his female customers. Zmarai's sexualized and rageful behavior was accompanied by physical changes. He looked more angry, hunted, more than usually unshaved and unwashed, and he cracked his knuckles as if barely controlling punches. Spat out in manic exhaustion, his words made no sense. If the immobility of depression was rage turned inward, this was the opposite—a rageful, euphoric, yet powerful gesture of moving to destroy the world (and himself). Insofar as it became a strain to maintain communication with Zmarai during these episodes, this research followed the temporal patternings of his immobility, rather than his excessive mobility.

Conclusion

Reflecting on Zmarai's problem from multiple perspectives allowed me to enrich my view on his painful state—without claiming to know his problem better than he did, or worse, offering psychotherapeutic insights. First, through reflections on *khapgan*, the chapter developed a particular lens on the mobile turn in critical theory for considering a multiplicity of elements, scales, and forces in the formation of migrant suffering and subjectivity. Nurturing long-term intimacies with field informants can allow for a richer mine of intersubjective interpretation that can challenge myriad misunderstandings that can arise from taking a narrative at face value or reverting to assumptions of trauma. While immobility revealed some everyday contours of "normality," it also provides insights into the "fragility of relations and of experience that is revealed when madness cannot be absorbed into the everyday" (Das 2015, 84). Dreams and life histories are both highly selective research products. Shared in the context of biography, dream stories illustrate the personal uses of culturally influenced symbols and imagery—here, desires to be king, for the company of men, the fires of deep passion, the beauty of youth, to find a green resting place, to simply stop moving, or to be left alone, as the romantic saying expresses: *Pridā chey gharzam lewanai pe ghroonou* (Leave me to wander around the mountains in my craziness). They provide fertile ground for analyzing subjective and intersubjective encounters with surprising versions of one's self, history, culture, and world.

To revisit the figure of the king with which the chapter opened, I turn at last to Widmark's (2011, 160–70) analysis of Pir Muhammed Karwan's short story in Pashto "De Lar Kali malang" ("The Wandering Mendicant of Lar Kali Village"), written in exile in Pakistan in 1994. According to Widmark, the narrative follows an unknown protagonist who describes a *malang* who descends into insanity after being bitten by a rabid dog. In the *malang*'s maddening pain, he dreams a dream in which he, too, is insane. In it he encounters two kings of his homeland *(watan)*: a black-clothed king leading a large army in a funeral procession who, possessed by a black jinn, brings "grave disease or intractable mental illness"; and has a flashback to "real" king, possessed by a white jinn, who visited his village in his childhood. The *malang* tries to attack the king, demanding why his countrymen are driven insane by mad dogs. The protagonist sees a reflection of the *malang* in the king's tears, but it is not him. He wakes screaming with bloodstained hands; the neighbors shout that he is a madman. Widmark puts forward the possibility that the two kings are one; imaging power, and authority, turning bad. In observing the disintegration of a society, while people deem him insane, the *malang*'s madness is imbued with wisdom (169).

This story was written around the time Zmarai's family sought refuge in Pakistan. Its themes of exile and madness have obvious pertinence. The mendicant's frustration caused by people's indifference to events in the country, and the accusations put to the king, reflect so many Afghans' frustration at the relentless violence destroying their land and the inability of politicians or the world to stop it. Zmarai's distrust in the media may be a symptom of paranoia, but paranoia here is also institutional and political, and a "sane" response to the distortions and manipulations of the news media, the lies and broken promises of politicians, and the endless circularity of war. The protagonist's bloodstained hands, the neighbors who point out his madness and his defiance (the attack on the king), likewise implicate madness as a bid for freedom from oppression, the inability to bear oppressive reality, and ways that oppressive reality can constitute forms of madness. The two kings suggest the difficulties of living with two inseparable people inside him, one "real" and one mad.

Finally, if immobility expresses resistance to the ways that Afghans are defined within migration contexts, it is an ethical act of faithfulness *not* to enclose Zmarai's story within the limits of any one explanation. The research work, too, became a shared support for bearing, without escaping or assuming, the load of cultural and economic obligation entailed in migration. It is nonetheless rooted in the indefatigable labor of survival. Zmarai often cited the idea in Islam that life is a test from God that one must endure—and that the afterlife will signify the end of suffering. As he often told me, in Afghanistan suffering is considered part of everyday life in all aspects; the ability to endure suffering is manly and honorable *(ghairati)* for both men and women.

Thus the grief and hopelessness of a continual falling short, of moving and never arriving, which also constitute the fundamentally human pain of the unfulfilled life, remain oblique, so ensuring the continuation of kin relations organized around the material reproduction of existence. Immobility is about ambivalence, self-protection, and self-destruction. Yet even when there is "no solution," life moves in uncharted directions. Still, Zmarai wonders (hope by now a word too definite for his amorphous feelings), even if he is aging and becoming less capable himself, that perhaps through his sons there may still be a chance to set things right and start again. After all, *Harwakht chey maiee le obou rawunee say taza da* (Anytime you catch a fish from water, it is fresh). This for him is the enduring pull of life.

4. FOOD, WATER, AND WHEREWITHAL IN THE TIME OF CROSSINGS

Claude Lévi-Strauss's essay "The Doldrums" in *Tristes Tropiques* ([1955] 2011, 73–80) tells the tale of Old World navigators whose ship became stuck at sea while in search of the New World. It is evocative of relationships between sea and sky, air and water that become turned the wrong way up in a situation wherein, despite the lack of wind or air to propel the ship along, the seamen's urgent sense of needing to escape impending death is pressing:

> If one looks at the vista the wrong way up, a more likely seascape appears, in which sky and sea have changed places. Across the horizon, which appears closer because of the passivity of the elements and the relative dimness of the light, occasional squalls can be seen lazily moving, like blurred, short-lived columns which still further diminish the apparent distance between the sea and the overcast sky. Between these adjoining surfaces the boat slips along with a kind of anxious haste, as if it had only a short period of grace in which to escape being smothered. (73)

Lévi-Strauss moves us on in this chapter from the oneiric world, sleep travel, and stories of death on the Jalalabad river, to other travelers' journeys across sea, land, and air in search of refuge and new beginnings. It is also germane to ways that immobility, longed-for movement, and unexpected reversals are stitched through the traveler's discovery that the awe-inspiring new world bears no relation to his imagining, the maps he was given, or the stories he was told—and shifts our focus toward other earthly, watery, and imaginative worlds encountered on the way.

Drawing, inevitably selectively, on thirty-four interviews conducted in Sussex and London between 2009 and 2012, twenty in Peshawar in 2010 and 2011, and many conversations and observations gathered between 2009 and 2017, there follows a series of storied fragments from everyday life that are loosely linked by ideas of movement and migration, food and water, and terrestrial and aquatic crossings. Practically, the chapter encompasses three interrelated crossings. First are those from war in Afghanistan to Pakistan which transformed Afghans into refugees. Second are those circuitous crossings across land and sea which made British asylum seekers of Pakistani refugees. Third, since the 2010s particularly, are Afghan repatriations from Pakistan which raise the bizarre specter of Afghans returning in reverse direction, like refugees to their own land.

The chapter weaves ethnographic fragments with conjunctions of time, subjectivity, and movement. It crisscrosses explications of larger physical and geographical border crossings involving migrants with everyday insights into labor mobility and its aporias; the interplay of hostis and hospitality in food as emblematic of the refugee condition in England—from home cooking and commensality to the dementicating humiliations of government food vouchers—and everyday border regimes that shape trajectories of mobility and immobility for Afghan refugees in England and Peshawar. These evoke multiple tangible and intangible exclusions captured in Etienne Balibar's (2002, 78) claim that the border is "everywhere and nowhere." They also indicate some social and classed processes of defining difference within Pakistani, Pashtun, and Afghan difference.

Writing Fragments

Rather than provide thematic comparisons, whole narratives, or a chronology of events, this chapter presents fragments that remain phenomenologically important in people's tellings. These subjective pieces, snap-shots, and discontinuous narrations shape new realities, fictions, life-worlds, and disjunctive temporalities. They also implicate some historical and temporal modes of Pashtun storytelling; the ethnographer's role as scribe in translating experience; and ways the retellings of memories ripple and create new textual and oral imaginings of migration.

Building on the book's fragmented approach, a short "fragmentog-raphy" perhaps, the chapter returns to questions about the power and limits of words to express the slow-ticking mundanity of life, its tran-quil moments, its sudden ruptures, and its immense chasms of loss and devastation. It builds alliances with work by writers who have employed literary devices very differently to make lucid and visceral the illucid, or to retain its illegibility, or to affect the senses with the extreme limits of experience, or a sense of the ordinary, and anything and everything in between.

Rosaldo (2014, 102) offers a haunting account of the death of his wife during fieldwork in the Philippines in 1981, using free verse and *antro-poesía*, what he terms "ethnographic poetry," to capture the traumatic shock of "a harrowing experience, the moment of devastating loss, the personal realization of mortality." His explication of the writing process occurs toward the book's close. Rather, he allows the poetry to gradu-ally reveal "not so much the raw event as the traces it leaves" (102). His poetry does not evade deep emotions, but instead "brings things closer, or into focus, or makes them palpable. It slows the action, the course of events, to reveal depth or feeling and to explore its character. It is a place to dwell and savor" (105). Rosaldo uses ethnopoetic writing about grief to create "deep feeling through the accumulation of concrete particulars" and a shared intersubjectivity with his reader, while seeking to "render intelligible what is complex" in "the uneven and contradictory shape" of powerful experiences and perceptions (107).

In a ludic, literary, and quite different approach, Berlant and Stewart (2019, 4–5) deploy hundred-word multiples in which "words sediment, next to something laid low, or they detour on a crazed thought-cell taking off," in "an experiment in keeping up with what's going on." In their poi-esis of the ordinary, speed and motion centrally feature in the "relation of scenes to form, observation to implication . . . figuration to what sticks in the mind . . . prehend [*sic*] objects as movement and matter, retains a scene's status as life in suspension. . . . Our styles move in proximity to currents. . . . We enter a public through capture by its circulations; we become ourselves both more alive and tired at all kinds of speed" (8, 28). They likewise dispense with introductions: "Honoring the contingency of the experiment, there is no introduction upfront, but distributed commentary throughout the book, plus reflections in many spots about how the writing attempts to get at a scene or process a hook" (x).

While fragments of ethnographic multiples arguably require a slower cooking in regard to this book's aims, Stewart and Berlant provoke ways that tempo and motion inserted into short pieces might transport us differently into the rhythms of everyday life, as it is arrested or propelled by the specificity and nebulae of traumatic intrusion. This element can enrich literary approaches in anthropology, for example, which advocate that "perspicacious presentations, juxtapositions, analogies, poetic images, epiphanies and anecdotes may best do justice to the character of experience and carry us into those penumbral regions where the unnamable begins" (Jackson 2009, xiv). It can disrupt the certainty of explanations, unhook certainty and legibility from their theoretically informed anchors, and representations of migrants from any single dimensional terms of identity, culture, affinity, or purpose.

This short fragmentography may similarly work to undo the colonial gaze, but fragmented thinking and writing involves much more. For example, it may accumulate impressions of fragmenting time, space, and ontology within single subjects; but also reassemble external fragments into new interactions, forms of life, and possibilities (Caron 2019, 454). I propose fragmented writing as an ethnographic process of discovery, of making lucid small umbral or evanescent moments, or details that might easily pass unnoticed. Fragments grapple with tentacles of memory becoming entangled with everyday musings, consciousness, and the intersubjective realm of nuanced intuition and sudden realization. Here I neither focus on immense grief that overwhelms, nor on what specifically constitutes the everyday. The starting point is crossings; and ways people move across tracks of cohesion and undoing, geography and affect, fracture and liminality—as they assume variegated size and proportion in consciousness and experience. Insofar as severe and tentative journeys across divides between the ideal, and what is actually lived, shape the human condition, crossings make migrants of us all.

The Mosque Is a Ship

Given that Afghanistan is landlocked, it is unsurprising that Afghan imaginings of the sea should assume, as for Lévi-Strauss's Old World navigators, a fantastical quality. This sense is captured in *Teashop in Pol-e-Khomri* by Magnum photographer Steve Curry (Curry 2007, 24–25). Taken at a time when many Afghans journeyed across the world as refugees, some in ships aboard which they first set sight on the sea, the photograph depicts the dark interior of a teashop outside Kabul. It draws the eye to a man, the owner or a passing customer, staring at the crude painting on the wall of a black transatlantic ocean liner from which four white funnels belch smoke, as the ship approaches a luscious green coastline populated with unclear forms, perhaps sheep or haystacks. The motif of travel through foreign time zones also appears in the fantasy images of modern skyscrapers, cityscapes, and futuristic imaginings of planes and flying cars stitched into war rugs by refugees in Pakistani camps—woven images of Afghanistan's "nightmare of modernism" (Mascelloni 2009).

The fantasies and wonders of foreign exploration across land and sea have a long precedent in Afghan literature—for example, in the writings of the Pashtun intellectual and politician Mahmud Tarzi, who traveled across Europe to establish Afghan embassies following independence in 1919, and who pronounced on the strange, inscrutable British. Likewise, at times during this fieldwork, while driving and enjoying pleasures away from everyday routines, illuminations of the strange and fantastic intruded unexpectedly.

For example, over a period of several years Hamid and I occasionally drove along the Sussex coast to visit a Pakistani *pulao* restaurant where on Sundays dishes were half price, and we could eat and talk at leisure. This dark night, we were returning along the coastal road that followed the high, windy, and unforgiving cliff face where, local lore has it, witches once ruled and godless locals met with the devil in open mockery of God's name. Jokingly, on this stretch of road I would frighten him with stories of witches who could fly through the car window, enter his nostrils, ears, throat, and make devil's work in his body. Becoming scared, Hamid would drive faster, talk louder, and mock me in return.

Continuing some miles, a large rectangular-shaped building would invariably impress its aura into the night sky. Its bright dome shining alternately green or gold habitually reminded me of a mosque I knew in West Malaysia, where my aunt lived. The "mosque" sighting usually served as an invitation to finish the game, imagining ourselves safe from evil influence and traveling through a faraway landscape. This day the "mosque" glowed golden. For the first time we decided to drive closer and inspect. The approach led us along a smaller track to the shore, where we discovered not a mosque, but a cross-Channel passenger ferry docked in port.

We were both awestruck as Hamid uttered, "But the mosque is a ship!"

The Storyteller's Bazaar

Peshawar is one of South Asia's oldest cities, capital of the ancient Khushan and Durrani empires, a Mughal-era trading center, and Frontier headquarters for the Raj. Within the ancient walled city lies Qissa Khwani, the old storyteller's bazaar. Attracting merchants from all India, traders would stop in Qissa Khwani's many teahouses and exchange stories, creating a living tradition of storytelling.

Oral traditions remain central to Pashtun social life. The scribe *(areyza nawees)* also plays an authorial role in Afghan society. Transitioning boundaries of literacy and illiteracy, and oral and written worlds, in Peshawar he is found peddling his penmanship outside government offices, seated at a small table in the company of other scribes. An official writer, his role is to assist the illiterate with official matters. He may also wait outside the passport office near Rahman hospital in Hayatabad. Or, outside Kacha Roh (the registration office for aliens), he may draft an invitation letter for relatives in Britain who need a visa to visit home. Or he may be found outside any other government office or ministry. He can explain what he has written, so the person can sign with a thumbprint. At the telegraph office he can transcribe your missive or write an important letter with the proper mode of address. He may even have connections in the office you are appealing to, and help expedite your case for an additional sum.

One of the first writing lessons Afghan pupils learn is letter writing, typically a formal absence letter addressed to the school principal. Teachers are exacting about the placement of dots and correct calligraphy. However, not everyone who leaves school can write, or indeed attends school, and the scribe is crucial for unlocking the debarred mysteries of written words. Whereas in times long past a pigeon carrier served as an emissary for royal dispatches, and before the postal system letters were delivered between Afghan towns and villages by cycle, now mobile phone technology and the internet offer instant communication regardless of literacy. Nonetheless, in Peshawar's Mohajir schools children continue to learn and recite a rich oral tradition of Pashtun poetry. Even if they cannot master the verses exactly, a valuable appreciation for the sweet language may ensue. This literary appreciation among the illiterate is exemplified in the tale I heard, recounted by the Sussex driver Wazir, about a cobbler from Khogyiani district in Nangarhar who recited such beautiful poetry of his own making that when he died his neighbors gathered to remember his poems, bringing with them a scribe to preserve his verses.

Anthropologists also both collect and write about human stories, and sift and analyze official and legal documents. I was also charged with "writing work" many times. As Raouf declared unceremoniously upon asking me to write his appeal letter for government housing, "Why should I come to you if I can write it myself? That's your *job*—to write in the correct words."

If moving around provides multiple pathways into a community, ethnography and storytelling provide inroads to the gestalt of a life. They create a kind of immortality with one's interlocutors, and spaces where suspense and unpredictability are tied to a dream or dance; or for taxi-driving, migration, and anthropology to meet, and writing stories to become a practice of mutuality. Anthropology does not just tell stories about actually existing events. This would be a narrow phenomenology that cannot integrate the discontinuous transition between experience and reality (Lévi-Strauss [1955] 2011, 58). Anthropological storytelling is powerful precisely because it dissolves divides between here and there, familiar and strange, reality and fantasy, and creates the emergence and disappearance of the universe. Hence it smacks of the magical. Following Malinowski (1954), if words and sounds can affect the world, and presage physical or other changes, storytelling is a mode of magical thinking. For Freud ([1913] 2013), storytellers are practitioners of magic who can project their mental states onto their surroundings, and even change the world for their listeners by their words or spells.

Anthropological storytelling may draw us to the Freudian uncanny—the *unheimlich,* or unhomely—where beyond the familiarity of the actual historical event, a stranger, more chromatic encounter and fundamental revelation with experience can occur (Freud 1919). For Freud, the uncanny belongs to all that is terrible—to "what arouses dread and horror" (219). It is not clearly definable, except insofar as it coincides with dread about the unknown, and is opposed to everything familiar, native, and of the home (220). Regarding migrant lives in motion, storytelling might illuminate fears of meandering in the borderlands between life's passing, and creative or terrible rebirths into other forms. While storytelling may produce an encounter with the real, and invite the spirit of transformation, its potentiality is not always necessarily emancipatory, as many instances show.

Rather, in collapsing distinctions between human and migrant, war and peace, and multiple layers of the past and present, migrants' stories may communicate the experience of living in the border regions of death-in-life, of being "stuck" in the endless time of extreme suffering. This temporal element reminds of Levinas (1987, 69, 78), who views extreme suffering as a form of radical passivity that destroys all possibility of refuge, and or assimilating or fleeing from the world: "It is the fact of being directly exposed to being. It is made up of the impossibility of fleeing or retreating." However, as this fieldwork reveals, any sense of being immobilized in time is still transitive and transmutable.

Regarding time and subjectivity, Das's (2006) work on violence has been highly influential. Through her sketch of a girl, Manjit, who had lost both parents and was abducted during Partition, Das illustrates how these events came to nurture for her a sense of time as a powerful agent that can strike down or heal (95). She criticizes sharp separations drawn by anthropologists between physical and phenomenal time. The task is not to focus on a series of "nows," but to recognize ways the *whole* of physical and phenomenological past is actualized in the present—for example, as a sense of pastness, recovery, or blockage (96–101). In the form of words gathered during fieldwork, the relation of time to stories about life's passing expresses something of what I try to convey. As fragments they shed light on ways experience lives not always coherently, but transports speakers into strange worlds that convey shifting relations of pain, desire, impossibility, and the immensity of political events.

WORDS FROM EVERYDAY LIFE

A Tear

"How is Mubeen?" I asked Ashraf of his youngest son.

A tear sprung sharply to his eye, which threatened but did not overspill.

"Fine," he nodded in reply.

"Is he in school?" I pressed.

"Yes," he nodded.

"Are your family all in Peshawar?" I pressed further.

Again he nodded, "Yes."

In this short elliptical exchange I was inquiring, he understood, without wanting to pry, upset, or shame him, about his family's safety in the forced expulsions of Afghans from Peshawar in 2016; whether his children's school registrations, like many others', had been revoked; and whether his parents had safely returned from a family funeral in Kabul.

"What is there to say?" his resistant stare communicated. "You are concerned, but I am more so. If something terrible happens, I prefer to think about it then."

Water at Home

After Fazl had twice scalded his son with boiling water, the government removed the child from the family. "Now the boy does not even belong to his own father anymore," described Ramin in a tone akin to outrage. "This country is so bad."

A Dream of Wales

"What is more heavenly than to wash your face and hands in cold, cold, icy mountain water, and to picnic with friends, away from everything. Did I tell you? A group of us are planning to go to Wales. I heard the fresh water and mountains are beautiful there, like Afghanistan."

Seasonal Comforts

For migrants who confront themselves through everyday failure and abjection, cooking may assume the hue of escape and reinvention, the magic of becoming somebody who labors creatively and successfully—a producer of comfort and happiness for oneself and others. Following the seasonal patterns of the year, of driving time, the pleasures of cooking create their own annual cycle.

In the winter storms of 2016, Awalmir worked little. January was quiet. There were few customers and too many taxis on the road, and in any case he was depressed.

"Work a little," I said to encourage him. "Make some rent."

"No," he replied. "I'm at home with my brother. I will cook us *qurut* and *shola*. It's good home food, especially if you are ill."

There followed a recipe.

"To make *shola* cook rice and green mung beans together in lots of water to make a porridge-like paste. Then serve with *qurut* [dried yogurt curds, sometimes salted]." Awalmir used "proper" homemade *qurut* his cousin had brought from Afghanistan. He continued, "Then fry onions and pile them in the middle of the dish. Such delicious winter food." Warming home-comfort food to buffet cold taxi-drivers against the hard English rain, the heartless gale blowing outside.

The Strict Delivery of a Recipe

Winter inevitably ends, officially with the spring festival Nowruz. This dish is served at Nowruz but, Gul Nabi insisted, you can make it anytime. Wazir's reserved elder cousin, Gul Nabi, cited his recipe as a mode of instruction. His stern delivery jarred oddly with the sweet dish he described.

"*Take* some dried apricots, walnuts, almonds, mulberries, raisins, sultanas for the best taste. Wash and soak all overnight, in a pan in some water. The next afternoon, put everything into a dish. *Then* you can eat the softened fruit and nuts and drink the juice. The juice *will be* sweet and delicious."

The Stillness of a Flock of Birds

By summer, driving jobs are more plentiful, the city is full of visitors, and London friends travel to Sussex more frequently to enjoy the good weather, picnicking on the expansive Sussex Downs or the stony beach abutting the sparkling sea. By chance one Sunday, walking with a friend along a quiet part of the beach, we noticed around ten taxis parked. I recognized the license plates as belonging to Afghan drivers. We approached the wall to the beach, meaning to scramble over, and encountered a large group of about forty Afghan men and, Aman told me afterward, their London visitors picnicking.

Sitting on blankets, spaced between them shopping trolleys full of supplies, relaxing and motionless while enjoying the bright sunlight on the beach, presumably replete after good food, they appeared like a mirage in the refracted sunlight off the sea, a strange flock of human seabirds so still and peaceful that, notwithstanding we would have felt embarrassed disturbing a large group of men, we changed our minds about tentatively intruding.

Cold Comfort

Compared with the comforts of home-cooked, shared food, the British government's food voucher program was humiliating, even maddening (Brown 2000).

"Food vouchers killed people," asserted Amanullah in 2009.

"They were so shameful; the shop assistants looked at me badly, sometimes I sold forty vouchers [worth £40] for £30 to avoid using them. One guy worked in a newsagent and saved his vouchers, £800 worth. He sold them for £600. No one cared about losses. The vouchers made you feel so ashamed; they didn't trust us to even *shop* for ourselves."

Here continued, "Since, I've worked as a cleaner, porter, chef, security guard, bouncer, washing cars, and a delivery driver. *Still* my family has nothing. I'm sending nothing. They borrowed money to send me here. Now they are eating snow."

On Maddening Sustenance

Sipping coffee after work one afternoon with a city social worker, whose caseload included many asylum seekers, this dedicated woman offered her tale.

"In the mid-2000s, I had a case of an Afghan father and son, both suffering serious physical and mental health problems. The son had severe brain injuries following alleged torture, and the father was suffering"—she described carefully—"the kind of mental health stress you might expect of someone who'd lost their home, their family, then traveled to the UK across many countries with his brain-injured adult son."

While waiting for the outcome of their asylum application, the son was given full-time residential rehabilitative care, and the father housed. Finally, it was not the terrible losses he sustained that broke him, she continued, but the food vouchers. His desperation and sense of humiliation "took on a life of its own," propelling him into dark paranoia and desperation. He became obsessed with return, with wanting to erase recent events, and applied to the Home Office for repatriation.

His social worker's team even sought to invoke the Mental Health Act[1] to keep him in the country against his wishes. "It was one of those cases where you do too much," she continued. He was repatriated with his son. It haunted her that after six weeks he telephoned from Afghanistan imploring her help to return—inevitably too late.

A Storage Problem of Fifty Fish

"I *believe* I will buy fifty fish for the Eid party, like last year, as an extra dish to complement the meat *pulao* and chicken wings. It's not too costly; they will expect some specialty from me as chef." Returning along the coast road from the fish market, Sher Agha telephoned me. "But I have no place to marinade and store them. Will your family agree if I use your fridge?"

"Alright," I agreed hesitantly, "you can use our fridge. We can marinade them together. I'll be at work tomorrow, but somebody will let you in to collect them."

When he arrived we washed and gutted the fish, smashed garlic, coriander seeds, green chilies, cumin, added the juice of fresh lemons, olive oil, powdered spices, and he left them in my fridge. When I returned from work the next day, I found a spotlessly clean fridge and kitchen, and a small note written falteringly on ripped newspaper in the floriate style of students taught to write English in Pakistan: 'Thank You a Lot.'

Become a Shopkeeper

"My wife called to say that my father says if I cannot send more money I must come back. He will get me a shop. I can be a shopkeeper."

The tone of confused disbelief that Zakiullah adopted to relay this information suggested his father may as well have invited him to Peshawar to be a brain surgeon. His surprise jarred with his unexpected discovery that he did not want to leave England after all, despite his dreams of return.

Trust Nothing, Nothing Is as It Seems

Many migrants in Britain, like Ihsanullah, grew up during war in Afghanistan, witnessed killings, believed politicians' broken promises, saw their homeland destroyed by international powers, and felt betrayed by treacherous dreams of mobility, freedom, and refuge. Many became susceptible to depressive, traumatic, anxious, and semi-psychotic states, where they understandably took nothing at its word, seeing double meanings and double-dealings everywhere. Like an underground river that murmurs beneath the earth, revealing its force only through small fissures and cracks, these states intruded unexpectedly into conversations.

As I drove with Ihsanullah along the A23 road from London toward Sussex, he pointed to a stack of large cylindrical pipes waiting to be inserted into the ground as part of a roadworks expansion project.

"They must be for water," I mused.

"No," he responded. "They're for spying. The government will use them to store weapons and spy on people."

He was immoveable. I could not dissuade him.

Another occasion, we were sharing food in an Afghan eatery. He gazed up and, pointing to a large blue bottle fly on the wall, startled me when he said, "That fly is a government camera spying on us. You cannot convince me otherwise. I believe it."

The Family Boat: In Case of Flooding or Disaster

Malalai had arrived from Kandahar to join her new husband, an engineer and good match, but he complained she was neither tall nor beautiful, and now she lived in a domestic violence shelter. I met her some months earlier at some workshops I delivered to women at an Afghan community organization in London. We remained in contact outside the sessions and she often called me for advice, or just to talk and pass the time. She had "shamed" her family, they ostracized her, she was lonely, and she missed her mother keenly. Her ally and younger brother was an asylum seeker in Germany, but his travel restrictions prevented their meeting. She described a crushing pain that had followed her from Afghanistan to England.

"Marriage is unlucky," she declared as we relaxed on my sofa which, I joked, was our family boat. In the case of flooding—if, for example, the sea should break its shores, engulf the house, and end the world—we could jump onto the boat and float safely away with blankets wrapped warmly over us.

"As a child in Kandahar, my eldest brother was violent until I left home. When I think about the beatings and the hurt, a physical pain starts in my wrist and travels sharply up my arm. Even when I was ten years old or younger, I desperately dreamt of suicide, of a way to escape, and murder: how I would kill him, and what story I would tell the family. Now, I would never visit his house. When I have children, I will never allow them alone with him. If my children are daughters, I will worry about how to keep them safe from men, help them find freedom from the terrible violence of men that is worse than any war, that has followed me through all my life. When the pain comes it is like a freezing sharp knife, or icy water stabbing deep inside my arm. Like an icicle. I cannot move my arm."

Then more accusingly, "At the workshop you talked about violence. I already know enough about violence. I'm more interested in how to get freedom."

Like a Mama

"When my youngest brother came to England from Peshawar," described Wali gently, "he was so young he still slept with my mama at home. So he slept with me. To put him to sleep, I would play with his ear. Like a mama."

He continued, "When I visit my home in Peshawar, I do not see my wife first, or my children. I go straight to my mama's room to sleep beside her, like a child returning after my long journey."

A Good English Mother

Many child refugees with relatives in the UK are placed in foster care—especially if relatives are not deemed to have suitable living conditions. Zirgul, whose teenage son had recently arrived from Calais and claimed asylum, described his foster family within an Afghan family idiom. "Sorabh is living with a very good Pakistani family now. The women wear hijabs, they're good Muslims. His English mother allows Sorabh to visit us in Sussex and nobody tells the social worker. She visited our home in Peshawar. From an English viewpoint it's not good. From an Afghan viewpoint she's very kind. A good woman."

A Mashki Like a Mother to Water the World

In November 2016 I attended a creative writing workshop at the Royal Asiatic Society in London titled "Writ in Water." The attendees were introduced to photographs and objects extemporizing on the theme of water. Preoccupied with thinking through this book's material, I was drawn to a full-length studio portrait of a water carrier from nineteenth-century India hauling his inflated skin of water over his shoulder, and sketched the following:

See in the scratchy back of the water carrier's *(mashki)* sack, here where the free flow of the river or mountain stream is become full like a uterine caul, with bovine scrawn made again fat and watery and newly alive with dark internal lappings bitter with their tang of the tannery, or dried fat perhaps, or the carceral taste of a lifetime of chewed and masticated chaff, or wheat, or maybe rubbish. The skin from the old buffalo's broken back, pulled downward to an open point, points like a nipple, offering mother's milk. O freighted men who nourish their mothers by watering the world; their progress through the streets driven by strange new currents, along cobbled riverbanks, through the seasonal eddyings of such unnatural traffic.

Later, I canvassed information about water carriers in Afghanistan. Saifullah responded readily. "When I was a child," he remembered, "a *mashki* [Dari] would come to family weddings. *Mashkis* were often from the Panjshir valleys. They transported water in a calf skin, dispatched it around homes and shops or, in the case of a wedding, sprinkled it over the dusty floor to ensure guests would be comfortable and clean. This was when villages had no taps or water pipes, just a well. It's traveling work, like taxi-work."

On the Work Men Do for Women

"This verse is from a very *sweet* old Pashto wedding song," continued Saifullah on another occasion. He had snatched time from work to enjoy the sun in a walled garden backing the seafront. Seeing me by chance, he called out and I sat down. In the leafy shade of a fig tree, watching other visitors relax, I asked about his recent wedding in Peshawar. He recalled a childhood memory instead, which presaged fears of new responsibilities.

> *Shah Dramana zoora wura day Shah Razi kala day waley ourana wala!*
> *Shah Dramana.*
> *Shah Dramana pe khre spoor key, magkh yey pe toor key, koor pe koor*
>   *yey girzawe.*

Powerful Shah Dramana why did you destroy the house of Shah Razi.
Shah Dramana.
They forced Shah Dramana onto a donkey, blackened his face, and paraded him from house to house.

"This verse from a wedding song," he explained, "describes two big chiefs in Afghanistan. Women add the second verse to raise laughs. Now mostly only older women sing it, mothers and grandmothers. They stand and sing with their hands over their ears to concentrate on the *sound*. They're already old but deliberately make their voices sound even older. People enjoy the sound more than the words. When I was a child in Kabul, so young I sat with women not men, I heard women singing this *very early* one morning at dawn. A beautiful sound. In those days weddings were very simple. Women just washed their faces, wore a dress, and attended the wedding. Now they wear too much makeup and change dresses every two hours. They want money to show off. It's horrible."

What We Need

"We need three sheep, two sacks of onions, fifteen kilos of rice, three boxes of chicken wings, fifty big pieces of bread, and everything else.

We'll be outside with no running water. Do we need twenty-five or thirty water bottles to do *wuzu*?"

CROSSING WATERS: ON THE SHORES OF ACHERON

The ancient Roman Virgil died before completing his epic poem, the *Aeneid*, which recounts the founding myth of Rome, through the wanderings of Aeneas who voyages across land and sea, and into the underworld to speak with his father's spirit. Virgil's biography, as the undistinguished son of a Gallic farmer and migrant to Rome, resonates through the poem's keynotes of sorrowful lamentation, exclusion, and exile—now synonymous with the Virgilian style. Book 6, "The Shores of Acheron," evokes a scene by a river in the underworld where the newly dead are crowding the shores and begging to cross (1956, 156):

> Here all the concourse of souls was hastening to the bank, mothers and strong men, high hearted heroes whose task in the body's life were done, boys, unmarried girls, and young sons laid on pyres before their parents' eyes. As numerous were they as the leaves of the forest which fall at the first chill of autumn and float down, or as the birds which flock from ocean-deeps to the shore when the cold of the year sends them in rout across the sea, and sets them free to fly to sunshine lands. The souls stood begging to be the first to make the crossing, and stretched their arms out in longing for the farther shore. But the surly boatman accepted now these and now those, and forced others back, not allowing them near the river side.

Aeneas's hellish wanderings are pertinent to many young Afghan men who must deal with mercurial agent boatmen to cross sea, land, and air to reach Europe in hopes of renewal and a better life.[2] They describe how developmental pathways are shaped by war, migration mobility, and managing encounters not with ornery boatmen, dead souls, or a multi-headed Cerberus, but unscrupulous smugglers, asylum bureaucracies, detention, and deportation regimes. After 2015, many arrivals in Greece were trapped in camps there in appalling conditions when the surrounding countries tightened their borders (*New Humanitarian* 2017). By 2017, European countries had hardened policy approaches toward Afghan asylum seekers. European countries rejected almost ten thousand Afghan asylum seekers in 2016, around triple the numbers in 2015 (ibid.): 33 percent first-time Afghan asylum applications in 2015, compared with 54 percent Afghan asylum rejections in 2017 (Eurostat 2016b, 2018). Alongside falling recognition rates, returns increased significantly. An agreement between the European Union and Afghan government in 2016 allowed the "near-unlimited deportation" of rejected Afghan asylum seekers (*New Humanitarian* 2017). Alongside that, Afghanistan faced more civilian deaths and casualties, deepening instability, a resurgent Taliban, and an Islamic State–aligned militancy. "Returns," the Migration Policy Institute stated at the end 2017, "dominate Afghan migration patterns at one of the most insecure and unstable times in its recent history" (ibid.). Notwithstanding, many deportees repeatedly attempted the journey in a carousel-type situation of simultaneous forced and voluntary returns, new and reattempted departures from Afghanistan, leading to over thirty-eight thousand new Afghan asylum claims in EU countries in 2017 (Eurostat 2018).

Correspondingly, attention in refugee studies shifted during the 2010s from crisis and disaster focused on countries of origin, toward treacherous border and maritime crossings in Europe (De Genova 2017). Migrants' journeys could very easily take a year, much longer, and be punctuated with months of waiting, fear, and exploitation. I heard firsthand stories of migrants killed by border guards, at sea, who witnessed deaths, experienced violence, hunger, were cheated or stranded by fraudulent agents, packed into dangerous boats, had claims refused, were detained, forced to live in refugee camps, and subjected to cruel, low-paid work. Families likely sacrifice a lot to send a son. His failure to arrive, or his deportation, brings him enormous shame. In turn, many arrivals negotiating tough passages, risks of deportation, and first-time separations from their family, are dismayed that Europe differs so dramatically from their expectations.

Might a wider cartography of maritime, watery, or fluid relations contextualize the political conditions of governance and affectations that shape England's relation to Europe, the Mediterranean, and wider waterscapes of refugee migration? Might this vocabulary produce critical thought around the human geography of citizen–refugee divides, and colonial and postcolonial connections? If the refugee and a nation's borders exercise fluidity, should they not also address geographies that are literally fluid and circulatory? Many social and political geographies tend to prioritize the enclosed, terrestrial nation without considering how maritime, fluvial, and aquatic landscapes shape social borders. Bose (2006) reflects on forms of belonging found in oceanic borderlands. Mapping the interregional arena of the Indian Ocean as a radical space for understanding identity and society *beyond* continental or national identifications, he conceives of shared water rims as places for political and personal affinity, another kind of frontier, cultural borderland, and imaginarium. Correspondingly, the contemporary journey through water, ports, and surfaces to the island state, and isolated states of refuge, is a topography that can offer fresh concepts for citizenry as well as national divides.

Water is central to the British national character, seas, and irregular migrant transit. Gedalof (2007, 79–80) deploys ideas of "leakiness" to analyze governmental dilemmas about immigration: "One of the key tropes animating the British/English imagined community has been water— the mythical language of an 'island race,' and the perceived dangers of 'swamping' and 'opening the floodgates,' are familiar manifestations of the preferred element when thinking about belonging in British terms." Ahmad (2011) emphasizes the perseverance of human smuggling across the Mediterranean, and ways that vertiginous risk-taking by migrants feed the booms and busts of Europe's restrictive economy. He riffs on Braudel's pioneering study of seas as historical units of analysis, rejecting "contemporary imperialist mythmaking portraying the EU as heir to some ancient and medieval lineage" arranged around the Mediterranean, through the provocative image of "the bloated black or brown corpse, swirling off shore from Italy, Greece or Spain" (128–29).

Additionally germane, Hurd, Donnan, and Leutloff-Grandits (2017, 3) use the metaphor of a tidemark to describe ways that crossings leave behind "layers of embodied memories of movement and emotion." As part of "border temporalities," tidemarks are nonlinear, concurrent, parallel, and synchronic; past, lived present, and imagined futures coexist in experience and imagination, and shape possibilities of future lives as people manage, shape, and represent borders across which they move or are stopped (4). Hence, through tidemarks we might think of becoming sensitized to the temporal rhythms of migrant lives as *not* implying a forward motion or transcendence that can redeem life from the frontiers of destruction. Rather, tidemarks acknowledge the lapping and overlapping violences that shape moments, days, and years of failure and loss in the task of enduring. This means seeing success and failure not as absolute, but conditions people move in and out of. It means blurring distinctions between borders of reality and unreality, the mundane and the fantastic, dominant epistemes, and subjective experience. In other words, accepting the uncertainty that comes with the natural waxing and waning of forces *across* "thresholds of life," while allowing these components to remain in "unresolved, nondialectical tension" (Singh 2015, 122–23). Crossing herein is not a movement from location A to B, but an indelible part of moving backward and forward through life.

Like a Deadly Storm at Sea

Although during the nineties most Afghans arriving in Britain were granted asylum prima facie (i.e., on first application), journeys tether exhaustion with illness and terror.

"It was months later, 1998, after we'd worked in Moscow for six months and saved enough to travel again. Another agent took us from Holland to Belgium. From there we came overland. It was *unbelievably* difficult. We walked for miles without sleep for days. Our feet were swollen. We were totally exhausted. One night we stayed in a tiny cheap hostel so close to the train station the room shook all night with the movements of the train. I was sweating with a fever. It was like being on a ship in a black and deadly storm at sea."

A Pakhtun Woman Pushed to Her Limits

As if to make real to himself the immense challenges facing migrants who place their faith in untrustworthy agents, Mujibur relayed this story. More than the journey's physical difficulties, his words conveyed a sense of crossing over into a more dreadful space of dispossession and alienation, without his risking personal vulnerability.

"When we eventually saw our friend again in London, he told us his agent had abandoned them in Belgium at a petrol station. He just left them, about twenty refugees, exposed to view. They froze with fear, but had to quickly decide. They ran straight through the cars, across the busy motorway, into the fields and deeper into a thick forest to hide, but no one had any idea which direction was correct. That night a black storm came, bringing strong lashing rain and lightning. They were terrified, freezing, and drenched in that forest—women and children, too. One Pakhtun woman removed *all* her clothes to wring out the freezing water. Imagine, *a Pakhtun woman!* I've heard much worse, of agents who kill babies, throw them overboard, abandon them halfway because they cry and draw attention, or of people on small boats who drown and nobody helps."

Just Waiting, the Deadness of Time

Migrants en route endure long months of waiting. Sustained by the dream of Europe, they inhabit a space where time apparently freezes like a sleeping corpse, or murders motion, all the while boys travel through developmental space and become young men.

"We traveled to Malaysia and to Tanzania, from Tanzania to Turkey, and from Turkey by sea to Greece," Ajmal described. "In Malaysia we waited for months. We walked everywhere, looking in the shops, waiting, not moving, just killing our time."

A Celebration Moved the Station

Upon arrival, an unreal, incredible sense of freedom may initially overwhelm, as all life's immense possibilities suddenly rush into reach and, after months of traveling against the tide, a shift in gear ushers in a strange, new forward motion.

"We were three Afghans, all Pakhtuns traveling across Europe, in 1999, plus a married couple. When we arrived in Amsterdam we panicked, we knew nothing. I begged the agent to take us to the train station. I called a friend in Rotterdam.

"He said, 'Take the train directly, be brave, no need to hide in this country. When you arrive I'll dance the *attan* for you!'

"The Pakhtun couple *begged* us to take them to their relative. We agreed because they were Pakhtun. We lost four hours finding the correct train, taking them to another city. They didn't even say goodbye. As Pakhtuns they should offer us food, tea, at least *water*. Then back to Amsterdam. *Very* luckily we caught the last train to Rotterdam, feeling very strange. We were hours late.

"True to his word, my friend was waiting on the platform.

"He placed a big tape recorder on the floor and began dancing an *attan*! He was young, handsome, with beautiful long hair. We danced together, so happy! Two of us lived with him for ten months, he didn't ask for one penny. He fought with his family because he was studying, not working. Now he has a good job in Geneva, can you believe it? He deserves his luck. I can do anything for him."

It Would Be My Fault

The immense pressures to reach Europe are reinforced by ruthless traffickers whose promises may be interrupted or vanish. Soon after we met in 2000, Marwan described his journey from Pakistan.

"I was very young, maybe sixteen. It was 1997, I traveled with my cousin. My agent insisted my fake Russian passport was legitimate. It would be *my fault* if I failed. I should say I was from Dagestan Republic where nobody speaks Russian. I trusted him. We flew, a group of Afghans, from Peshawar to some Russian airport. The immigration officer stopped us. It was terrifying. He said, 'I know you're illegal Afghans but can't prove it.' Finally he shouted, 'Go!' I had paid the agent around US$1,000 up front, but in Moscow he disappeared. It was very scary.

"For one month, we stayed in a hostel alone. Later we discovered some Afghans also traveling to Europe. Then we enjoyed ourselves, walking around, having fun. I stayed six months, working on a market stall selling bags. My friend settled there, but my cousin insisted London was better for my future. Finally, my uncle found another agent. We lived in a big guesthouse with around thirty-five Afghans, also waiting to leave."

After Sighting the Beautiful Sea

Zia's youthful tale is permeated with a sense of abruptly snapped possibility.

"In summer 2005 we made a trip to the sea. I'd never seen the sea, it was *so* wonderful and beautiful. I was bored in Southall, so I moved here. I found friends. We worked in a big seafront hotel, around fifteen Afghan boys in the kitchen. One fought with the supervisor and we all left. Then I worked in a twenty-four-hour shop for four years, twelve hours a day. I was still young. When they got their alcohol license, I left. I didn't want to sell alcohol to drunk people. Those years gave me severe back problems. Twelve-hour shifts on my feet, all through winter, unloading heavy deliveries, then straight to an evening job in a pizza kitchen. My room had no kitchen so I couldn't cook. I ate takeaway, burgers, chocolate, and sweets. When I didn't work, I watched cartoons and Hindi films. My dream was to make a fantasy film about Pashtun culture, with music and dancing. When I told my father he said, 'No, your idea is too shameful.'"

Waiting and Wanting

Another occasion, Zia solicited me to help move his belongings in my car to new accommodations, a soulless windowless basement beneath a Kurdish kebab shop. Wafi had invited him to stay temporarily while he found his feet. Ramin was desperate to visit his family, but without gifts to display a returnee's success he could not do so. Slowly he did amass aftershaves, perfumes, and other sundries, assisted by his brother in Greece who posted him mobile phones for the parcel of gifts he was preparing. One morning Zia phoned me, despairing. Wafi had been smoking heroin secretly, defaulted on the rent, and hightailed with his possessions and Zia's parcel. He had betrayed his friend without compunction. Gradually Zia withdrew, seeing betrayal and spies everywhere, convinced strangers were stealing his mail, possessions, watching his home, conspiring to undo him.

The Contingency of Working Age

During the nineties, young Afghan asylum seekers sought work routinely. Since then, tightening restrictions have prioritized the rights of the child to protection. This resulted in many applicants claiming to be younger than their age, in contrast to the earlier years, when young applicants pretended to be adults so they could work. Attaullah remembered.

"Finally we reached England. I was fifteen, but said I was nineteen so I could work. I said the Taliban were forcing boys to work, and I refused. Most like me got asylum, six months' permission first.

"After my cousin arrived, I joined him in London, Southall. I met two boys from my village. It was like Asia, not a feeling of Europe. Like all new boys, I stayed in Southall, three years. I'd never worked, what a shock."

Growing Pains

Childhoods may be difficult and painful everywhere. Individuals migrate for many reasons, no reason, because they are told to, or in order to leave troubled families. Reasons for migration are never singular. Migration may be undertaken unthinkingly, or be expressive of a traumatic reality infused *not* with motivation or intention, but a fundamental illucidity, confusion, sense of disorientation, moving without purpose.

"I was born in Jalalabad, in the Russian war," Zahir began. "My mother said it was a dangerous day. She had no doctor, no medicine, bombing and fighting were everywhere. It was so bad, later our whole family went to Peshawar as refugees. We stayed ten years.

"In my family, there were problems. I have around fifteen brothers. My father preferred our other mother's children. Her sons treated me badly, I always ran away. When I was thirteen, my parents tried to engage me for marriage. I cried and went to Peshawar to live with my brother, but he treated me like a slave so I returned. That was the Taliban time. At first the Jalalabad people invited them, we wanted security and schools. But later the Religious Ministry became so strict, they forced boys to work for them, one from every family. My family didn't want us to join. After a year, my father said I should go to England, send money, because Afghanistan is so poor—no schools, security, no *water*. Just like that I left, with no plan, no desire even."

Just Deserts

Hanif works hard as a London taxi-driver. Every few months he visits Sussex. He refuses invitations to stay with local Afghans, which Zahir finds odd enough to tell me. Rather, he books a room in the smartest hotel on the seafront, with full service. "That's my pleasure," Zahir up-turns his hands in incredulity as he reports what Hanif said.

Immigration Interviews

The British immigration screening interview will, to filter out applicants from Pakistan or Iran, check a person's knowledge of the locale in Afghanistan they claim to have fled. Intimate knowledge about the interview constitutes an advantage. Yet many applicants hide details of their personal sufferings, which involve feelings of shame, persecution, wariness, painful memories, and violence. Instead they invent dramatized or alternative details in their interview. Their silence also serves the interests of a government unwilling to acknowledge asylum seekers' suffering. For Najeeb, knowledge about the interview was a point of pride. He delivered it in the style of a taxi-driver who has met the knowledge requirements for licensing and additional testing: "Immigration has added extra questions about local knowledge. If you claim you come from Kabul, they ask, 'How would you make tea, where is Darul Aman palace, where is the Arg [Presidential Palace], where is Feroz Ghar, Shar-e-Naw, what are Kabul's famous places, its sites of interest? What is your currency, what do your notes, your coins, one hundred Afghanis look like?' You should know every note has a city photo on it. When they ask, 'What uniform do soldiers wear in Kabul?' you should know each foreign country dresses its soldiers in its national uniform. Or they ask, 'What color is local *niswar* [chewing tobacco]?' 'What is the name and location of the big cinema?'"

Vital Movements

Haji Zaman's son traveled in England by special envoy—a coach departing the Calais Jungle migrant camp to display the British government's generous "rescue" of especially selected unaccompanied migrants aged fourteen to seventeen before the camp's forcible closure in late 2016. Haji Zaman's son and nephew sped along to Croydon, to "Lunar House," head office of visa and immigration affairs. The boy's father, like his paternal uncle, scrabbled together the money for smugglers to fly his son directly from Peshawar to France. While the son's confidence stopped with his first sighting of England that loomed as alien as a moonscape, his depressed father, despairing of ever being relieved of his responsibilities, and worrying for his much-loved son, began moving again, his blood now flowing more strongly with the boy's arrival.

IN PESHAWAR: CROSSINGS AND OTHER MOBILITIES

Migration trends for Afghans in Pakistan are geographically shaped. Most Afghan Pashtuns in Peshawar come from southeastern Afghanistan; Afghans from central and southwestern Afghanistan have established communities of origin in Islamabad. Karachi, the world's largest Pashtun city, receives all, as well migrant and Pashtuns displaced from fighting in Pakistan's Khyber Pakhtunkhwa province and the tribal agencies (Rehman 2017). Most Afghans in Peshawar are Pashtun. Peshawar's Uzbek, Tajik, Hazara, and Turkmen communities largely hail from Herat, Mazar-e-Sharif, or elsewhere in northern Afghanistan and live peaceably, running businesses, including manufacturing and selling carpets in Shoba and Khyber bazaars in the old city. Afghans live in all areas of Peshawar—in Tahkal, Board, Tajiabad, Hayatabad, Shahin Town, Saddar, Latifabad, Zaryab colony, Hayatabad, Tehkal, Afghan colony, Afridiabad, in Sethi Town and poorer enclaves along Charsadda Road (Turkmens and Uzbeks). There is an Afghan musicians' quarter in Dub Garai in the old city. During the Russian war Pashtun families settled in Kacha Garai, Nasir Bagh, Shamshatoo, and Jalozai refugee camps and others across the district.

The wealthiest families live in the older areas, such as Shahin Town near the old American Club. Many nouveaux riches reside in Hayatabad and, some joke, buy ostentatious houses that they then paint bright colors to loudly signal their wealth. Others drive lorries, buses, taxis, and rickshaws, are mechanics, or teach English to would-be migrants. Musicians, singers, and chefs cater for weddings and functions. Poorer Afghans push carts, work in small kiosks and shops, sell cigarettes and bags, are porters and gardeners, work in homes, polish shoes, collect rubbish for burning or selling *(kabadi),* or are street hawkers. The very poorest come seeking good families to hire their daughters as household help.

Afghans in Peshawar represent a formidable trading force and have connected Pashtuns across the border since before independence. Trading across borders, Afghans import, for example, cars and car parts, lorries, trucks, cigarettes, textiles, electronic and electrical goods, refrigerators, washing machines, house paint, building materials, carpets, and myriad other goods from China, Russia, Iran, Afghanistan, and the Middle East. They export rice, teas, dried fruits, spices, cooking oil, sports clothes, leather jackets, and almonds, and conduct transnational trades in trucks, lorries, and cars. Peshawar's sprawling *kar khanou* (work factories) market, where most traders are Afghan Pashtuns, expanded from trades in marble in the nineties. Now traders pitch up in large warehouses to sell containers of everything—refrigerators, tires, fabrics, batteries, radios—or conduct business from *kar khanou*'s many offices, or trade in its small shops. Saddar's more sedate shop rows trade carpets, hand-stitched dresses, and everything else, while Darra market backing onto Hayatabad serves eclectic trades in drugs, guns, and kidnapping.

I conducted fieldwork trips to Peshawar in 2010 and 2011 when I accompanied Afghans on visits home and visited Pakistani Pashtun friends. I stayed with friends as well as at a small hotel managed by Afridi tribesmen who, my interlocutors informed me, would protect me from the police and in my vulnerable position as a lone woman. I was not new to Peshawar, however, having lived and conducted fieldwork in Karachi at various times between 1993 and 2008 and having visited friends several times previously.

Driving along the Way

As Baryalai drove us out of Peshawar toward Shamshatoo camp, a generous commentary about the route combined biography with local folklore.

"Afghans live all along this route. To reach Shamshatoo, we'll take three roads: the Grand Trunk Road passing Board where richer Afghans live, then toward the perimeter; next the Ring Road, the stop for large trucks from Afghanistan. We won't take the turning for Kohat, but follow the road to Ziandai.

"This is a road to cure illnesses. Our car will pass Pandu Baba *ziarat* [shrine]; people say if you touch it, you can be cured of any ills. Then onto Ziandai. There is nothing here, this is a 'no place.' We lived here with my uncle when we fled Kabul, before we moved to Kacha Garai in the city. The road continues through small towns and villages where the Daulatzai people live. They are mostly Pashtuns who fled northern Afghanistan. Then to Khattak Puhl where Khattak tribespeople live. People swear the mullahs here can cure jaundice and yellow fever. This land was given by the government to Hekmatyar; most people here support Hizb-i-Islami.

"Let's continue, past the tall, smoking brick kilns where Afghans work for Pakistani bosses. Now past Shamshatoo town, into the camp. The camp is semiprivate. It's like a small town, controlled by its own militia. They do not give it to Pakistan. It has its own private houses, markets, schools, and even a jail. It's very safe to live here."

Established in 1982 by Hekmatyar, since this visit the camp's population of around eight thousand people diminished significantly when many returned to Afghanistan after 2016.

Do Not Trust a Researcher: In Shamshatoo

"I grew up here in Shamshatoo camp," said Allah Khan before offering this cautionary tale, a veiled warning to me perhaps, after we passed the militia at the camp's entrance in his Suzuki taxi, and parked past the shops and homes at the upper corner.

"Here in Shamshatoo, most people support Hizb-i-Islami. Hekmatyar has many men. In 1992 he surprised people when he signed a peace agreement with Ahmed Shah Massoud, his old enemy. One 'Hizb-i' called some supporters together.

"'Listen,' he said. 'Hekmatyar is very bad. After fighting jihad so long, he became Massoud's lackey; he sold us. Everyone knows Massoud made deals with Russia, France, and General Dostum. After so much jihad, all our fighting comes to nothing.' Everyone agreed Hekmatyar was bad.

"The next day when all reconvened, he changed tack. '*No!*' he shouted. 'I spoke lies yesterday. Gulbuddin is a hero. He lost his brothers, family, country; he left Afghanistan for Pakistan. Day and night he thinks only of jihad. He's not Massoud's slave, he played a game to destroy him. He's a true hero.' And everyone agreed.

"*Finally,* he turned and said, 'Yesterday you believed Gulbuddin was bad, today he was a hero. You must *think.* A clever [educated] person can make magic on you. Don't trust anyone. People can exploit you.'"

A Good Son

One windy night our group, a mix of English returnees and their local friends, liberally ordered barbecued lamb, meats, and salad at the Habibi restaurant opposite *kar khanou,* which was owned and staffed by Afghans. We arranged ourselves on the rooftop, enjoying live *rubab* and tabla music.

From his indigent beginnings in Kacha Garai camp, almost opposite the restaurant, Toryalai reclined into a tale about his brother in London whose son was granted a "leave to remain" visa following a long, legal process of establishing paternity. Having omitted his son from his original asylum application, he met with skepticism, a DNA test, and many months of anxious waiting.

Toryalai continued expansively, "'Congratulations,' the case officer finally proffered, 'He's your son!' 'Thank you,' his father replied crossly. 'I've told you so for months.'"

Reunited, father and son were thereafter assigned government housing. The tale ended happily: "The son helped his father get a home. He is a good son. He served his father."

Don't Tell My Name

Family honor and reputation are at stake in men's ability to protect female relatives at home. Mubeen was filled with shame upon recounting his mother's terror, humiliation, and flight during Kabul's civil war.

"After Najeebullah's government fell, Kabul imploded during intense factional fighting. I was hiding on our roof with our family, a very young child, with firing all around. *Pow pow,* so loud and terrifying. My father screamed I was sheltering on wrong side of the house. '*Move,*' he shouted, 'or the bullets will kill you.' My heart was pounding.

"That same night, with still pounding hearts, we all ran, taking what we could and hiding the rest. We fled down the narrow alleys that separated houses in our neighborhood to avoid the main road. My mother put her wedding gold around her head and tied a scarf tightly to conceal it. It was so terrible and shameful. The rest we hid.

"You can write this story, but don't tell my name. That's how we arrived in Peshawar."

The Dance of Blood

The war against the Taliban braided English local life with the circulation and repetition of rumors and stories, half true, exaggerated, and awful.

"In Kabul, near the end of Najibullah's time," began Razi, "the Hazaras made breast soup from Pashtun women, and forced Pashtun captives to eat it. They raped old Pashtun women. Worse, in the North, in Mazar and Balkh, they say Dostum cut the necks of Taliban fighters, poured gas inside the wounds, and lit it. The burning body would dance in pain, with fire and blood pouring out. They called it the *rakhs e khun*, the dance of blood. That's why we're here. Never trust Afghans from the North."

On the Incredible Discovery of a Snake

After the Indus burst its banks in 2010 and drowned all of Pakistan in flood water, Torylai became overwhelmed at witnessing the deathly force of nature which, unleashed, could evidently upturn the world. As we drove outside the city he expanded on that idea.

"In the floods, all the riverbanks burst and all Afghanistan's water flooded Peshawar in a roaring deluge. Here at Zahelo camp in Aman Ghar everything was totally destroyed. Many animals and people died, their bodies left rotting and unburied for days. The stench of corpses lingered for weeks after the floodwaters subsided.

"They discovered a dead snake there, only native to Afghanistan, a snake never found here. How *unbelievable* an Afghan snake should be *here*, dead with the refugees, hundreds of miles from home."

Lines of Return

In the following song lyrics by the celebrated Pashtun singer Naghma, the word *kadey* denotes travelers packing up their tents and belongings to move on. Deploying the plural case, here it implies the mass return of refugees from Peshawar to Afghanistan. Riding in Mati's taxi to the airport, he sang along.

Wus darna zama Pekhouwara
Da Kabul pe taraf
Zemunga kadey nun bareegi

Now I'm leaving you Peshawar
For Kabul side
We're loading up all our belongings today.[3]

A Difficult Offer

In June 2016, payments for Afghans to repatriate increased from US$200 to $US400 per person. For large households, such as those with over fifty members, the incentive was tempting.

"My father is in Afghanistan," stated Wali flatly, in October. What he could not say easily was that his father had left to find a new family home in Jalalabad, that their ancestral lands there had been appropriated by the provincial government for returning refugees ("We can give them that at least," he said, rationalizing the loss, "they are poor"), that Pakistan had closed the Torkham border and was not readmitting undocumented Afghans (or even those with documents), that he was fearful about his father's decision.

"*Never mind* the winter snow. *Never mind* having to sleep outside. How can they send people back to *fighting*? It's not *safe.*"

Youw Mazadar Glass Chai

Wandering through the small lanes of *qissa khwani* in Peshawar's old city, Hayatullah and I climbed a narrow, sharp-turning staircase to enter a rooftop teahouse where tea-makers brewed a huge vat of strong, sweet milky chai for workers and passersby.

Moving to a corner, we were the only customers apart from an older man who, eager to know who we were, and correctly claiming to recognize Hayatuallah's tribal origins from his face, started a conversation.

To allay any awkwardness about any unseemly exchange, he cited his version of a famous verse by Rehman Baba:

Ke dey pe zrekey guna nawi, tesh pe katoorkey guna nishta

If you have no sin in your heart, looking at someone is not a sin.

In his late fifties, he said, Gul Rahim made a living nearby in "handwork" *(de las kar),* selling from sacks of dried fruits and nuts on the roadside. His wife and sons were in Afghanistan. He visited infrequently. He had spent eighteen years in Mecca, so long because he was cheated by a labor agent who sent him with a group of Pakistanis for construction work. Holding an Afghan Mohajir card issued by the mujahideen, he found upon his arrival that he could not work. Working illegally, to save money, he slept near the Grand Mosque—in deep trouble, but in Allah's holy city thanks to God.

Happy at this spontaneous conversation, we exchanged stories and ordered pot after pot of tea, in the steam of which Gul Rahim moistened cheap, dry cigarettes. As we prepared to leave, I offered to pay. He protested, "Please give me this problem to pay for the tea. I will love it because I'm Afghan."

Not wanting to allow him to pay for tea we had liberally ordered, we engaged a complicated negotiation, which ended with Hayatullah's successful plea: "Please, you have given us more with your stories than we have given you."

Based on one warm chance meeting, Gul Rahim offered his story. Not knowing him in any meaningful sense, I was partly minded of Tagore's character the Kabuliwala.[4] I wondered how Tagore's allegory about the delayed gratification of wishes, waiting, breaks with reality, time, and unconditional love might apply to this fruit and nut vendor, and other Afghan laborers in Peshawar and England.

Saki Jan's Reluctance

Accompanied by two Pashtun Afghans, one returnee and his friend, in 2011 I visited a crowded neighborhood of Tajik-speaking refugees to meet a local Herati family introduced to me by a friend in Britain. Upon our arrival, Saki Jan articulated his disapproval of foreigners, especially educated ones.

"Foreigners take your knowledge, then push themselves ahead. Be scared of three countries: the English pen, Pakistani corruption, and Iranian sweetness."

Hekmatyar and the General

The Pakistani authorities' antipathy toward Afghans in the 2010s contrasted starkly with the Soviet–Afghan war when Pakistan's General Zia ul-Haq sponsored mujahideen groups against Russia, and welcomed Afghan refugees into Pakistan like brothers. Driving in a taxi with Zmarai around the old city, our driver explained that history wistfully.

"In Hekmatyar's time there was a blast in a cinema near here. Afghans across the city were rounded up and jailed. Hekmatyar was furious. He went to the jail, and released them all. Nobody stopped him. This was during General Zia's time. Zia loved Hekmatyar. Now nobody will release Afghans from jail."

Urdu Graffiti on the Khyber Pass

Amrikey ghulamey aur goonda gardi jät ke liye

[Unite against] American slavery and their gangster activities.

In Ten Peshawar Taxis

In 2011, talking to taxi-drivers as we hired lifts around Peshawar, accompanied by returnees, I collected many stories. These drivers drove small unlicensed Suzukis. In those cases where the drivers and my companions were Afghan, our conversations centered on Afghans' experiences in Pakistan, migration to Britain, and police intimidation in everyday life. All Afghans, British returnees included, experienced police harassment, arrests, confinement, and document checks, as did lower-class Pakistani Pashtuns, non-Pashtun Afghans, and all drivers of low-end transport vehicles, bicycles, and rickshaws (Alimia 2019). Alimia (2019) writes of Afghans who are stopped and subjected to searches, as well as the petty corruption of police at the hundreds of checkpoints networking Peshawar's cityscape. The biopolitics of profiling a group under pressure to leave Pakistan means just looking Afghan may cause one to be stopped, arrested, or deported.

Bestrewn with checks and constraints, the anonymous taxi-ride lends itself to shared personal divulgences, stories of work, struggles, pleasures, and family disputes. The scenario of returnees traveling in taxis with a British woman lent itself to many such exchanges with taxi-drivers who spoke openly, were happy to stop by the roadside to talk further or be interviewed. One, hearing Zmarai speak, declared, "I recognize your Jalalabad accent. I like Afghans from Jalalabad." In this case, the returnees led the way.

Another relayed the difficulties of driving work in Peshawar.

"Sometimes I take damaged secondhand cars to Jalalabad for Rs 1,500 per trip. I can take three, hooked onto one another. If I leave Aman Ghar near Naw Kar at 5:00 a.m., drive to Jalalabad, and hand over the car to the customs [*gomrak*] there, I can be home that night. Those jobs are not enough."

As we passed a Turkmen market in Shoba, another offered his perspective.

"Turkmens are happy here. They're peaceful, they don't make problems but do make excellent *kāleen* [carpets]. They live mostly here on the road to Charsadda. Uzbeks also produce *kāleen* and live on Charsadda road, but they fight, for language, power, just nothing. Uzbeks got rich here through fighting."

Another shared his predicaments.

"We have land in Khogyiani. When it was distributed among our relatives, my brothers refused me. They said I've become Pakistani, I no longer keep *murrai-zwandai* with them. I sent the argument to a *jirga*, who said, 'Brothers may fight, but they are still brothers.' The old people in the tribe came and decided in my favor. Soon I'll claim it. It will be difficult, but I'll do it."

Taxi-drivers are at the front line of violations of Afghans' rights and dignity in Pakistan.

"I was born in Chaman camp near Quetta. I lived in Islamabad and worked for the Serena Hotel as a delivery driver. I could go to all the top hotels without being stopped—Afghans can't usually enter. Now I live near Nasir Bagh *thana* [police station], last checkpost before FATA [Federally Administered Tribal Agencies].[5] I'm eighteen now, I left school after class [grade] 3. I have an uncle in London and a cousin in Birmingham. I'd love to go, [but] I can't get a Pakistani driving license here. I'm scared at the checkposts, very panicky. If the police are ahead, I'll drop you before the checkpost. They'll charge me Rs 600."

Discrimination and hostility affect Pakistanis, too.

"I'm Shinwari, not Afghan, but the police treat both badly. They're worse to Afghans, and non-Pakhtuns—for example, Dari speakers. The army are better, they don't demand money. From A to Z the police are bad. My brother-in-law joined, but saw so much harassment he left."

Many Afghans in Pakistan use illegal economies to acquire paper citizenship as Pakistanis (Sadiq 2009). Notwithstanding, an interesting reversal of mobility capital underpins Afghans' greater possibilities of European travel and citizenship than Pakistanis whose applications to visit Europe are highly restricted.

"I come from Khost. My father has a saloon there, cutting hair. Previously, I worked four years in Dubai driving for a bus company. I bought a house in Mohmand agency, where many Afghans live. Mohmands and

Afghans are brothers. I'm happy here. I don't want to return to Afghanistan while there's fighting. I have no problems because I look Pakistani and Afghan. I have a Mohajir card and a fake Pakistani *shenakhti* card. The police think I'm Pakistani. Afghans immediately know I'm Afghan! Afghans understand because they travel more, see the world."

Young men are arrested wholesale.

"We were fourteen friends, cousins, in two cars, setting out to enjoy. The police stopped us and took us *all* into the *thana*. We shouted very loudly to annoy them, but they beat us separately in turn. I think they did worse to one. When my turn came, I shouted that my uncle is friends with your intelligence chief, you will lose your job if you touch me. Meanwhile my brother phoned my uncle. Luckily, they didn't touch me. We were finally released, that day. I was afraid we might be there for days, with nobody knowing."

Drivers spoke of desires to migrate, prohibitive costs, and of ways that migration creates differences in opportunity within families.

"I'm from Kunar but was born here. My brothers are in Ostend and Holland. One is waiting for citizenship. Here they don't grant taxi licenses to Afghans. I have four mothers—my father was educated, he worked for the Pakistani post office, he died long ago. I want to go to Holland, but it costs US$18,000, cheaper by land. It's US$25,000 to go to the UK because people must cross the sea—but my brothers can't pay either."

Still others pointed out sights, or thought aloud, spoke trivialities, or told jokes to make the journey more cheerful.

"If you take Jehangir Rai road here you reach Khan Dera, a *beautiful* river spot with running water. A Pakhto recording studio makes music outside here, the proper way."

Allah Khan joked about himself.

"I had a regular job to collect a college girl each day, Fariha. I really liked her, in my mind and heart. I kissed her seat when she left my taxi. One day I telephoned her and said, 'I love you.' She said, 'You're stupid, don't call me, you're making problems.'"

London in Chowk Yadgar

Stopping in the money changers' quarter in Chowk Yadgar, I was surprised, perhaps naively, when a dealer addressed me in a London accent.

"I work here helping my cousin's business for half the year, and as a mini-cab-driver in London for the other half. I live six months here, six months there."

Conclusion

The circuitous routes that migrants took to England crossed continental Europe, Asia, and Africa. Some appear to have used heroin-smuggling routes through the North Caucasus, and cocaine routes through Africa (UNODC 2017). They highlight under-researched connections between human and drug trafficking in the ways that opioid use diffuses out across Afghanistan's borders alongside migrants and refugees, and also the use of heroin by migrants.

Since the mid-2010s, and the withdrawal of foreign eradication programs, opium cultivation in Afghanistan has increased exponentially,[6] bringing burgeoning mass opioid addiction and challenges for neighboring, transit, and destination countries (UNODC 2018). Estimates cite 3.6 million heroin addicts in Afghanistan, including a million women (Constable 2017). Pakistan supposedly has the largest number of heroin addicts in the world—over four million—with an estimated forty-four tons of heroin consumed in Pakistan annually (Quigley 2014). Peshawar borders opium fields in Badakhshan, Kunar, and Nangarhar provinces, and heroin-processing labs in Khyber agency.

The chapter also elucidated crossings of multiple material and existential borders. These returned us to reflect as anthropologists on our trade in words, and to ways our perceptions of life and endurance lay rich ground for enlisting an "ordinary ethics" of speech and reasoning that can question social life (Lambek 2010) and help make bearable others' difficult journeys (Kleinman 2014). Ethnographic stories, or pieces of stories, also invoke "timeliness" (Rabinow 2007) in the ways that time works to create the moving subject, and moves both chronologically and phenomenologically through what people remember, struggle to assimilate, or use to deflect or to entertain. Recognizing multiple pasts and presents in controverted interactions between people, polities, and political visions shape writing and interpretation as political acts, and Afghanistan's political and historical territory as reaching beyond national borders.

The chapter also raised questions about the ways people are stopped or propelled into motion, when nothing is moving in the direction it should be, or vistas appear upside down. It pointed to refugees in Peshawar who still feel estranged after thirty years, Afghans in England whose attachment to their families after twenty years of separation remains strong, and the dual plane of wonder and de-rooting shaping children's passages through Europe. Their stories highlight marginal transnational lives shaped by global inequalities, fracture and liminality, and losses and gains in confidence.

Involving the ethnographer and the observed, fieldwork and friendship, and enactments of kinship and exchanges of care, ethnographic fragments illuminate the ontology and temporality of crossings. Migrants' passages through land, sea, and physical and psychic metamorphoses create new tactics for bearing life. They insert life into text and, to return to the book's prelude, respond to the call "We are more than history or mere parchment, insist the crying corpses—we are human! Bring us alive!"

Finally, I return to Das, for whom storytelling bears on the literal struggle to hold corroded lives and worlds together, and attempt a deeper relation between violence, hurt, and different writing experiments. She argues that anthropology can act on the double register to contest the official amnesia that makes violence disappear, but also attend to "poisonous knowledge that is digested, eaten, swallowed, contained, but still needs attention so that it does not become a curse on the world" (2015, 386). Anthropology provokes attention to what cannot be eaten. It also dares us to imagine different realties, although we should not imagine the ongoing task of renewal and redemption, of rewriting fragments and remaking worlds, can be complete.

As when she visited my home, Malalai expressed this directly: "I know enough about violence. I'm more interested in how to get freedom."

5. BARTH IN SUSSEX

Community, Feasting, and Immobility Revisited

Chey na kar, alta tse kar?—If you have no work, what work is there for you? (i.e., do not involve yourself in something if not essential).

Khpel sifat da khpelay khulay na mazaa na kari; bulbulan ba de sifat kari ka ta gul shawe—Praise for oneself from one's own mouth is not in good taste; the songbirds will praise you if you become a flower.

Ka Mohammed Pakhtun wa, tola Pakhtana ba kafirān wa—If the Prophet Mohammed was a Pashtun, all Pashtuns would be nonbelievers.

This chapter's focus is on collective mobilization and immobility in regard to Afghan Pashtun community organization in the Sussex field site.[1] In doing so, it engages the work of Fredrik Barth, which has received scant attention in regard to recent studies of Pashtuns both in- and outside anthropology, despite his substantial contribution to understanding Pashtun political leadership (Edwards 1998; Hanifi 2016). First, it examines the extent to which, in terms of Barth's (1959b) seminal arguments about segmentary opposition in Pathan organization, community politics in Sussex described a two-bloc system of competition and conflict that maintained a curious balance: "The relative stability of alliances, and the continued relatively peaceful coexistence of the two parties . . . seems puzzling. One would rather have expected a chaos of constant realignments and a disintegration of the bloc organization" (14).

Second, it reflects on the political significance of collective immobility in wider community politics in Sussex, developing on similar adaptations in Afghanistan (Coburn 2011). It shows that those who refuse political participation (who despite their interests in acquiring community power, do not make overt moves to formal leadership or power) emerge victorious—albeit that individual and group power shifts fluidly between fairly equal blocs. Formations of immobility establish competitive social hierarchies, ensure that conflicts do not erupt (too far), and cohere local Afghans around shifting formations of superiority, power, and difference in a fluid context of recent migration and settlement. These factors of social and political organization converge to signal, in Barth's terms, less ethnic fragmentation and a lack of cohesion in the diasporic context, as ways that Afghan Pashtuns in a small English city are "playing the same game" (1959b, 15).

Third, by way of expanding on Barth's anomaly of finding stability where conflict might be expected, and of neither simply applying Barth's model wholesale nor reducing actors solely to instrumental political players or to men of action, the chapter expands on previous discussions of hospitality, commensality, and food. It moves from the indignities of the food voucher system and its bitter lesson in cultural citizenship for marginal and excluded asylum seekers, and the contrasts of the men's commensal food practices—their group picnics on the Sussex Downs, group meals at Afghan kebab shops in town, and their refreshment of the sensorium of eating on pleasure trips undertaken in Pakistan and Afghanistan—to the significance of their collective political struggles occurring over the flashpoint of the Eid-ul-Fitr feast and religious festival. Certainly the political hot coals of this event also involve opportunities for shared enjoyment, religious fidelity, and cultural practice between ethnic compatriots. They also have relevance for competitive feasting in comparative contexts (Bloch 2005; Bourdieu 1990; Dietler 2001; Herzfeld 1987; Ortner 1978; Shyrock 2012). They bear particularly on Barth's (1959b) theorization of hospitality as a prime mover of highly dynamic political relations, which acts simultaneously as a stabilizer of community through games and conflict. Additionally, on his position that ethnic identity is not only about social boundary processes and the use of culture as a political resource, but also about the meanings of eating, joking, and sharing pleasures (Eriksen 2015, 108; in Lewis 2017).

Since the millennium, Afghan community politics in this city reveals a picture of intense competition, movements of formation and dissolution, and quelled leadership bids. These activities formally separated Pashtuns from non-Pashtuns (although informally separations were less pronounced) while also leading intense rivalries to emerge and play out between taxi-drivers, mostly Pashtuns. After 2010, attempts to formalize a Pashtun "community organization" gathered intensity, involving local political manipulations that in Fredrik Barth's terms describe a "variety of game" (1959b, 15) with certain characteristics.[2] The city's Pashtuns became divided into roughly two groups: the "new" community organization, and the "original" community leaders organized around a crude narrative opposition between "modern" and "traditional" values, tribal and regional origins, and status based on economic success and length of time spent living in England. The two groups' leaders were among the first to settle in the city. These groups were organized around two families *(khel)* and their allies, whom I pseudonymize as the Gulzai and Shinzada groups, respectively.[3]

While Barth's model apparently describes a predictable arrangement of Pashtun organization and opposition, for Barth there are no fixed social structures, underlying Lévi-Straussian models of the human mind, but rather the core issue is the observation of humans in action: motivated individuals who maximize and calculate the odds in various social situations (Eriksen 2015). Barth did not search for abstract rules, but rather investigated the knowledge, sentiments, and interpersonal realities existing at moments of political, economic, and social decision making. Introducing some reflections on im/mobility within a longitudinal approach may account for formations that disrupt ideas that the two-bloc system will always prevail as a stabilizer of conflict. It reveals the dissolution of the two-bloc organization over time, and their incorporation into the factionalized interests of a single community organization. Nonetheless, within the group conflicts occur between individuals over the leadership of sporting, educational, and religious–cultural activities.

The chapter also raises questions concerning ways religious identities provide mobile and immobile trajectories in variegated relation to community formation, competition, and Pashtun political organization. It also queries some limitations of mapping different kinds of relationship of patrilineal and matrilineal descent within the family with, for example, different kinds of affect, to account for bondings and conflicts within the family that thwart or bypass these expectations (Jackson 2009, 61). It brings this to a critique of the paradox in Barth's arguments and the question of why, despite conscious individual ambitions to power, these are almost always thwarted, or achieved only temporarily, and the stabilization of conflicts within an acephalous political system is maintained.

Last, the focus on im/mobility raises broader conceptual questions related to the vulnerability of structure to process in temporal processes of transformation, the extent to which structure and process may align commensurately in community politics, and the potential significance of prioritizing a processual ontology over a genealogical reading of migrants' political organizations.

The Gulzai and Shinzada Groups

The core Gulzai grouping comprises four full-sibling brothers and many nephews, close friends, and kin from their *khel* and larger *quam* in London. This group originates from Nangarhar, with younger members who were born in Peshawar and had never lived in Afghanistan. To recap, a *khel* refers to a smaller strand or segment of the larger *qaum* that may "only" go back five or six generations. For example, "Sabat" *khel* was formed by one of three brothers several generations back, who each formed segments based on their names or *takhalus* names (e.g., *Yaad khel* and *Nazir khel*). Over time segments "separate" or grow to the extent that members are not involved in each other's affairs. Instead, the literature maintains, parallel agnatic collaterals compete (Ahmed 2004; Barth 1959b). Thus, while Sher Agha, Hamid, and Hashmat share a grandfather two generations back, their families are effectively now separate. They are distant enough to be friends without the interference of structural tension.[4] Sher Agha and his brothers are proud of, but wary of forming reciprocal or close relations with their direct agnatic collaterals, whose father boasted extreme wealth in his lifetime and operated a global trading business from Dubai. Hence, when this uncle offered to buy them a shop in Sussex after Sher Agha acquired British citizenship, they deliberated but refused for fear of igniting future agnatic hostilities. Their closest relative–friends are a core group of around twenty Southall relatives more distant in lineage terms (i.e., not the children of their paternal or maternal uncles), but of similar financial status insofar as all are remitting migrant taxi-drivers.

Some of this group made the journey from Pakistan to Britain together to claim asylum. Their friendship bonds are stronger than those the brothers shared with their distant cousin and half brother in Sussex— neither of whom, to avoid taking sides or direct confrontation, were involved in community politics. Later, as the Gulzi brothers' nephews arrived and were successful in their asylum claims, this group swelled. While as minors the nephews lived with foster families near the main asylum seeker processing center in nearby Croydon, they frequently visited Sussex and correspondingly aligned themselves with their uncles and supporters, approximating but not exactly mirroring a father–sibling brother–son model (Barth 1969a, 1969b).

In terms of social, cultural, and economic capital, the Gulzi brothers were disadvantaged in terms of newer values placed by Pashtuns on education and literacy, but advantaged in more "traditional" forms of status insofar as theirs was a respected wealthy *qaum* with political influence (although their strand's wealth had declined over the past decade). These brothers' wives and children lived in Peshawar. They claimed status from their relatives' involvement in fighting with mujahideen groups in the nineties—and their wealthy uncle's patronage of the Taliban subsequently in exchange for permission to conduct business. Hashmat boasted that "he donated one hundred Land Cruisers to the Taliban," and that former president Hamid Karzai had attended his funeral. The brothers' attitude was "We don't *want* Pashtuns from an inferior tribe and area to be our leaders—it's shameful here, and back home." Hence, in leading the Gulzai bloc, they drew support from unrelated friends and taxi-drivers into competitive interactions over transnational family status, and tribal and personal reputation. They justified these in terms of desires to preserve traditional values in a foreign country, wherein they recognized that the values and meanings of Afghan Pashtun identity were not fixed but in transformation and flux.

Their core rivals, the Shinzada group originating from Wardak, comprised five brothers, plus one half brother, and many growing sons. They claimed a respectable family history of high learning and education. They boasted that their region had produced a number of notable military and government officials. While the Gulzai group reiterated the aspersion that people from Wardak were politicking social climbers, the Shinzadas derogated the Gulzai bloc for their "backward" attitudes (meaning that "their minds are like concrete, they will never change"—*harshey chey kham shi pakheygi, kho insaan chey kham shi bia na pakheygi*—which literally translates as anything raw can be cooked, but if a person is raw they cannot be cooked). I first met the brother Haji Waleed working in an Asian supermarket (work beneath his education and qualifications) when he arrived in Sussex in 2000. He joked regularly about my personal background, teasing me by saying "A Chinese–English–Pakistani— what's that?!"

The four full-sibling brothers initially leased a restaurant business. Eventually all became taxi-drivers and driver–owners. Some acquired mortgages. All performed Haj and Umrah pilgrimages, and took the respected moniker "Haji" as a prefix to their names. All eventually married and settled their wives in Britain. Nonetheless, fraternal tensions characterized this group, and when Haji Inayatullah sought to establish himself as a community leader, his brothers were not always supportive. Haji Waleed's children all became university educated, including his daughters, who set a precedent for Afghan Pashtun women in the city, and augmented the family's status narrative of educated professionalization. Their differences from the Gulzai bloc to an extent arguably characterized the idiomatic opposition between *kalam aw kalashnikov* (the pen and the gun),[5] a symbolic representation of opposition between education and violence, democracy and warlordism, progress and tradition, and changing migrant class-consciousness in Britain. They reflected ways that education as a route to social mobility, autonomy, and financial security have become progressively more valued among Afghan Pashtun families over tribal standing, political power in Afghanistan, or the sole acquisition of wealth through business. Flourishing Pashto and Afghan university student societies were instrumental in this shift—as education has assumed increasing value for the children of migrants from Afghanistan and elsewhere. Britain's post–World War II history of immigration from the colonies to the heart of the imperium saw many children of immigrant parents from across Asia, including myself, achieve social mobility through education and professionalization.

Barth in Sussex

The tensions between the two groups characterize in Barth's terms a two-bloc organization of conflict and competition. While I cannot do full justice to Barth's exposition in a short chapter, I summarize some key points. Barth's (1959b) main premise concerning Yusufzai Pashtun patrilineal descent groupings in the tribal areas of North-West Pakistan is that these structural arrangements do *not* translate in an equivalent manner in political action. Certainly structural arrangements that determine the fusion of the interests of fathers, sons, sibling brothers, and their descendants constitute a typical descent lineage system *(khel)* or segment, and an implied Durkheimian form of "mechanical solidarity," to which Yusufzai Pashtuns align (6). The same might be said of the full brothers of the Gulzai and Shinzada groupings. Rather than mobilize to merge descent segments together (Fortes and Evans-Pritchard 1940; Radcliffe-Brown 1950), Barth proposes that Pashtun genealogies are important in political action *only* insofar as they define rivals and allies in a two-bloc system of opposition. Close descent groups are consistent rivals. This directly contradicts the fusion of smaller related segments in opposition to larger segments that one might expect in a "classic" lineage system (9). For Barth, twofold Pashtun political groupings depend on a combination of individual leaders and individual strategic choices. These are shaped by forms of equivalence between full-sibling brothers, and structural rivalries with patrilineal cousin brothers (involving intense factionalism and competition for status, power, patronage, and leadership).[6]

In sum, the "persisting opposition between collateral agnates prevents their interests from fusing even *vis-à-vis* outsiders" (11). The system of two blocs does not depend on a recognition of the nature or function of duality; rather, it emerges through individual self-interest. In addition, structural ties between fathers and sons, sibling brothers and their sons/children, supersede those of half brothers or maternal relatives—and segmentation between groups of half brothers may occur, when groups carry the names of their respective mothers (8). Barth's model depends on an equivalence between the two blocs, wherein lies its pertinence to the Sussex scenario. However, Barth does not expand on the processes by which blocs of equivalence are formed in the first place, or on variations that occur when they do not.

Barth is relevant for explaining why the cousins and half brothers of both the Gulzai and Shinzada groups were *not* part of their core bloc, but why the Gulzi brothers' Southall friends, more distant geographically and also in kinship terms, *were* reliable allies. His arguments are also relevant to Sher Agha's ability to make leadership bids without the jealousy of his brothers: that is, there was a strong sense of fraternal unity in this particular family who considered themselves "one bone," and there were no individual leadership interests among the other brothers. While his argument that self-interest is self-limiting because of the equivalences between two opposing blocs constitutes a limitation—certainly in the case of larger national political contexts (Edwards 1998)—it has pertinence in the smaller Sussex case nonetheless.

Barth (1959b, 20) calls for the study of Pashtun lineage organizations, group solidarity, and games for political power "in conditions of change"—which here concern the political organization of Afghan Pashtun migrants; their mobilization into two persistently opposed "community" blocs; their behind-the-scenes lobbying and strategic manipulation that ensure neither bloc becomes overly dominant, but oppositions still persist; and ways dynamic relations between full brothers, strategic allies, and other kin move in and out of these alliances and oppositions. This raises questions regarding ways such structural arrangements are commensurate with highly fluid conditions of change—in a very different situation facing Pashtuns to that described by Barth.

First, according to Barth (1959b, 15), the primary conflicts occur in the field of government. These involve political manipulations that characterize a variety of game, wherein "the simple nature of the opposition encourages the formation of a two-party, not a multi-party, system" (16). Within each bloc, meetings of core members are ostensibly egalitarian spaces for making strategic decisions around joint action, resolving conflicts, and collective leadership. In Sussex these might include meetings to organize large-scale feasting events for religious occasions; sporting activities involving friendly and competitive football and cricket matches; and decisions on group membership and strategy. These conflicts were subsumed, as before, into a division between the Shinzada "community organization" and the Gulzai group's opposition to its leadership pretensions (over them). They were partially stayed or maintained in balance insofar as the Gulzai group held its dominance in the political–religious sphere of feasting—due to Sher Agha and Hamid's culinary skills honed in local restaurants—and the Shinzada group in activities such as children's sports sessions (the Gulzi brothers' children were not in Britain anyway) and football matches against outside teams. While within each bloc consensus was sometimes grumblingly reached, it was "sufficient" in Barth's terms "to merge the interests of one corporate group against the other" (9). Notwithstanding, over time the two blocs would eventually merge into one leadership coalition with influence assigned equally to five nominated leaders.

Blocs function to protect members by "exerting underhand pressure, by working together in councils, and as armies in the case of fighting" (Barth 1959b, 13). Balance between blocs is maintained by the cupidity of individual politicians. Thus Sher Agha, a skilled sportsman, sometimes coached the Shinzada "community's" football team or played for them during matches against outside teams—reminding them of his value and prowess while ensuring rivalry did not disintegrate too far. These activities aptly contradict any conception of political activities as pure self-interested opportunism (14). That is, that competition, rivalry, and conflict serve to *maintain* structural arrangements and the exercise of power within a broader-based system of political organization (13–14)—and do not allow supremacy to reside permanently with any one leader or "king."

Regarding the relation between structure and anti-structure, chapter 2 examined how *chakar* simultaneously establish and dissolve structures through the illusory freedom of travel and movement. Bringing this paradox to analyze the conditions at stake in community politics can generate further insights into this relation in a way, I suggest, that does *not* involve jettisoning Barth's arguments about structural organization for alternative readings that prioritize process. Rather, they push us toward a reading of ways both interpretations coexist, even if equivocally. The idea can be fruitfully brought to analyze another dimension of community conflicts and organizations, in the interplay between mobility and immobility. This bears on immobility and its workings as a strategy or political tactic to stabilize conflict.

Immobility as a Political Tactic

A closer inspection of Afghan community history in Sussex reveals multiple tactics of switching alliances, hedging bets, open hostility, threats, public pronouncements of unity, appearances of inaction compared with furious behind-the-scenes work to form alliances—and designs on dominance and power shaped around masculinized aesthetics of tribal and family superiority, individual reputation, and coerced loyalties.

To illustrate how immobility might work as a political tactic, and to complement Barth's model, in 2000 an Afghan community organization was established by two brothers of the Gulzai group, Wazir and Sher Agha, although with little support among the city's embryonic Afghan community; following Wazir's deportation for spending a lengthy time in Pakistan during his asylum application process it dissolved. Two separate attempts to formalize a community group followed by brothers of the Shinzada group between 2000 and 2005, Razi and Inayatullah. These were sabotaged by Sher Agha and his brothers, who spread rumors that they were earning money for the local government as British spies—harsh, but an accusation sufficient to inspire suspicion given many knew of British Afghans who had worked as informants during the 2001–14 war. Thus, while the city council provided many services for "vulnerable migrants," they eschewed engagement. They rejected the derogatory category "refugees" and a "host" country warring in Afghanistan. Rather than "assimilate" as promoted in local government agendas for Muslim migrants, they instead developed diverse forms of collectivity that simultaneously assimilated, accommodated, and resisted English and Western influence.

That is, in relation to formal partnerships or relations with the city council, nothing moved. Through the strategic adoption of "collective immobility"—by decisively *not* acting to form an official Afghan community organization that could serve as the mouthpiece in communications with local government, and by blocking opponents' initiatives—they created opponents and stability in the process. This allowed them, paradoxically, some freedom of movement to negotiate identity, citizenship, and progress on their own terms: to create alliances, maintain boundaries, pursue forms of "community engagement" as it suited them, and quell leadership claims.

Collective immobility was directed toward subverting dominant practices of citizenship, creating autonomous critical pathways to social cohesion and peace, and also described a strategy of the Gulzai brothers to block the Shinzada family from claiming dominance over them. In 2009, an attempt by Inayatullah of the Shinzada bloc to form an Afghan Taxi-Drivers Association was thwarted by Sher Agha, leaving it active only nominally. Informally, a similar pattern emerged. When in 2010 a group of taxi-drivers arranged a meeting to discuss the possibility of collecting funds for charitable endeavors in Afghanistan, the idea was initially met with enthusiasm— "It'll be our choice [*khpel waq*], not the government's"—but these became beset with arguments about who should be "leader." In their subsequent meetings they enviously attacked Inayatullah's plans to collect funds to build or rent a mosque. "Why do we need an Afghan mosque? There are three mosques in the city. This is his *personal* ambition, not Islam."

So the idea dissolved, as did the grouping—and the years 2009–14 characterized a hiatus in formal and political activities. This served to germinate the relative strength of two blocs that would subsequently emerge. Informally these years were characterized by an increase in the city's Afghan population and a growth in community parties, football, volleyball, and cricket training sessions—occurring alongside the si-multaneous rise of the Afghan national cricket team. I followed similar sporting developments in 2011 as part of a community–university en-gagement research project.[7]

In the sense communities either cannot or will not move, immobility's passivity is ambivalent, and may have positive, negative, and ambiguous valuations. Immobility may encompass "positive" strategies of active re-sistance, or an active mode of refusing to move toward assimilationist so-cial processes (Lakha 2009). Through adopting "collective immobility" in relation to formal organization, these migrants strategically avoided, and engaged, divisive conflicts based on ethnic, regional, or political identity.

This behavior bears similarities to the strategies of "masterly inaction" described in Coburn's (2011) ethnography of a Tajik-majority town in northern Afghanistan in the post-2001 period. Coburn queried why, despite high levels of political tension, feuding, and factionalism, local politics remained peaceful. Rather than "traditional" categories such as tribe, clan, or state, he emphasized shifting alliances based on tribes, but also on patronage and shared loyalties to modern commanders, political leaders, or nongovernmental organizations. These flexible groups con-stantly competed for power, creating not Hobbesian war and violence but temporary peace and stability (6) and prevented the emergence of a single leader (29). Coburn's analysis suggests that "collective immobility" in this Sussex city may indeed describe a response to migration and a potentially hostile host society. It reflects an older adaptation for coping with political and economic instability, with its roots in multiple hierarchies, allegiances, and divisions in Afghanistan—and shifting loyalties based on forms of social and cultural capital that may include one's tribal origin, religious leadership qualities, status based on age, length of stay in England, culinary and sporting expertise, the ability to organize, and more recently educational achievement and literacy.

By 2014 many Afghans were more established in English life. Inayatullah's and his brothers' children were thriving educationally. Sher Agha and his brothers' families were living in Pakistan, and they still bore the burdens of remittances. At 2014's end, Inayatullah successfully formed a city "Afghan Community" organization and hosted a launch party attended by around thirty local men, where prayers for the group's success were offered. Outnumbered in this case, the Gulzi family members and supporters did not attend, although they observed events closely. They refused an invitation on principled grounds: "We want autonomy and peace; we neither want relations with the English council, nor divisive politics in this city. Their organization is like a political party."

Behind the scenes they made concerted efforts to meet with council representatives and sports development officers, and to attend council refugee forum meetings; they made plans to use council funding for a regular football club, distributed housing benefit and immigration advice leaflets, and agreed to assist the city police with information on human trafficking. However, these initiatives disintegrated—mostly due to the members' lack of commitment beyond their rivalry with the Shinzada group. The same year a separate group was established by Dari speakers (mostly Tajiks, Hazaras, and Uzbeks), whom both Pashtun groups derogated because some openly drank alcohol, and two of their leaders had "shamefully" divorced non-Muslim wives within a year of marriage. This group also established their own annual Eid party, which has continued, separate from the Pashtuns.

High Stakes: Islam, Pashtuns, and Small and Large Wars

Edwards (1998) engages three of Barth's principal critics—Talal Asad, Akbar Ahmed, and Michael Meeker—in order to assess the relevance of

Barth's work for an analysis of the different stages of war in Afghanistan (1979–98).

Edwards prioritizes Barth's argument in *Political Leadership among Swat Pathans* that political relationships are formed primarily from decisions people take in response to circumstances; that "society" emerges as the aggregate of individual and collective choices which subsequently shape, *intentionally and inadvertently*, people's life histories, and those of people around them (713). First is Asad's (1972) critique of Barth's notion of free choice as the central operating principle in Swat society. Asad argues that it was not free choice but the landowning class, within the agrarian class structure, that was key to political leadership—in short, that Barth neglected the influence of the landowner class who could exploit and dominate those without land (Edwards 1998, 714). Second, Akbar Ahmed (1980) criticizes Barth's neglect of the rise of the state system within Swat, which centered on the charismatic and beneficial leadership of the Wali (ruler). For Ahmed, Barth failed significantly to differentiate between *nang* (honor-bound) and *qalang* (rent-paying) Pakhtuns. Whereas *nang* societies are poor, acephalous, and segmentary in nature, and codes of conduct bound by traditional codes of honor—*qalang* societies produce marketable goods; and their interactions are asymmetrical and shaped more by patron–client relations than by Pakhtunwali. For Ahmed, Barth *overemphasized* conflicts between the ruling class and their subjects. Ahmed also criticizes the Marxist and Barthian model of the Pashtun man as a maximizing entrepreneur who "confronts the material world, comprehends it, and wishes to possess it"—and he criticizes Barth for neglecting the influence of local saintly lineages and wider Sufistic traditions of Islam (Edwards 1998, 715). Third, Meeker (1980) disagrees with both Asad's and Akbar's criticisms. For Meeker, Barth is limited by a vision of society as a self-balancing structure with interlocking functions, and misses the forces of organized violence within institutions that stabilize injustice (Edwards 1998, 715).

Proceeding to analyze various stages of the war in Afghanistan, Edwards finds obvious rapport in Asad's argument regarding the class underpinnings of the Marxist Khalq party's coup in December 1979—likewise, in Ahmed's argument that Islam provided a binding force against the corrosive competition of the khans between 1980 and 1989 when the seven Islamic political parties controlled the anti-Soviet resistance from

Peshawar. That is, recognizing the limitations of Afghanistan's rivalrous politics to confront a powerful foreign occupier, "people looked for unity and leadership among charismatic individuals and religiously based political formations" that transcended local contexts, and fostered a sense of connection to "larger patterns and institutional arrangements in the Islamic world at large"—not through miracles and saints, but rather "the promise of immortality and eternal paradise" (Edwards 1998, 719). Edwards locates much significance for Meeker's pessimistic diagnosis in the decline of the resistance parties and the rise of local warlords and commanders. He sees in the Taliban movement an anomaly to each of the positions established by Barth and his critics. That is, far from Barth's depiction of the unifying role of Islam in Swat, Islam in Afghanistan has been as divisive as it has been unifying (Edwards 1998, 720). Edwards sees the Taliban's success in transforming from a madrasa to a militia movement in their ability to build a popular base, rather than imposing themselves on the people, and by condemning the Islam of the political parties by identifying with the purist culture and Islam of the villages (725). Notwithstanding, the Taliban became incorporated into Afghanistan's national political apparatus, and continue to enjoy support from a war-weary populace.

How do these critiques aid this analysis of community politics in Sussex? Regarding Asad's emphasis on class differences, these are not significantly pronounced among this stratified but nonetheless fairly equal community comprising taxi-drivers and blue-collar workers. Neither do differences in status and wealth involve economic interdependencies and attendant possibilities for exploitation. While they may produce envy, they do not in themselves determine political authority.

Certainly, in the forceful individual strategies for supremacy in the matters of community feasting and religious celebration, there is value in Meeker's argument that "heroic identity" intentionally deploys personal strategies based on force and coercion. In this geographically delimited field site, the intensities surrounding individuals' ambitions for leadership are perhaps more amplified than in a large metropolis like London. In this situation Islam is used as a tactic, perhaps unsurprisingly given that many members supported the Islamic resistance parties in Peshawar, and later the Taliban's ideological vision—but without experiencing firsthand the violence of the movement's ascendance.

To pursue Edwards's point that religious education remains an avenue of social mobility of young male refugees in Peshawar, in Sussex religious observance serves to demonstrate integrity, traditionalism, trustworthiness, readiness to work for the community, and suitability for community leadership. While British Afghan Pashtuns are typically espoused strong believers, who may practice Islam in a variegated manner in everyday life, they recognize the strategic importance of public religious observance as a political tactic that cannot be trumped—although they vocally deride the perceived hypocrisy of those who publicize and boast about their religiosity (e.g., by making multiple Umrah pilgrimages that not all can afford). In sum, the uses of Islamic identity are strategic, and put to the interests of securing relative advantages based on Pashtun conflicts around hierarchy and personal competition. Islam's egalitarian principles are drawn on to mitigate conflicts between Pashtuns becoming out of control. In this sense the interplay between Pashtun and Muslim identities appear more aligned with Barth's original arguments than with Ahmed's critique.

Hot Coals: The Battle for Eid-ul-Fitr

Let us consider these arguments in regard to the community context of the formal annual religious feast on Eid-ul-Fitr, which follows the fasting month of Ramadan. The event has become established in the Sussex site as a highly condensed symbolized representation for the manipulation of political relations and power in friendship, kinship, and community solidarity. Formal hospitality is not involved; the event is advertised by word of mouth or mobile phone group message midway through Ramadan; and guests pay a fee to attend. During Ramadan, taxi-driver friends invite one another for iftar (a meal to break the fast) at each other's homes, or if working share iftar at the mosque, or at local food outlets. Most drivers fast, even if it means changing routines—for some, sleeping all day, waking around iftar time, and working at night. To avoid disapproval, those who neither fast nor pray do not advertise it publicly.

On Eid morning, hundreds of the city's Muslims[8] congregate for Eid prayers in the local mosques, after which the Afghan organizers begin preparing food in earnest for the party, which begins in the afternoon and continues late into the night. The feast represents the culmination of drivers' efforts to collectively maintain religious practices in a powerful Afghan and Pashtun cultural idiom and, following a month of collective fasting and related religious activities, represents a high point in their annual calendar.

Public commensality events like this can be converted into a form of what Bourdieu (1990, 112) calls symbolic capital, or "commensal politics," wherein the food ingested at a ritual feast comprises a literal embodiment or incorporation of the social relations or debt it engenders (Dietler 2001, 73), or a mechanism of social solidarity that establishes a sense of community via relations that define status, social superiority, inferiority, and indebtedness (Mauss 1990). Unlike the mundane commensality of meal breaks that punctuate taxi-work, the shared pleasures of picnics on the Sussex Downs to celebrate births, visas, or simply good weather, or the avowed equality enacted on the *chakar,* these are politically charged events designed to demonstrate culinary expertise, confidence and flair, and organizational excellence in the authoritative modality of the religious feast. The power they produce confers the temporary status of community leadership, and apparently suspends competition while affirming the special rights and leading roles of the organizers in its very practice—as well as the decision of participants to pay fees to attend. As such, the Eid barbecue barely conceals what Bourdieu (1990) describes as the equal importance of the labor required to conceal the function of the exchanges. It is, in Dietler's (2001, 73) analysis of feasts, an expressive trope of shared community that creates and reproduces relationships that "encompass aggressive competition by effectively euphemizing it in a symbolic practice that encourages collective misrecognition of the self-interested nature of the process"—although in the Sussex context, self-interest is hardly concealed.

Imbued with high religious and political significance, the annual feast also assumes importance in Barth's (1959b, 14–16) terms as a zero-sum majority game wherein, in a series of victories and defeats between opposing parties, one opponent's loss is a gain to the other. In this case, "the stronger party, corresponding to a 'majority' of players, gains the victory" (13–14). As before, power is not the exclusive aim. The event involves all the pleasures and collective enjoyment of outdoor commensality and good company in the shared celebration of a religious festival; fun and games; and opportunities for children to participate in Afghan Pashtun culture as well as to affirm continuity in Pashtun's high moral standards through the ingestion of good food imbued with the sustenance of distancing themselves from England's polluting culture and perhaps earlier deprivations of the food voucher system.

What key events and processes produced the Gulzai group's dominance in the annual Eid feast, and their limitations outside this sphere? In 2012, Sher Agha and his relative's nephew Raouf, from the Gulzai group, organized a larger Eid party than in previous years. It was attended by over sixty guests, mostly taxi-drivers, and supported by relatives from London who drove down for the occasion. The party was a resounding success. For the first time, they rented a pavilion in a local park with access to water where guests could perform *wuzu*. Considered a political coup, this marked the transition of an ad hoc, disorganized event to a larger, more official one.

After a sumptuous picnic the guests formed a line and prayed on the grass. They took photographs, which they shared on social media with pride, and then played volleyball and cricket and sat talking late into the night. Their seating arrangements reflected friendship groupings and social hierarchies. The two organizers cooked, solicitously cared for their guests' needs, and hardly relaxed. Their closest friends and allies sat around long carpets nearby, while other groupings formed on the basis of relative social distance from their hosts. Some who wanted to drink alcohol clandestinely sat farther afield. The hosts' furious activity contrasts with the feasts of wealthy Afghans where the best cooks are employed to produce the best dishes and the host will just sit or recline, his immobility reflecting his high status. If he is extremely important, a host may not eat at all but simply survey his guests enjoying his bounty.

Following the Gulzai group's success in 2012, expectations intensified the next year. Sher Agha's relatives were visiting Pakistan so, regrettably, he "worked alone." Not wanting to seek assistance from unrelated supporters he asked me, as a supposedly disinterested outsider, if I would draft an invitation "in good and perfect English" that he could transmit to their mobile group app, help him shop for halal meat and good-value sundries, and calculate for him the costs and amounts.

Specifically, we shopped for three sheep, one sack of onions, green tea, spices, twenty-four six-packs of water bottles, ninety tins of Coca-Cola, twenty juice cartons, sixty bags of sweets, one roll of black rubbish bags, one sack of rice, a kitchen roll, one hundred fifty plastic cups, two hundred plates, fifty plastic spoons, two bottles of cooking oil, one bottle of lemon juice, six bags of charcoal, eight cucumbers, three cabbages, three boxes of chicken wings, one bottle of olives, six lighter fuels, raisins, twenty bread packets, and three bags of kindling. He wondered about buying fresh fish from a local market to marinade in spices and fry—a "surprise" dish that would gain him admiration. Therefore the day before Eid we drove to a nearby fresh fish market on the sea and bought fifty gutted whiting fish local to the southern coast.

He had collected fees in advance and invited male musicians. Alcohol was forbidden. On the day itself, guests arrived wearing traditional *salwār-kameez* and *weskots*. Women were forbidden to attend. This attitude toward women constituted an obstacle to applying for council funding for community events, which Sher Agha considered and then rejected, invoking an argument about moral relativism in regard to the "British values" of pluralism, tolerance, gender mixing, and democracy. "We need equality. It's not fair if somebody sees my women, and I don't see his. If we ask the council for community funding, they will insist women come. That's *their* equality, not ours," he asserted. That year, I helped shop and draft the invitation but did not attend. In 2014 the group organized similarly well-attended events at which women council workers and managers, drivers' daughters, and I were present. Subsequently it was agreed by the leaders that Afghan women could also attend, but gender segregation would apply, as with weddings and parties.

By early 2015, the Gulzai group's reputation had weakened. Financial problems and their relative economic immobility had raised the stakes in the political–cultural–religious sphere, particularly around the Eid festival. Rivalries came to a head involving plans during Ramadan that hot summer when the Shinzada "community organization" decided to host their own Eid party. Sher Agha retaliated threateningly:

> I have organized this Eid party for years, I *will* do it this year.
> Your community organization is barely three months old, you
> are hijacking my party. You *will* stop your party, pay your fee,
> and attend mine. This is *not* a shared event. I am *not* involved in
> community matters. Build your mosque, organize your activities,
> do not disrupt my plans. If your members are unhappy, I will

visit their homes personally, ask for forgiveness, and ask them to attend *my* party, not yours. The same for the elders. I am not your rival. I don't *want* to be a community leader. But I warn you, I have more supporters.

This strong response put the Shinzada group in a predicament. They had already distributed leaflets around local universities. If they proceeded, they feared people might boycott the event to avoid taking sides in what had throughout Ramadan assumed the intensity of a local war. To cancel would involve shame and humiliation.

Following Barth's thesis, groups will call meetings—between themselves, or they will attend those called by other blocs; or occasionally they will seek "neutral" (contested) mediation. Councils, *jirgas,* and local blocs may reach a decision at meetings through "debate, threats, compromise, and occasional use of force" (1959b, 4). An emergency meeting was called by the five community leaders. Sher Agha was invited but, fearful of being outnumbered, he sent excuses in his place. Instead, he visited one elder behind the scenes who agreed he could run his party, and then he informed the community. "Elder" in this context refers to those older Afghans who were interested in community affairs—which not all "older" and long-settled Afghan Pashtuns were. The leaders were unhappy with this "deal." Seeking to resolve the deadlock, the following evening Sher Agha dressed formally in *salwār-kameez* and set off with trepidation to an iftar meal (to break fast) with the community leaders. In turn, they each invited Sher Agha to share in the community party, and offered him an "official" leadership role—which he refused. The discussion became serious, escalating to threats of violence.

Fast action ensued. The following day, *two* public invites were issued. One, posted by Inayatullah on the community Facebook page, called for a local "effort to unite Afghans and establish a recognized community, and improve unity and affection among our people." The other, a message sent by Sher Agha to the Afghan drivers' mobile app, stated, "Respected brothers and elders, *assalamu alaikum.* We would like to continue our tradition of hosting the local Eid party. . . . This will be our sixth year *inshaAllah (God willing)."* Learning of the Facebook post, Sher Agha and friends confronted Inayatullah, with the result he backed down and agreed to hold his party a day later. In the zero-sum contest around who would organize the Eid party, the "community" bloc lost. Other issues were at play. Inayatullah had previously impressed as a devout leader, having made several Haj and Umrah pilgrimages. He had been encouraged by relatives in a nearby city to collect funds for a mosque, and dispatched around £5,000 in donations. Seeing no material results, the other leaders became angry and demanded their money back. Now taking advantage of his defeat over the Eid party, they ousted him and Inayatullah found himself in the cold.

Because he was insistently *not* a community leader, Sher Agha now had the upper hand. He swiftly calculated that he could enhance his "win." Emboldened, he hired the pavilion in the park, and enlisted as many relatives from London as would travel. On Eid day it rained heavily, but a steady stream of celebrants, allies, and those simply curious to observe the unfolding of the dispute totaled as many as ninety people. They enjoyed *kabuli pulao,* kebabs, curry, and cricket; all agreed it was an unparalleled success. The success of the Afghan national cricket team, mostly Pashtuns, who qualified the same week for the T20 ICC World Cup 2016, contributed an extra flavor of celebration. The next day Sher Agha attended the Shinzada party to demonstrate a victor's benevolence and friendship.

Sher Agha, in a strong position, now began politicking seriously against the other group. Support for the "community organization" dwindled. One founder removed his name from the council's list of official members. Others agreed that a community organization only caused problems. Inayatullah's half brother Rafi attended both parties. Rafi likely gave occasional loyalties to both groups to prevent his half brothers from becoming too powerful. Thus, as a result of weak support among his opponents' brothers, disunity among the Shinzada leadership, and his own determination to not lose, Sher Agha found himself surprisingly gaining power.

Similar events occurred in 2016, when locals benefited from invitations to two parties, from both the Gulzai and Shinzada groups, respectively. By 2017, the situation had changed yet again. Sher Agha returned during Ramadan from a visit to Pakistan to find the new community leader Faisal on an Umrah pilgrimage and his own nephew Raouf seeking to augment his personal reputation, arranging to host and cook the Eid barbecue for the Shinzada group instead! Furious, he threatened and insulted Raouf (*Mashkook!*—You trickster/cheat!). Raouf shamefacedly obeyed his uncle. The very night before Eid Raouf canceled the barbecue, giving no reasons, but muttering excuses about loyalty to the "original organizers." The Shinzada barbecue was postponed until the second day of Eid. Despite the advice of his London relatives, who were at a loss to understand his doggedness ("It's just a community barbecue for God's sake, not Afghan politics"), Sher Agha sent his own message inviting all to the "usual" Eid party in the park the next day.

Many attended, including his London relatives, and Sher Agha triumphantly led the communal celebration. Tired with the conflict, people complained, "It's a local barbecue, not the Afghan presidency." Rumblings increased. Still Sher Agha hung on, determined to "win." Wanting to swell his numbers and dent the "community" effort, he issued an unprecedented invitation to some Tajik drivers ("We are all Afghan brothers")— who indeed attended. Some of Sher Agha's bloc also attended the "community'" party, as did Sher Agha briefly, while others visited friends and family. Thus, while his dominance over the Eid celebration continued, it extended only to the barbecue, and people's resentment appeared in verbal attacks on their role of servitude: "Sher Agha and Raouf are our cooks—they are illiterate, uneducated, cooking is all they can do."

Certainly the situation, serious to those involved, resembled a comedy of errors to observers. On the third day of Eid, I was invited by some local Pashtun women for lunch—relatives of taxi-drivers also privy to these events. We enjoyed numerous dishes, tea, and joked, "They think they're politicians," inventing different episodes of an imagined TV sitcom, analyzing the situation as female receivers of shared gossip about male community life—where women's celebrations are largely confined indoors to the domestic sphere, and the men's took place outside.

While we joked, Sher Agha's "fight" about reputation and leadership was no small issue. Having suffered so many personal losses of economic status, upward mobility, homeland, and a future for his children, it concerned his fundamental human value and worth—a worth not based on financial success, but one for which, ironically, he spent money buying impressive foodstuffs he could ill afford, which far exceeded the sum of the guests' fees.

Following Sher Agha's weakened position, in 2017 the Shinzada bloc called a meeting and issued another collective invitation: would he kindly join their group, manage the annual Eid feast (to which they would invite women), and coach the football team? Community conflicts would cease, and he would have an assured leadership role. Their group would maintain separation from the Tajiks, and represent a strong Pashtun force. Sher Agha considered it. Together with his brothers and nephews, on whom he could rely for absolute loyalty, his chances of maintaining his non-formalized "original" leadership position outside the Shinzada community organization were strong. On the other hand, he could shore up power within the community group. His brothers and nephews would boycott any match or barbecue if requested. And so he agreed to join—and thereby seemingly ensured the ongoing bi-factionalization of interests from within. At the meeting's end, all prayed together for the agreement's success.

Whatever further changes may ensue, Sher Agha's dilemma illustrates Barth's argument that the two-bloc system depends on the relative equal strength of both blocs—here the weaker bloc was subsumed into the stronger one. Additionally, in the dissolution of the model it also demonstrates the vulnerability of structural arrangements to contextual change, to processes of transformation that prove exceptions to the rule, and to the vicissitudes and unexpected outcomes of individuals' ambition, intention, and resentments.

The exploding local partnerships, power plays, and competitive high stakes surrounding the annual Eid party have some resonance with politics in Afghanistan. During the civil war years Dostum repeatedly changed sides; after the Taliban seized Kabul in 1996, the staunch enemies Hekmatyar and Massoud twice made alliances—a tactic perhaps mirrored locally in Sher Agha's decision to form a coalition with the Shinzadas. Among most taxi-drivers, a sense of weariness with Afghan politics prevailed. Many preferred the assured pleasures of the outdoors barbecue to the minefield of Afghan politics even though, we have seen, organizing the former is, so to speak, no picnic.

Unexpected events arose to cohere their coalition. Some months later an anonymous text message arrived in drivers' WhatsApp group chat accusing the leaders of welfare benefit and tax fraud as well as drug use. Widespread unease ensued. In a damage limitation exercise the leaders removed the Facebook page to close the group to outside scrutiny, and in response to the crisis of trust they organized a collective Umrah pilgrimage to Mecca and Medina. Hence their uneasy alliance continued. As the proverb says, *Dunya haghou oukhwara, chey haya ne peyzanee* (Those people who eat [enjoy] the world, cannot keep their standing; i.e., good character is lost in satisfying appetites).

Conclusion

The Eid feast involves local political power struggles that resonate in part with larger battles in Afghanistan. However, unlike wealthier Afghans, many migrants (the Gulzi brothers particularly) live hand to mouth and even as leaders must "serve" their guests—their adaptations demonstrating strategies of the indigent, and changing practices of hospitality in diasporic contexts. In addition to the specific stakes of power and status centered on religious feasting, such tensions reflect these Afghans' move toward a stronger "grounding" in British society. These are reflected in changing community dynamics, new kinship lineages, a greater willingness to formalize community activities, and shifting values around social, cultural, and economic capital.

While their organizations around British electoral politics were less fraught, and overall less invested, in the 2011 local city council elections some forty or fifty drivers pledged their support to the Green Party, whose MP had supported some individual Afghans' asylum claims. Their vote also constituted a protest against the Conservative Party's hostile policies to asylum seekers.

Analyzing these processes allows some reflection on intellectual shifts from structure to process, to shifting identity politics, through the cultural and mobilities turns, toward a process ontology approach and philosophy—wherein we might go beyond a view of mobility or immobility in terms of tactics of blocking or propulsion within existing structures, but see them as part of a motile logic in which structures are considered *part of* a motile approach to life. That is, again, rather than jettison structure for process, immobility for mobility, or separate individual and community politics, might we not hold both together? Rose's (1992) notion of the "broken middle" posits such an effort as an ethical endeavor.

These ideas are important because they reiterate the co-imbrication of both individual and collective forms of immobility in mobility (this seems obvious)—or let us say process within structure—largely as a solution to the problem of dichotomy. In short, it is not clear that immobility exists without real or imagined mobility, that structure exists without process, or indeed that we are talking about one to the exclusion of the other. Collective immobility serves to cohere groups through bifurcation, to stabilize conflict, and to prevent any individual from becoming too powerful.

Regarding Barth's analysis, the political two-bloc system and analysis of lineage alliances therein cannot be applied wholesale and universally to Pashtuns in Sussex or anywhere else. Derived from a system of strategic choices of allies by individual landowners in North-West Pakistan, the choices it describes refer to factors implicit in a relatively small number of features of Pathan organization. This does not mean it bears no relevance to English migrant contexts. Rather, it offers an opportunity to assume the mantle of Barth's call to examine how games for political power are configured in changing conditions, as well as to an extent how to dismantle it.

While these taxi-drivers seem far removed from the agricultural interests of Yusufzai Pashtuns on the Pakistani Frontier, their situation in this small city nonetheless demonstrates to an extent "the relatively peaceful coexistence of the two parties" (1959b, 15), with continued relevance for Barth's exacting analysis of lineage organizations, group solidarity, and Pashtun strategies for power. This is not a society on the brink of war (as Meeker senses in his analysis), although it does shape individual and collective histories with fractious and sometimes disturbing individual attempts to establish supremacy. However, these former refugees are overall more concerned with achieving stability and success than introducing more conflict into their lives. It is also not clear whether the community organization and its leadership actually enjoy the support of the city's Afghans, or whether people are avoiding to become involved (Edwards 1998, 726). There is much relevance in Sussex for Barth's analysis of ways that highly dynamic shifting allegiances depend on the fortunes of individual leaders. However, while Edwards (1998, 724) found that the loyalties of Afghan refugees to place, descent group, tribal ancestor, village, and tribe were less than for previous generations, I found that these ties were particularly strong for men separated from their families, and unable to return to Afghanistan—and also kept alive by parents with children in the UK.

Certainly Barth's (1969a) observation that the ethnic boundary is a social boundary is pertinent to shifting formations and reformations of Afghan community politics in Sussex. The task I propose is to work toward unearthing the social lines, processual dynamics, and networked connections that *do* produce real transformative forms for people in terms of belonging, identity, and global and community citizenship—and to explore *which* theoretical perspectives are important for understanding ways that practices, policy, and politics regulate or enable transformations in a variety of settings; relationships between political, social, and personal transformations; and ways that individuals' ambitions and intentions are enabled and thwarted.

This, I argue, requires that we consider shifts in theory, identity, and politics in the fields of migration and mobility studies, as we encounter shifting and problematic notions of truth, experience, and consciousness in relationships shaping forms of social–political transformation. And last, it requires that we also consider ways that action and processes move across situational fields and are entwined without being fully collapsed within the practices of transformation, political engagement, and governance under examination—and reflect on what opportunities and limitations these create for rethinking collectivity among Afghan migrant communities as they face complex fractures.

ENDLINES

An Aporia of Freedom and Suffering

Recall for a moment the iconic portrait *Pathan Man*, captured circa 1919–20 by the British imperial photographer Randolph Bezzant Holmes in his studio in Peshawar, garrison city at the frontier of the British empire in India. The black-and-white portrait depicts a ragged but nonetheless magisterial Pathan tribesman, poised with a long rifle in his right hand, his right leg resting atop a large fake boulder, his right elbow on his right knee, cradling his head in his right hand, his left leg obscured by the folds of his dress, which fall in a classical Roman style. Rather than any preparedness to act, the frame arrests him in deep contemplation, in the endless time of action not-yet-begun. Given the year is 1919–20, perhaps he is contemplating Afghan victories over the British, or their losses, on the Khyber front of the Third Anglo-Afghan War, which reestablished the Durand Line border between Afghanistan and British India. Next, disrupting the carefully composed vertical alignment between left foot, rifle butt, right forearm, and head, imagine the fingers of his left hand curled around the rifle now unfurling and unfolding from their prone position, and his inclined right forearm—tensile with the strain of over a century of held pose—now stretching and raising itself into a simultaneously upward and backward movement that opens out his trunk into a long expansive curve. Imagine that, by moving his right arm sideward through lateral space, and twisting and turning his body in order to propel it into a circular motion of acceleration, he steps away from the rock and, following the arc of movement he has drawn through the photographic space, releases the rifle, turns fully on himself, and decides to leave the scene altogether.

This study sought to shift the fixed posture and British–European artifice of Afghanistan—and the still life of the proud Pathan tribesman and master of tradition arrested in perpetuity—toward an alternative reading of Afghan life as a moving, contingent, changing, and fully contemporary force. It followed the inexorable movement of Afghans in England over almost two decades as they transformed from refugees to remitting migrants, settled citizens, and became more embedded in multiple transnational, community, and entrepreneurial spheres. While these temporal shifts are variously represented in political discourse in terms of the overarching values of freedom and autonomy, the book showed that they are also fractured by suffering and ongoing structural, political, and symbolic violence. It underscored the gap between contradictory and idiosyncratic forms of individual migrant life and hegemonic forms of discourse, and the sense of dislocation, duality, and forms of effacement this produces in migrants' lives. In its focus on unheroic, mundane, blue-collar Afghan labor, it accentuated the shadow side of the migration dream, and the silences, gaps, and repressions of memory and feeling that living in these spaces entails. Of those men whose voices and stories feature in these pages, many can track changes in their lives from their first arrival when their families required their remittances to sustain their livelihoods, to a less freighted time when they could build sufficient capital to relieve their families' pressures in Afghanistan and Pakistan, and also establish their own households in England. Notwithstanding, the logic of global capitalism means that certainly not every migrant's labor is sufficient to secure a

FIGURE 2. Pathan Man. Photograph by R. B. Holmes. Copyright Royal Geographical Society (with IBG). Reprinted with permission.

livelihood and future—and the study also accorded recognition to many who still remit, or else struggle or fail to, after many years.

Through its organizing frames of language and life, history and temporal transformation, movement and mobility, and an empirical and imaginary field spanning England, Pakistan, and Afghanistan, the book revisioned questions about what it means to be Afghan, Pashtun, Muslim, and a remitting or working migrant in the contemporary world. It approached migration as an ongoing process that resulted in Sussex–Peshawar–Afghanistan becoming a simultaneously single, multiple, fractured, and fragmented field of interaction, and taxi-driving as a quotidian and mundane setting that could provide valuable information on the transnational lives of Afghan migrants. Through the book's stories of life journeys into the aftermath of war, it also mined some dispossessions of land, personhood, bonds of kinship, and their recasting in migrant subjectivity as sources of ambivalence, impossibility, and impasse. This revealed ways the labor of life for Afghans in England is shaped by loss and mourning, and by experiences that stand in critical counterpoint to the seductive neoliberal vision of unfettered progress and wealth accumulation.

Life and everyday living were thus prioritized over an inquiry into ways that migration and struggle might emerge from historical events, cultural codes, or symbolic forms. Attending to the myriad ways that Afghanistan lives in England, a key aim of the book was to disrupt the persistent fixed gaze of the colonial ethnographer on the British military man's egregious encounters with the unconquerable Pathan, Anglo, and Afghan ideas of a brave unyielding Pashtun culture, and Afghanistan's ongoing "refugee crisis" as a radical disjunctural moment in the country's history of mobility and migration. Rather than reprise the story of Anglo-Afghan relations through the historical travels of British armies, explorers, and anthropologists who journeyed from the center of the British empire to its frontiers in Afghanistan, it explored the stories of Afghan migrant taxi-drivers (journeymen) aspiring to class mobility and respectability. Thereby it challenged some resistant colonial myths of Pashtun traditionalism, obscurantism, and isolation, and generated some fresh understandings about Afghanistan, war, and exile.

Changing the direction of travel, and transporting in Anglo-Afghan relations back to the scene of the imperial homeland, does not mean constructing a mirror image in reverse. As an Afghan in England, the Pashtun taxi-driver neither becomes English, nor is he finally subordinated to or free of British imperialism. Rather, he is confronted with a side of everyday life shot through with the memory traces of contemporary war, the imperial ruins of England in Afghanistan, and a post-imperial England trying, like himself, to reassert itself on a world stage, more feebly than in the past. In this theater, migrant subjectivities evolved through mobility undermine hegemonic understandings of the imperial center and its unruly margins, and remake and undo Anglo-Afghan relations in the process.

Reviving Kipling's themes of imperialism, corrupt power, colonialism, and the fractured image of Alexander the world conqueror, migrant subjectivities also evoked the alluring and deceptive specter of colonization in the present. They revealed ways that political, moral, and epistemic orders shape modernist notions of disorder (Good 2012). They disclosed contours of continuity, interruption, and immobility in ways that imaginings of a whole and unconquered people and homeland, and a strong sense of place, permeate migrant lives, bodies, and labor; as well as ways that migrants both resist and accommodate a pervasive sense of difference, being a stranger, on the outside, and in different kinds of inside.

Next, in moving the fixed pose of the Pathan man into life, and giving metonymic voices for example to the crying souls buried on the Jalalabad river, the study brought the body with its sensual, somatic, and cultural consciousness back into discourse and interpretation. Many studies of movement, the body, and embodied movement have provided advances to anthropology's traditional emphasis on the spoken and written word— even though our earliest memories are preverbal impressions, senses, and emotions not yet brought into language.

Correspondingly, the book also encompassed an interpretive movement or exploration that described a sensual, bodily, oneiric, and existential departure: a journey made by moving, driving, dancing, dreaming, and wandering, wherein incompleteness and fragmentation describe a loyalty to the book's subjects. This also comprised an ethical endeavor to recover various epistemological forms of effacement in writing, and to embed deep perceptions of life and endurance into anthropological theorizing and engagement (Kleinman 2014). The approach invoked multiple literacies of orality, storytelling, argument, and wistful imagination as social practices (Street 2006) of the road. It questioned the relation of words to pain, desire and impossibility, and the ways words live in the body and take their speakers into worlds other than their own, into departures from themselves and unusual or unexpected returns. This led to an exegesis of fragmentation for imperial subjects caught in the forward motion of living Anglo-Afghan relations as if for the first time. It also shaped some alignments with calls for academic discourse to work with the "capricious, inchoate, contingent and chaotic forcefields that surround and underlie our socially constructed orderings of the world" when seeking to capture the shifting relations between person, locale, and the vastness that surrounds it (Jackson 2013, 277). Therein it prioritized fragmentation as a writing style that could pinpoint the disordered excursions of quotidian experience through prose poem, thought experiments, and "captions, punctums, catalogs, autopoetic zips, flashed scenes, word counts" (Berlant and Stewart 2019, 28–29). That is, like Pashto literature, writing about Pashtuns can link "multiple aesthetic worlds outside of, and arguing against, the fixity that imperial processes of bordering and ordering seek to impose" (Caron 2019, 446).

In doing so, the book also drew attention to regions between waking, imaginary, and otherworldly worlds of travel that have concerned scholars of Afghanistan—for example, to Caron (2016, 3), who argues for juxtaposing archival knowledge of Frontier history with knowledge generated by other spiritual and ethereal words, in order to institute forms of historical knowledge production that build through plural and more democratic uses of the social networks they constitute.

Fragments and fragmentation likewise offered valuable interpretive tools for anthropologists and historians seeking to understand past and present-day Afghan internationalism. Particularly valuable to the arguments in this book were works that introduced the voices of Afghans into a critical disruption of the Great Game paradigm, and spatial and ideological framings of Afghanistan's past (e.g., Green and Arbabzadah 2013; Green 2013, 2015; Green 2016). These revealed that internal versions of Afghan history to be just as divided, fractured, and oppressive as colonial models (Green 2016); ways that small fragments of regional and localized difference indicated dissonances and shifts in everyday social registers of culture, religious life, and political disposition in the Afghanistan–Pakistan borderlands (Marsden and Hopkins 2011); they pointed to the historical mobility of Afghanistan's literary traffic in revealing a connectivity of overlapping empires, mobile people, and cross-regional languages (Green 2016); as well as the influences of British imperialism and Russian, Pakistani, and Indian regional power (Wide 2013b). In challenging the primacy of Western colonialisms as the starting point and epistemology for studies of Afghanistan, these works also provided some balm to Hanifi's (2016) passionate call to debunk the British imperial reasoning that impugns Pashtun ethnicity for both creating and destroying Afghanistan—typified in ideas of the destructive Taliban movement's putative radical refusal to "move" away from "traditional" precepts of culture.

Outside of scholarship on Afghanistan, relevant literatures on new materialisms have also criticized the anthropocentric view of human subjectivity. Regarding the body and its embeddedness in the world, the physicist–feminist Karen Barad (2007), for example, extends Maurice Merleau-Ponty's view of bodily sensations as the gateway to knowing the flesh-of-the-world, in an active, embodied, relational, and creative process. Barad likewise sees the world as dialoguing on the physical level rather than solely within the body or mind. She usefully links Merleau-Ponty's ideas of fleshiness to materiality, both as a matter of the body, and of ways the body links in dissonant and concordant relations to the constitution of politics and the world in discourse. These linkages bear fruitfully on the impossibilities embodied by Afghan transnational migrants who are represented in political discourse in terms of the values of freedom and individualism, within an implicit civilizing mission, but who in their required assimilation into regimes of kinship obligation, work, and integration appear caught in a double bind—and a stringent biopolitical regime that contradicts the generic principles of freedom.

In troubling some divisions between life and death in order to understand ways that migrant life after war is imbricated with forms of living death, the book also reached for the language of sleep and dreams, for a reckoning in terms of "a configuration of sleep, dreaming, and death, as both eclipse and an awakening" (Pandolfo 1997, 9). It mined ways the relief and oblivion of sleep, and the half-waking worlds of dreams, fuse a person's words and their imaginings with those of the world (Freud [1953] 1975). It uncovered alternative forms of knowledge about life and history, and revelations that jarred against images and utterances recalled in the telling of dreams. The semiconscious state of sleep travel, and the incoherent motion of dreaming, also revealed some painful forms of impasse related to the life course, as well as the exchange between personal and collective experiences of war, displacement, and the loss of a sense of home or belonging. These revealed the commingling of the past and present as particular formations of fracture, wound, contradiction, refusal, and nightmare. Following these paths of understanding highlighted some predicaments of madness and love in everyday life, the forceful breach of displacement and war, and the value in pursuing a certain roving off familiar maps. This made possible some understanding of the question of "What have taxi-drivers or picnics to do with suicide?"

As it revolved around an axis of identity, difference, loss, and exclusion, the book examined the imbrication of these elements in a cleavage of experience that makes life both livable and impossible. Thereby it also addressed a central preoccupation with Afghan diasporic and exiled society—namely, the tentative uncertainty of identity, and the paradoxes of Pashtun patriarchal family and cultural idioms that emerge in migrants' experiences of being hemmed within unwanted worlds of dispossession, partition, violence, and war. It revealed therein the prospect of an endless migratory journey that offers temporary respite, but no return (of Pashtun lands, an august and unvanquished homeland, an undivided family, an intact sense of hope).

Therein the book reached beyond identifications and categorizations of class, context, colonialism, and culture—and Western definitions of Afghanistan and its people which, rooted in power and history, reiterate the boundaries of who a person is, and might or might never become. It took "migrant," "refugee," and "asylum seeker" (likewise globalism, transnationalism, and internationalism) as provisional metaphors that marginalize and disempower through the judicial, bureaucratic, clinical, and legal regulation of refugees, or infer individuals are more determined by cultural codes of kinship and behavior than they are. Going beyond manifest boundaries, or spatial distinctions between nations, metropole, and periphery, East and West, it also challenged some practices of classification and interpretation that typically divide on the basis of stasis and movement, such as local indigenous, bordered (socially, economically, nationally, classificatorily), and sedentary or "placed" people, versus the transnational or global citizen who transcends spatial and categorical borders, tangible identities, and the socially situated nature of the world. These framings enabled the study to go beyond contemporary languages of emergency and crisis, and the tendency to view all Afghan life through the prism of suffering, war, or the result of an aberrant culture at odds with the contemporary world.

It is still important to remember that these migrants are not from longtime-settled communities, of established cross-border traders, mobile entrepreneurs, or international businessmen such as characterize Afghan populations elsewhere. While their transnational kinship networks, and biographical, family, and national histories extend far beyond the borders of Afghanistan and Pakistan, it *is* as refugees that they came to England, in *new* flows of refugees, in relation with which they built new Afghan communities as if from the beginning, and new knowledge along the way.

The study conceptualized the multiplicity of their social, economic, and cultural building practices as foreign to a predetermined understanding of geographic knowledge. Forward-blind, it emphasized ways that Afghans in England created new social cultural and economic pathways as they moved through space, rather than following predefined space, thereby forming a "migrational or metaphorical city" (De Certeau 1984, 112). Within this framework of cartographic deviation or detour, the book's focus on migrant mobility was tasked with overturning the boundaries of existing knowledge. It shifted the onto-epistemological focus from genealogical to motile epistemologies, not by introducing new maps, but by developing a view on building, life, and knowledge as unfinished business, one that is constantly re-created in the movement of its own expansion.

Ellipsis . . .

The book differed from British studies of Asian diasporic communities, which have largely been published in sociology and geography, and which primarily locate their analyses within Britain's racialized, postwar history of postcolonial immigration from the mid-twentieth century onward (not central for Afghan refugees arriving since the nineties, during the age of the global war on terror), in theorizations of class, race, ethnicity, Islam, integration, and exclusion. Rather, it aligned itself more with anthropologists who have made questions about how to represent human experience and marginality in ethnographic writing central, with historians, and with anthropologists of Afghanistan working in different contexts.

Regarding the book's focus on language and life, geographical space speaks in this book not only to literatures on nation, diaspora, and transnationalism involving migration from Afghanistan. It represents place as a moving "space of enunciation" (De Certeau 1984, 115): not a map of collected statements or descriptions of events, but an interlocutionary space of articulation and expression that exceeds territorial boundaries, wherein subject positions can reconstitute and recycle themselves as stories. Thereby it links to other works that have sought to grasp the elusive journey that is human life, and its physical and sensory experience into the errancies of language. These have, for example, engaged ways that liminality is forged into textual forms of exiled Afghan personhood (Olszewska 2015); ways that violence in regions of the past becomes actualized in the present (Das 2006); how life can be renewed when worlds and lives are shattered (Jackson 2013); and ways that the transitoriness of migrant life appears ever more acutely within a transnational paradigm (Napolitano 2015, 4).

Underscoring the value of retaining a sense of incompleteness in the task of representing the figure of the colonial other in writing, Pandolfo (1997, 5) emphasizes the trace of a "polymorphous figure of alterity, ever present and elusive, alluded to and never surfacing in full shape, recurring in personal and historical narratives, quotidian speech, and philosophical speculation." She proceeds to describe "a polysemic concept at the limits of representation and thought, mark of an intractable difference, fracture, rift, schism, disjunction, or separation—separation from oneself—the figure of an exile that is constitutive of the position of the subject, as both a possibility and a loss" (5). She points us usefully toward ways the Afghan journey in England impinges with temporal visions of imperial ruin, remains, and to the return of colonial and personal pasts within present experience—and to the presence of these visions in academic, political, and community discourse as silences, gaps, and unspoken feeling and experience. These contrast with the incredibly rich use of Pashto proverbs and idioms to demarcate a more socially and culturally acceptable form of everyday spoken language.

The book's interlocutors raised historical memories that could resist the effacement of Afghan Pashtuns and their territories by four decades of war and conflict, and border politics and policies toward refugees in present-day Pakistan. For Afghan refugee families and returnees to Pakistan, nostalgic versions of the preeminent past, including idealizations of long-dead heroes such as Ahmed Shah Durrani and the poet Rehman Baba, served to provide respite and to create new future-oriented forms of colonial resistance to the dispossession and violences of the present (Battaglia 1995). For returnees to Pakistan, these imaginings were key in shaping social and mobile constitutions of kin and friendship relations as they undertook journeys into lands, places, and areas of the past that had circumscribed their paths through life. As they traveled through the lands around Peshawar and into the past, they reimagined new futures, and they reinscribed new memories into the landscape. These were made more sensually potent through the practices of preparing and sharing food in the landscapes through which they traveled, and pleasures they ingested along the way.

Exemplified in Zmarai's words "I have two people in me," the book also gestured to the dual forces of energy and stasis, mania and depression, life and death, and ways madness is shaped by individual resources and limits, the possibilities of the environment to provide and nourish, and the dual opportunities and impossibilities produced in migrant life under neoliberal work regimes. Doublings as well as crossings through time and space additionally implicated borderline states in the crossing of state borders between normality and abnormality, war and peace, past and present, and trauma and healing in relation to the processes, practices, and limits of recovery or renewal available to these Afghan men. They additionally revealed ways the body of a migrant community becomes sundered, split, and transformed into a theater of repeated warfare and eerie return, wherein the violence of multiple pasts is scattered through the urban landscape, becoming readable through the tidemarks of half-erased tracks of former displacements, settlements, and upheavals. These forms of textual and ontological displacement generated new possibilities for transformation and being.

At the level of political behavior, identity politics, and leadership, the book also revealed tactics of mobility and immobility, and impetus or restraint, which provoked new reflections for Barth's arguments about Pashtun lineage alliances and the two-bloc political system of organization. Examined within contemporary conditions of change and over time in a diasporic community, these highlighted ways that Pashtun games for political power in migrant contexts simultaneously reaffirm his arguments and dismantle them. Neither fragmentation nor suffering are totalizing conditions. The focus on worlds of Afghan mobility and the connectivities this establishes beyond dominant reasoning about Afghanistan, and Afghan bordering practices of culture and history, stand in "counterpoint to imperial fragmentations, even if this counterpoint enjoys less global visibility" (Caron 2019, 447). Mobility can thus also comprise, as Caron argues, "part of what stitches together fragmented networks into new, and less-violent, kinds of cartographies" (454).

The concepts also raise questions regarding the extent to which imperial and other textures of war and violence in refugee and migrant life are usefully viewed through the trope of suffering and upheaval. These tropes invite a consideration of their flipside as well as the concept of freedom; and the ethics that the exercise of freedom furnishes in different cultural traditions and social and historical contexts. This bears on the extent to which migrants can "really" be "free" within the restraints and possibilities afforded by contemporary historical and economic conditions, the structures and infrastructures built on illusions of free movement, and ongoing war. It bears, too, on ways these men's imaginary freedom is equivocal insofar as it enfolds melancholic tensions related to the losses of "traditional" Pashtun ways of living—for example, in Afghanistan, on ancestral lands, and within the large extended households many were born into—all the while retaining the ambivalence of these attachments, in their real and imaginary returns.

Crossings and Mobility

The tracking of migrants' land, aerial, and maritime crossings over the globe evoked an ontology of crossings and metamorphoses, of shattering and redemption, social and psyche, land and water, reality and imagination. Refugee crossings and repatriations additionally raised questions about the causal chains—human, legal, imaginary, and empirical—and the types of state incentive and coordinated infrastructure that govern moving people and the complex geographies and divergent temporalities of travel across borders. They shifted the focus toward an exploration of the points of change, stop, and continuity in ways that national and international events and crisis interplay with state and border infrastructures to create apertures, blockages, end points, origins, and choke points in the creation of a route, crossing, migrant, community, or a return. Since and before the Afghans in this book arrived in England, many other young men and families left Afghanistan. From 1981 to 2015 Afghans constituted the world's largest refugee population, with diasporic communities settling in Europe, Canada, the United States, Russia and the post-Soviet states, China, and across Asia. According to UNHCR figures, 2015 and 2016 saw an increase in Afghans arriving in Europe, namely 209,367 and 42,262, respectively, with over 38,000 in 2017 when Afghans no longer constituted the second-largest group (after Syrians) because of the increase from North and sub-Saharan Africa and the closure of the Balkan routes between Turkey and Greece in 2016 (Ruttig 2017). Thomas Ruttig categorized arrivals from 2017 into "the arrived but increasingly unwelcome; the stuck; and the still trying." More have tried the eastern Mediterranean route through Greece to Italy, and with the supposed closure of the Calais camp in France—and increased security resulting from the UK's hostile policies—been homeless in European cities (e.g., moved on by police for camping under the bridges and overpasses at Porte de la Chapelle and Aubervilliers in Paris).

Pakistan remains the world's largest host country for Afghan refugees. The entwining of Pakistan's history with British Indian history—not least in the creation of Pakistan's borders along the 1893 Durand Line—brings historical border disputes and past wars firmly into any contemporary analysis of Afghan–Pakistani and Anglo-Afghan relations. At the same time, the escalation of repatriations from Pakistan, which coincided with the escalation of violence in Afghanistan, neither bodes well for the international peace effort, nor for peace in the future. It also debunks the narrative of the success of the U.S.-led NATO invasion and occupation of Afghanistan in the global war on terror.

The 2001–14 war produced severe, unmitigated failures of intervention, reconstruction, and ideology on a massive scale. Partly, these failures resulted from the legacy of alliances and killings during and after the Russian war, and their continuation into present-day politics and social life. If the aim of the twenty-first century intervention was to rid Afghanistan of the Taliban, this failed, too. In the years following Afghanistan's mooted transition to democracy and peace, the movement acquired revived vigor and force. These failures, combined with an exhaustion of political will in Pakistan to receive more refugees, resulted in unprecedented flows of Afghan refugees to Europe, and a new field site and focus for research and for the study of people from Afghanistan.

The book tackled the complexity of Afghan migrant subjectivity and formations of personhood and collective identity in an English diasporic context. These Afghans enacted their ideas of what it means to be a certain type of citizen and person through the ordinary labor of taxi-driving. The drivers' expressions of labor and their tough physical forms of masculinity also inhabited Afghan British identity with conservative views of gender and ethnicity. The deep contradictions in the lives of men for whom the dream of upward mobility was a chimera served as resistance to dominant stereotypes regarding belonging to Britain as either citizens or refugees, and ideal-typic depictions of Pashtuns as brutal adherents to unyielding tradition and Muslim conservatism. They also have relevance for countering the mainstream discourses that vilify and homogenize Muslim communities in Britain, promote the discourse of the wholesale burden of Europe's refugee crisis, and for ways the prevalent global discourse on Islam and terror plays out in regimes of restricted mobility in international politics for Muslims in everyday life.

The global war on terror resulted in worsening relations between Pakistan and Afghanistan, and the deterioration of Afghan refugees' situation in Pakistan. Alongside the forcible expulsion or voluntary repatriations of almost four million Afghans from Pakistan since 2000; mass detentions, deportations, and everyday harassment; and tactics of bordering and restricted movement increased. While many Afghans returned voluntarily to a homeland suffering increasing violence and chronic insecurity, many others sent their sons to Europe, where immigration controls had tightened alongside an increase in anti-Muslim, anti-migrant populism.

Amid the malapropisms of the racialized post-9/11 climate that vilifies Islam as well as Muslim migrants to Europe, this story about humanity, struggle, and failure is an important one that collapses Muslim, Afghan, Pashtun, and British identities. Given that new Pashtun refugee and migrant groups across Western countries are living within similar social structures, burdens, and restraints, an in-depth study of a particular city and region also addresses a global picture. The study of Afghan Pashtuns in England can enrich work on Afghan migration outside Europe. It also complements other revisions of the narrative of Afghan's geographical and cultural isolation. By introducing Afghans' own perspectives on global travel, including around England, it jettisons in new ways the idea that Afghan societies and networks are based on integrated territorial entities. It also contributes to anthropological work on borders and crossings that integrates local, international, and existential levels (Donnan, Leutloff-Grandits, and Hurd 2017).

Last, the book brought a unique perspective on mobility to its understandings of Afghan migration and transnationalism. These involved political, economic, cultural, geographical, and human components in ways that mobility's relation to immobility is enfolded into migration; the international state system; global, local, and delocalized conjunctions of productive labor—as well as to ways that mobility and immobility may transform transnational and transcultural categories, praxis, imaginaries, and subjects living under conditions of war, migration, and neoliberalism. Afghan taxi-drivers in England are both expertly and hesitantly steeped in the migration apparatus. They are uniquely placed to offer new insights into migration's mobile and immobile infrastructures, its variations, senses, and resistances, as well as understandings of some pathological responses to the experience of being out of step, time, or flow.

Linking some manifest facets of mobility and immobility to political economic and historical conditions, the ethnography raised questions about the nature of these terms in all their diversity and vitality. Certainly, while immobility may be imposed, restrictive, and immensely painful, it is also deliberately regularized, as when migrant subjects assert their claims to a time and place to rest and create pleasure. In the particular contexts of their restraints and possibilities, which differ from the mobilities and circumstances of other eras, Afghan migrant taxi-drivers working and residing in England revealed im/mobility as a condition of being poised at the edge of motion and its cessation. Mobility, that is, is intrinsic to understanding immobility (Bergson 2002, 119). Rather than privileging a model of reality or ontological position where movement as freedom or its converse are seen as opposites in different contexts, or appear as alternately foreground or background in migrants' experiences, the book argued that holding both together allows two or more positions to be experienced at the same time, even if uncertainly. This epistemological dexterity can locate mobility and stasis firmly within an ontological space that is increasingly characteristic of twenty-first-century life—namely, as a condition that follows on the disaffected promises of global modernity.

Finally, in working through the vicissitudes of mobility and immobility in life and on the road, Afghan journeymen in England are and have been restricted by governing regimes of state, remittances, and taxi-driving mobility. At the same time they are highly adept at maneuvering through the interstices and opportunities of these regimes. Their experiences are germane in the current era, when mobility in the context of war and migration heralds dually as both universal force and illusion, at once dream, nightmare, and compulsion.

Dey lmar stirga pe youw ghwatta na pateegi (One finger does not cover the eye of the sun).

ACKNOWLEDGMENTS

If this book traces its germination to Afghanistan and Pakistan, it bore fruit in England, which many Afghans and generations of other migrants like myself call home—if even home is qualified with provisos, as it certainly is for Afghans granted refuge by a country that has waged war for so long in Afghanistan.

Starting points are amorphous. This story may well have begun two decades ago in August 2001 in Karachi when I traveled from the bus station outside the Pashtun-run Shah Zob Hotel to Quetta, capital of Pakistan's Balochistan province on the Durand Line near Iran and Afghanistan, eager for a break from fieldwork there and Karachi's relentless heat. The "fortress" city of Quetta nestles on the mountainous Bolan Pass that extends over Pakistan's border to Spin Boldak, Gulistan, and Kandahar in Afghanistan. For many, the border imposes peremptorily on Afghan land. Borders notwithstanding, many Afghans and Afghan businesses populated Quetta city (and likewise Karachi), alongside Baloch peoples, Hazaras, Brahuis, and a sprawling Pakistani garrison base. The Taliban offices of the Quetta Shura would be established here after the United States invaded Afghanistan in October. Pakistanis complained that Afghans had overrun the city; many were leaving. Properties were cheap. Abutting the center's expansive tree-lined avenues, crowded bazaars traded in goods from Iran and China. Agents here arranged passage for refugees into Iran and onward to Europe. Afghans complained that Quetta provided work but few prospects. I stayed in the Hamid Hotel behind the bus station and soon found an Afghan driver, Waleed, who proved a trustworthy guide.

En route Waleed suggested a trip to the Roghani, Landi Karez, and Dara refugee camps at Chaman to visit his family home in Kandahar. Weeks later, following 9/11, these camps provided emergency shelter to tens of thousands of refugees fleeing war. Rather than accept UN Refugee Agency repatriation incentives, many Afghans shifted instead to Mohammed Kheil camp, preferring the border town Chaman with its opportunities for casual work. Though after 9/11 travel on the road from Quetta would be curtailed, thanks to Waleed our passage at that time little concerned anyone, including the three youthful Taliban officials who waved us into the young Islamic Emirate. The border was open, and buses and cars crossed in both directions without apparent restriction.

The Afghan border town Spin Boldak revealed wide flat grounds of secondhand vehicles for sale, cars in ordered rows and motorbikes, including coveted Yamaha Enduro sport models that could be smuggled over the border to Karachi. Some months later, Spin Boldak would house over fifty thousand refugees fleeing American bombing in Helmand and Kandahar. Though by December 2001 the Taliban agreed to surrender Kandahar after heavy American bombing, they retained Spin Boldak and the border. While Waleed refilled his tank that morning, a car bearing young men drew up; they requested I cease taking photographs but, before speeding away, posed laughingly for the camera. We continued on through the sixty-odd miles to Kandahar across the desert, past vortexes of whipped-up, wind-funneled "twisters," rough-shod mosques where the occasional single figure prayed in the open, and modest roadside-eating places offering only bread and water. Eventually we entered Waleed's home on Kandahar's outskirts, a mud compound whose family rooms enclosed an open courtyard where a cow ruminated and women pumped water. For the next few days I rested there. The women and I quizzed each other about our differences—my look, my religion, their face tattoos, our respective marriages, our children—while their many children appraised me curiously. The keynotes of that visit—knowledge acquired on the road, border crossings, smuggling networks, Afghan transport economies, Afghan antipathies with Pakistan, Afghan refugee settlements in Pakistan, and excellent Pashtun humor and hospitality— would distill and reemerge in this project many years hence, by which time many Afghans who had crossed the border to Pakistan were now refugees settling in England and elsewhere across the world.

Likewise, it was not through any systematic series of decisions or well-laid planning, but transiently, transitorily, through an unfolding sense of moving, and being on the cusp of itself, that this book also wrote itself along the way—through backtracking, sideways steps, hunches followed on the hoof, and many inevitable blocks. If its genesis is not entirely certain, it thereby approaches the migrant condition of difference that sediments in the blood and heart for those of us who are continually made different by the onerous question "Where are you from?"

Anthropology is inevitably also about our own stories. If not explicitly so, this story also enfolds the echoic presence of my maternal descendants who migrated from their ancestral homes in central China and dispersed across the world during the immense upheavals and entropic losses of the nineteenth and twentieth centuries, including war and the retreat of empire. I lived in many places—London, Hong Kong, Karachi, Singapore, and California—before arriving in Sussex some two decades ago. Of Eurasian heritage, growing up in rural, predominantly white England, taught me a lot about my difference and its varied valuations, but it also freed me from many constraints of fixed identity. It drew me to deliberately seek out transitory, transient, and liminal ways of living and experience: in tandem with the carving out of fugitive paths, edges, outsides, and in-between spaces and interstices of mixed and multiple languages, cultures, and sensibilities: such places have become home, even if they are not necessarily comfortable.

In grasping new ways of living on and in new homelands, this book is centrally about the trade of learning to survive war, here the forty-year lag that has rendered the Afghan homeland unhomely and created the dual dream both of moving home and of unmoving houses, of finding intimacy with the unhomely, and with the everyday unknown as it passes through the realms of dread and imagination—as it does in the shared histories of my interlocutors and many other migrants and those affected by war. Capturing something of the way evanescent realities are inhabited by dream, and of what it might mean to redream history, is one preoccupation I tentatively explore in these pages.

There are many to thank for this book, which comprises an accumulation of relationships, innumerable conversations, and indebtedness. First are my Afghan interlocutors in Sussex, London, and Peshawar who will be named and unnamed; to Zmarai, Hamid, and Sher Agha my deepest thanks for your time and generosity, Zmarai especially. Thanks to Junaid Rana and Sohail Daulatzai, editors of the Muslim International series at the University of Minnesota Press, for taking a chance on a book about taxi-drivers. Thanks to my editors at the University of Minnesota Press: to Jason Weidemann for his expert professionalism in taking the book smoothly from initial review through to publication; to Zenyse Miller for work on the final manuscript preparation; and to Nicholas Taylor and Mike Stoffel for carefully checking the manuscript. For their valuable readings of earlier drafts, especial thanks to Kaveri Qureshi, Andy Smith, Stanley Thangaraj, and Veronica Doubleday. For providing critical insights, contributions, and encouragement, thanks to scholars, friends, and colleagues Nabi Misdaq, Mohammad Jamil Hanifi, Ghotie Ahmadi, Malalai Ahmadi, Valentina Napolitano, Jenny Shaw, Julie Billaud, John Baily, Antonio De Lauri, Farrukh Husain, Hannah Vincent, Zuhra Bahman, Rabia Nasimi, Sahar Khan for indexing assistance, the anonymous reviewers of previous iterations of journal articles, and to the editors and anonymous reviewers of articles published in *JRAI* and *Medical Anthropology*.

Thanks to the Asia Research Institute (ARI) at the National University of Singapore for providing me a visiting fellowship and time to write in the academic year 2017–18, and to the University of Brighton for a research sabbatical that made not only that visit but a longer period of uninterrupted writing possible. For helping me refine my thinking, thanks to audiences at workshops and seminars at ARI, to Mikkel Rytter for the invitation to an exciting workshop at the University of Aarhus in 2019, to Noel Salazar for an invitation to present at the ANTHROMOB group at the University of Lisbon in 2015, to seminar audiences at the universities of Sussex, Singapore, Brighton, and Bournemouth; to audiences at American Anthropological Association annual meetings in San Francisco, Chicago, Minneapolis, and San Jose between 2012 and 2016; at the biennial conferences of the European Association of Social Anthropologists in Stockholm in 2018 and the Society for Psychological Anthropology in Santa Ana Pueblo in 2019. Especial thanks always to Sappho Zakira and Sahar Khan for their forbearance, patience, and love. To mahma, whose history has journeyed powerfully through our family's generations yet in very few words, this book is for you.

NOTES

Prelude

1. The battle lasted from March to May 1989.
2. Misdaq (2006, 160–61).
3. Mostly Wahhabist fighters from Saudi Arabia, which supported the Afghan resistance (Misdaq 2006, 160).
4. Hamid Gul served as director of Pakistan's Inter-Services Intelligence (ISI) agencies during Bhutto's premiership, is credited with responsibility for planning the Jalalabad operation, and was sacked by Bhutto after it failed.
5. Aerial bombing had been the preferred policy of the Soviets fighting the mujahideen in Afghanistan (O'Ballance 1993).
6. River in Surkh Rōd district in Nangarhar province, eastern Afghanistan.
7. "Mother" in old Pashto. The common word for "mother" is *moor*.
8. In Islam, it is customary for women relatives to ritually wash the body of a corpse before burial.
9. Pashtuns in England often code-switched between Pashto, English, or sometimes Urdu or Dari for emphasis, humor, or communicative effect.

Introduction

1. Commissioned in 1787 and finished in 1822 as a pleasure palace in an Indian–Chinese style for the Prince Regent George IV.

2. The dilemma bears on a crude saying that makes the point directly. *Ne de deen sawe, ne de ghreen sawe*—literally "There is no benefit either for your religion [duty] or your penis [pleasure]"—referring to someone who neither supports his family nor pursues his own desires (i.e., is neither one thing nor another).

3. For discussions on codes and characteristics of Pashtunwali, and Pashtun tribal organizations see Ahmed (1980); Anderson (1983); Barth (1959a, 1959b); Beattie (2002); Caroe ([1958] 2006); Canfield (1988); Evans-von Krbek (1977); Glatzer (1983); and Lindholm (1982).

4. Ghilzai is the singular case, Ghilzi the plural.

5. Afghanistan has three major Pashtun tribal confederations: the Durrani, Ghilzai, and Karlani. The Ghilzai tribes (see Anderson 1983; Broadfoot 1886; M. Hanifi 2001) appear in historical readings as opponents of the pro-British rulers of 1880–1919, strict adherents to the Pashtunwali, and proponents of cultural and religious conservatism.

6. From 2001 to 2003 operations were termed "Operation Enduring Freedom." From August 2003 to October 2014 NATO took the lead of the International Security Assistance Force in the "War against Terror" in Afghanistan, with British forces remaining through 2017.

7. See Billaud (2015); Coburn (2011); De Lauri (2013, 2014); Edwards (2002); Marsden (2015); Monsutti (2010a); Nguyen (2011); and Thompson (2011).

8. See Monsutti (2005, 2010b); Olszewska (2012, 2015); Omidian (1996); and Oeppen (2010).

9. In 2013 the UN Refugee Agency confirmed Afghanistan as the world's largest refugee-producing country since 1981. Ninety-five percent of Afghan refugees live in Pakistan and Iran (*BBC News* 2013; Collective for Social Science Research 2006). In 2015 Afghans were the world's third-largest asylum-seeking population, after Syrians and Iraqis (UNHCR 2015).

10. By 1981, almost all refugees in the province were in the capital Peshawar; by 1989 over two million resided in Peshawar district. According to the 2005 census, the total Afghan refugee population in Pakistan's North-West Frontier Province in 1980 (including pre-1979 arrivals) was 1.15 million. Other figures suggest that between 2003 and 2006 over 2.5 million people of Afghan origin (including those settled in Pakistan illegally) repatriated to Afghanistan (CAR 2016).

11. Narratives of Pashtun incursions into Karachi downplay the severe hardships Karachi's working-class Pashtuns faced, and the unforgiving exploitation of young Pashtun men in Karachi's transport sector (Asdar Ali 2012).

12. UNHCR reports estimate that 340,000 people repatriated to Afghanistan in 2003; 350,000 in 2004; and 450,000 in 2005 (Alam 2012, 60).

13. See *Pajhwok News* (2016). Regarding Sharbat Gula's deportation see Azami (2017). The combined UNHCR stats for the repatriation of registered

refugees only from Pakistan shows a peak in 2005 dropping to its lowest level in 2014, followed by a spike in 2015 and 2016: 449,520 (2005); 133,015 (2006); 364,476 (2007); 282,496 (2008); 51,290 (2009); 109,383 (2010); 52,096 (2011); 84,423 (2012); 31,224 (2013); 12,991 (2014); 58,211 (2015); 381,275 (2016). By early 2017 an estimated 1.3 million registered Afghans remained in Pakistan, and over a million unregistered individuals.

14. See Saeed and Ferrie (2017) and M. Green (2016).

15. These data exclude unregistered and illegal migrants as well as asylum applicants. After the "Jungle" Camp at Calais closed in October 2016, around five hundred children were shifted to the UK, including young relatives of taxi-drivers. Since the Dublin Regulation of 2016, which required new migrants or asylum seekers to be fingerprinted and processed in their country of first arrival, many have been stranded in Greece—with up to forty thousand migrants, mostly from Afghanistan and Syria, trapped in camps on the five islands in the Eastern Aegean, in conditions designed for 20 percent of their number—for example, fifteen thousand on Lesbos in a camp designed for three thousand—with woefully inadequate medical and sanitation services (*BBC News* 2019). All, unaccompanied minors particularly, are vulnerable to sex and organ trafficking (Vulliamy 2016).

16. The appellation Pakhtun (versus Pashtun, Pukhtun or Pushtun) reflects regional differences in pronunciation. It is common in southeastern Afghanistan, Nangarhar province, and the Jalalabad region. Pashtun has a wider, more inclusive usage and, except where referring to a direct quotation, I use it to be consistent.

17. There are no official numbers, but estimates suggest around half of Afghan Pashtun families in this city reside in Pakistan, mostly Peshawar and also Karachi.

18. See Khan (2010, 2017a).

19. I spent many hours completing housing benefit and car insurance forms, taxi license renewal applications, parking ticket appeals, acquiring family settlement visa information, health and safety advice, translating information at medical appointments for my informants, or attending council and hospital meetings (with them, or on their behalf).

20. One speaks and does Pashto. Doing Pashto here refers to behaving according to the cultural precepts of Pashtunwali in front of one's brothers—for example, not smoking, not making sexual jokes, according respect according to age and behaving "appropriately," and not having unrelated female "friends."

21. Figures such as Mary Craven, Elizabeth Elgin, Florentia Sale, Gertrude Bell, and Hester Stanhope offer historical precedents of such familiarity as to be rather conventional. From an upper-class elite, and often involved in diplomacy

and political administration, rather than street-level research, they were viewed as eccentric admirable adventurers as opposed to suspicious or immoral.

22. As Arendt (1958, 26) tells us, sheer violence renders speech mute. For Scarry (1985), pain may constitute an experience that "destroys the world" of the subject while resisting expression in language.

23. The "minor discourse" was epitomized in Lévi-Strauss's *Tristes Tropiques* ([1955] 2011). The criticism of the "minor discourse," Kapferer (2013, 823) notes, is that it reproduces those dualisms of major/minor, East/West, primitivism/ rationalism, et cetera, that it protests.

24. They have drawn creatively from philosophy, psychoanalysis, and medicine in order to deepen understandings of how to move ethnographically between interior and social worlds. Studies have tracked the aftershocks of empire through the micro-ecologies of the psyche, the material debris of ruined matter, landscapes, disemboweled cityscapes, and infrastructure (Stoler 2008, 194); ways body and world are "severed or yoked together in pain" (Asad 2011, 657–58); explored suffering as a form of life (Biehl 2005); and what it means existentially to be subject to death (Desjarlais 2016).

25. My interlocutor's Pashto transliteration of this *tarāna* (acquired from a CD in his taxi) is as follows: "Afghana malk ke dey Angrezaan girzi / de peroon Angrezaan girzi/che zrelaweli we da sta nikunoo da / nun dey pe khowra wag daran girzi / nun dey ragheli di de dostey panaare / sta do watan de abadey panaame / meymanaan ne di mughbeyran girzi / de peyroon ourazi dukhmanan girzi / nun ye pe khowra biyar yarghal kurrai da / sta de wejelo ye att kal kuraai da / . . . Afghana paam kow dey khata dey neki / le khpel khadafna chey dey juda ne key."

26. A *landay* is a formulaic verse (comprising twenty-two syllables, nine in the first line, thirteen in the second) that is recited or sung by women to women, about love, grief, separation, the homeland, war, or sex.

27. Ahmad Shah gained Sindh and Punjab, then Herat, and Nishapur and Mashhad in Iran in 1751. By 1752 he controlled Kashmir and the Turkmen, Uzbeks, Tajiks, and Hazaras of the north, center, and west. In 1757 he retreated, leaving the Mughal dynasty to recognize his dominion—accepted by the British East India Company (Gommans 1994). After defeating the Sikhs in 1762, he returned to Afghanistan, leaving the British to expand. In order to forestall an Afghan invasion of British India, the British backed the Persian court (Misdaq 2006, 51).

28. The era produced a rich legacy of Pashtun poetry. The poet–warriors Ahmad Shah Baba and Khushal Khan Khattak (1613–89) exhorted Pashtuns to regain their honor and glory and vanquish the Mughals from Afghan land, while the peaceful mysticism of Rehman Baba (1650–1715) celebrated Pashtun culture and local life. Later came the self-searching Romanticism of Ghani Khan, and opposition to the incorporation of Pashtun nationalism and identity within Pakistan (Caroe [1958] 2006, 436).

29. Abdur Rahman's "pro-British" rule drove the less economically and militarily powerful Pakhtuns into peripheral areas, leading to an upsurge in radical Islamism and resistance to Western modernization such as Ataturk had imposed in Turkey in 1897 (Nojumi 2002).

30. Pashtun grievances, centered on discrimination in Pakistan, combined with other minority groups in the rapid rise in the late 2010s of the Pashtun Tahafuz Mahaz social movement, led by Manzoor Pashteen. Protests met with fatal violence by the army in May 2019, amid widespread intolerance for political dissent (Masood, Mashal, and Rehman 2019).

31. King Amanullah introduced many modernizing reforms, although opposed by Pashtun religious elites and the rural population (Nojumi 2002). King Muhammad Zahir Shah's long reign provided for parliament, elections, a free press, as well as roads and irrigation projects.

32. Under presidents Babrak Karmal (1979–86) and Najibullah Ahmadzai (1987–92), Afghanistan resisted Western influence, Pakistan-style Islamization, and Soviet communism. President Mohammed Daoud Khan (1973–78) courted both the Communists and Islamists, and aided Soviet designs (Misdaq 2006, 96). Pakistan armed the "Pashtunistan" forces that had formed in the 1960s, strengthening anti-Communist resistance. Notwithstanding, the 1978 military coup by the PDPA ended two centuries of Durrani dominance. The PDPA's attempts to turn Kabul into a modern, Communist, Persianate city (exemplified by "liberated" women) accelerated anti-Soviet resistance, and may have contributed to why the predominantly rural, uneducated Pashtun Taliban subsequently imposed their harshest laws on women (Mishra 2011, 367).

33. Attributed first to Saddam Hussein's regime in Iraq, in which tens of thousands of disappearances occurred, in addition to public executions and hangings during the same period.

34. The ISI supported the "Peshawar seven," comprising the mujahideen factions of Rabbani, Massoud's Jamiat-i-Islami, Hekmatyar's Hizb-i-Islami, Abdurrab Rasul Sayyaf's Ittehad-i- Islami, and four minor groups: Hizb Islami (Younous Khalis), Mahaz Milli Islami, Jabh-yi-Nejat Milli, and Harakat-i-Inqilab-i-Islami.

35. Taliban killings in Mazar-e-Sharif and Hazarajat (1996–2001) constituted a genocide; and the mass graves of between ten and fourteen thousand (depending on sources) Taliban fighters and supporters were discovered at Dasht-e-Laili, killed by Dostum, who transported them to Sheberghan prison in sealed containers (Rashid 2009, 93–94). Also see Jamie Doran's documentary *Afghan Massacre: The Convoy of Death* (2002).

36. Originally termed by the political officer Captain Arthur Connolly in 1840.

37. Examples include the 1975 film *The Man Who Would Be King*, directed by John Huston and based on Kipling's story; the 1971 film of Joseph Kessel's novel *Les Cavaliers* (The Horseman); Hollywood's *King of the Khyber Rifles* (1953),

North West Frontier (1959); the 1968 British comedy *Carry On up the Khyber*; and the 1992 Hindi film *Khuda Ghawa* featuring global superstar Amitabh Bachchan. Fyodor Bondarchuk's 2005 film *The 9th Company* was a hit in Russia, whereas the 2007 film of Khaled Hosseini's *The Kite Runner* was criticized for its neglect of the history that underpinned Western allies' sacrifice of Afghans in exercises of realpolitik. Andre Singer's *Khyber* (1979) uses anthropological filmmaking to recall British endeavors on the North-West Frontier, through interviews with Sir Olaf Caroe, the last governor of NWFP before Partition; Sir Claude Auchinleck, the last commander of the British Army in India; and Akbar Ahmed, a former political agent in the Tribal Areas.

38. Historical works document Afghan migrations to India from the thirteenth century; through the Mughal empire, the rule of the Pashtun King Sher Shah Suri, and Akbar the Great, who extended the Grand Trunk Road from Calcutta to Kabul; to the Durrani empire, the founding of territory understood as Afghanistan inside present-day Pakistan, and large-scale nineteenth-century migrations (Caroe [1958] 2006; Green 2013, 2015a; Green 2016).

39. Caron's border thinking synthesizes Deleuzean scholarship on modes of assembling knowledge, intertextuality, and other lateral rhizome-building alliances (2016, 329).

40. Arguably in development. As Marcus (2013) writes, if ethnography has long since abandoned a "retrospective orientation," it still not quite knows how to mine the anticipatory orientations of productive, parallel knowledge economies through which it moves.

41. To elaborate, maps, grids, charts, and diagrams are anthropology's illustrative means par excellence of depicting ethnographic research and field sites, and the mechanisms and arrangements of economic exchange, resource allocation, kinship, and alliances contained therein. Ceremonial, symbolic, and gendered exchanges, kinship genealogy, marital exchange, family trees, and models of lineage versus alliance (Gell 1999; Malinowski 1922; Rivers 1910) are all ideographically depicted in classic anthropological texts.

42. See Cresswell (2006); Greenblatt (2009); Harvey (2000); Kaplan (1996); N. Khan (2016); and Urry (2007). These analyses draw continuities with classic anthropological texts that detail the ecological, social, and cultural circulation of people, knowledge, objects, materiality, and time (e.g., Bourdieu 1990; Rabinow 2007; Malinowski 1954). Others study variegated imaginary, experiential, political–economic, legal, and cultural assemblages of movement, of "things-in-motion," mobility as a relationship through which the world is lived and understood (Adey 2010), and ways that capital, freedom, gender, immobility, motility, mobility regimes, infrastructures of mobility, and multiple, emergent, and poten-

tial mobilities may be ethnographically and anthropologically engaged (Salazar and Jayaram 2016).

43. "Ze yum da truck driver / nun Pekhaworkey, saba Lahorekey / pe youw sahat key, te mulkunou pana keygum / larakey rashee der hoteluna / pe key chergandee hum pulao-una / ze yum da truck driver."

44. These bear on motility as the potential and capacity to move; on links between driving, economic and social mobility, mobility capital, network capital, and mobility inequality (Schiller and Salazar 2013).

45. See also https://data.worldbank.org/ (accessed July 1, 2018).

1. Lifelines

1. Regarding the chapter's epigraphs, *tikay* refers to sung verses, whereas *musafer* may refer to a pilgrim, refugee, migrant, or other traveler.

2. The *surnai* is a double-reed aerophone.

3. Whereas transport for Ingold describes a preconceived "genealogical" movement from location A to B, a lifeless "movement towards terminal closure" (3), in wayfaring production adheres in action, *not* the end goal (6). Likewise, dwelling is not the occupation of structures (buildings, culture, categories) already *built*. Rather, dwelling emerges in "movement along a way of life" (12). Wayfaring captures being alive as an experience of continuous becoming, toward and beyond ends. It encapsulates the theoretical move from the problem and limits of perpetual time, to the opening up of time passing wherein life is composed of the lines of its own movement in time (14).

4. His "ontographic approach" describes "the method of extrapolating analytic abstractions from the ethnographic material, rather than, say, heaping Western philosophical concepts upon it" (87).

5. In southeastern Afghanistan, Pakhtu speakers might say *thlāl* (going) *aw* (and) *rathlāl* (coming), not *rāsha aw darsha,* which translates awkwardly as "come and move along." Strictly Pakhtuns from southeastern Afghanistan use the phoneme "s," not "sh." However, my informants' families also live as refugees in Peshawar, where "sh" is common. Hence *rāsha aw darsha* is a transregional, vernacular adaptation.

6. Those with "indefinite leave to remain" visas may not yet have been resident for five years, or able to afford the costs of the citizenship test and first passport application fee, which exceeds £1,000.

7. Pakistani Pashtun drivers in the city do not socialize closely with Afghans. They may occasionally play sports together, with other Muslim South Asians and Muslim groups.

8. The international policing of terrorist finance and money laundering

means that controls are strict on large cash amounts transferred legitimately between London, Pakistan and Afghanistan. They also keep remittances separate for income tax purposes.

9. A *jereeb* is equal to a hectare.

10. These investments secure the traditional value of land and property ownership in the context of highly mobile lives and chronic insecurity.

11. Since 2012, applicants must demonstrate an annual income of £18,600 to settle a spouse (£22,400 for one additional child, £24,800 for two, £27,200 for three).

12. Ghilzai denotes the singular, Ghilzi the plural case.

13. Loy Akhtar ("Big Festival") refers to the Eid-ul-Adha festival when Muslims sacrifice a cow, goat, or sheep; feast; and share food with relatives, neighbors, and friends. "Small Eid" is Eid-ul-Fitr, following the fasting month of Ramadan, colloquially called "Kuchney Akhtar."

14. There may be a tent, blankets, and sports gear crammed into the trunk, perhaps a thermos and gas burner; medicines, snacks, a *tasbee,* and sunglasses stuffed onto the shelf above the sun visor; water bottles and tissues packed into the driver's door pocket. A small pillow assists with neck ache, and music, TV, and social networks are all at hand.

15. The ability to buy one's own taxi (a license plate then cost around £50,000 in the informal market, because city council waiting lists are so long) confers status on the owner in this commercial "system of automobility" (Urry 2004, 27). Uber's entry into the city, combined with a long economic climate of political austerity, led prices to drop as low as £20,000 by 2019.

16. This was also identified by Catherine Besteman (2016, 235) among Somali Muslim Bantu refugees in Maine.

17. Also see Thangaraj (2015) for a study of South Asians in American basketball, and on ways masculinity and its contradictions underpin identity formations of sport, pleasure, power, and history in the socialization of U.S. ethnic communities.

18. Kalra examines the ethnicized character of local income generation, economic status, and ways that migrant drivers' lives are inflected with family separations and necessities to remit. The Pakistani drivers in his study are not refugees or affected by war.

19. *Murrai–zwandai* is similar to the Pashtu *gham–xadi* construct, where *gham* (sorrow) refers to the feelings, observances, and protocols (visitations, condolences, etc.) for dealing with life crises and loss, especially of life; and *xadi* to celebrations of happiness (especially weddings) and material, social, and symbolic gains (a bride, new social relations, a child's birth) (Grima 1985, 12–13).

20. I asked Ihsanullah about touching a dead body, which is supposedly ritu-

ally polluting in Islamic culture. Can only a *morda-shoy* ("dead body-washer" in Dari) touch a dead body? There is no Pashto equivalent label for this low-level, caste-like occupation. Many Pashtun tribes do not employ a *morda shoy*, he replied: "We wash our own dead to keep the shame of their nakedness among ourselves. Moving a corpse in war is helpful. Washing a body is different."

21. I interpret this story phenomenologically in terms of a connection of the psychic to the body. It does, however, implicate deeper layers of analysis at the individual, psychodynamic level, which I explore elsewhere.

2. The Taste of Freedom and Return

1. My ambiguous, shifting position as a female outsider proved well-suited to the quixotic, transgressive, liminal space constituted on the all-male *chakar*.

2. A Bollywood epic film.

3. "Such a river of life as nowhere else exists in the world" (Kipling [1901] 1993, 55).

4. This refers to Abdul Ghaffar Khan's funeral in 1988 in Afghanistan, attended by over two hundred thousand mourners, including thousands of followers and tribesmen from Pakistan, where Khan had been held under house arrest for agitating against the Pakistani government for Pashtun rights and unity.

5. Hospitality in Pashtunwali is distinct but related to *nanawatai*, meaning asylum or sanctuary, derived from *nanah watel*, to enter. *Nanawatai* signifies the asylum seeker's absolute inferior position with respect to the protector; thereby differing from *melmastia*, where relations are dynamic and more ambiguous. *Nanawatai* is a "disgrace" only requested in extremis, if for example one cannot pay one's debts, fails to honor formal dealings with another clan or tribe, or commits murder and then cannot face the consequences. The supplicant may send a relative to take *nanawatai* from the bereaved family, or take a sheep to the protector's door in offering (Misdaq 2006). Pashtunwali dictates he is given food and immunity, and his appeal accepted. Thereafter, financial or blood compensation (e.g., giving a daughter in marriage) may be arranged. In some cases Pashtunwali dictates that asylum should not be refused, as when Taliban leaders declined to hand over Osama bin Laden to U.S. forces in 2001.

6. Ideal-typic forms of Pashtunwali are romanticized in late nineteenth- and twentieth-century Pashtun poetry—for example by Ghani Khan, son of the Frontiersman Abdul Ghaffar Khan, "Fakhir-e-Afghan" (Pride of Afghanistan): "Custom does not allow protection to the breakers of custom. He stands alone and must pay the price. Even his friends will avoid the funeral. It is hard and brutal, but it works." ([1947] 2010, 26).

7. After Zahir Qadir's election to the Afghan House of Representatives in

2012, Gul Agha Sherzai opened his personal *hujra* in Nangarhar after every Friday prayers to offer food to locals as a sign of a leader's generosity: "While others are robbing Afghanistan for oil, iron, minerals, I'm giving people food!"

3. Immobility Dreams

1. These are Batemans, a seventeenth-century Jacobean styled house in Burwash village, East Sussex, where Kipling lived from 1902–1936—and North End House in Rottingdean where he lived with his family from 1897 until they purchased Batemans. Kipling's gardens beside his erstwhile home are now open to the public.

2. Zmarai chose this pseudonym, meaning "lion," a symbol of power. Asiatic lions (now extinct) used to roam freely over the mountains and plains of Afghanistan. The lion has more recently denoted military strength.

3. Single cases may destabilize political categories as conventionally institutionalized in relation to Afghans according to such overdetermined concepts as refugees, diaspora, transnationalism, citizenship, trauma, identity, and culture. See analyses by Biehl (2005); Daniel (1996); Farmer (1996); Gay y Blasco (2011); Jackson (2008); and Robbins (2013).

4. Phillips cites Freud's essay "Jokes and Their Relation to the Unconscious," in which Freud argues that jokes represent a momentary release from obstacles we have imposed on our pleasure (that like dreams, they are saboteurs of repression).

5. *Museebat* is an obstacle or blockage; the more literary term is *nakhwalay.*

6. This suggests a role for *khapgan* in the resignification of beliefs about ghosts in the neoliberal context.

7. *Badmarghee* may describe a grand affliction (terminal illness such as cancer, mental illness involving hallucinations, widowhood, divorce, or war and political afflictions); or other afflictions.

8. Although no suicide rates exist for Afghan migrants in Britain, the many cases of depression and suicide I encountered among migrant men compare with high rates of suicide and mental health problems among men generally—with men accounting for 75 percent of UK suicides overall since the mid-nineties (Office for National Statistics 2018).

9. Somatic symptoms are common among refugees and survivors of armed conflict (Rohlof, Knipscheer, and Kleber 2014).

10. This suggests a Pashto transliteration of the French *coup d'état.*

11. See Lindisfarne (2006) on exchange marriages between cousins.

12. Emily Martin (2007, 52) draws connections between psychiatric criteria

in the individual who "is *too* energized, or *too* immobilized," with historical anxieties around "simple exposure to the hectic pace and excessive stimuli of modern life," which co-occur with a depressive, fragmented, alienated consciousness, and isolation from the social.

13. Deleuze has engaged Spinoza's critique of the subject-oriented philosophy of Descartes, enlivening several debates relevant to immobility. Deleuze's concept "immobile intensities" (Deleuze and Guattari 2004, 381) addresses affect's less dysphoric relation to immobility: that the opposition of movement and rest create images of "immobile movement," akin to "spiritual voyages" effected without relative movement, but in intensity, in one place. Immobile intensities are not necessarily located in exterior space but, poised between other specific immobilities and mobilities, describe passing into states or feelings unavailable in travel— for example the "profound countries" of geo-music or geo-philosophy (381)—or, I suggest, dreaming.

14. See also Kracke (2003, 213).

15. In medieval Islamic scholarship, *al-ruya* referred to true dreams inspired by God; in contrast to dreams emanating from the devil, or from the *nafs* (the earthly spirit or soul), which were influenced by the dreamer's desires and emotions, and can be frightening (Qureshi 2010, 283).

16. See, inter alia, Abraham 1979; Basso 1987; Borneman 2011; Devereux 1951; Edgar 2011; Eggan 1949; Kracke 2003; Lohmann 2000; Nations 2013; Paul 1989; Poirier 2003; Tedlock 1987; Tylor 1871 (1877); Wallace 1958; and Williams 1936.

17. See Widmark (2011, 156–59) for a literary analysis of "dreaming while awake," hallucinations, madness, and hunger in a Pashto short story.

18. For Freud "Jokes and Their Relation to the Unconscious," jokes represent a momentary release from obstacles we imposed on our pleasure. Like dreams, for Freud jokes are saboteurs of repression (Phillips 2012).

19. Because the dream only offers a substitute fulfillment for an unconscious wish, it inevitably leaves a residual dissatisfaction, which may be experienced intensely.

20. "Condensation" refers to dreamwork that will "combine all the sources which have acted as stimuli for the dream into a single unity in the dream itself" (Freud [1953] 1975, 266).

21. An informal encampment built after the Sangatte reception center (1999–2002) was closed (it featured in Michael Winterbottom's 2002 film *In This World*). Many migrants from the camp entered the UK through the Eurotunnel or port. In 2015 the camp's population was an estimated 6,400 migrants, mostly from Syria, Afghanistan, Iraq, Eritrea, and Somalia.

22. Considered a food of the poor.

23. See Baily (2014, 119) on *bacha bazi* (dancing boys) in northern Afghanistan, and Pashto poetry extolling the beauty of young boys, as in lines such as "Across the river is a boy with a bottom like a peach. Alas, I cannot swim" (attributed to Khushal Khan Khattak; 109n7).

24. The relevance of the "Sussex" countryside scene may relate to the city of Brighton's reputation as Britain's "gay capital."

25. Cultural discourse disapproves of romantic love between spouses, which might threaten the structural requirements for gender segregation, lifelong marriage, and family patriarchy.

26. Zmarai occasionally visited my home, but more often we drove about or took trips in his taxi. We also had many conversations by mobile phone—mirroring communications he kept with his fellow taxi-drivers and his relatives in Peshawar.

27. Or Freud's "oceanic feeling," to revisit our watery theme. Freud introduces what he termed the "oceanic feeling" in *Civilization and Its Discontents* (1929). He uses it to refer to a feeling or sensation of "eternity," of something limitless and unbounded that is the source of religious energy but which also transcends it.

28. In Freud's terms (*On Narcissism*; [1914] 2013), "His Majesty the Baby."

4. Food, Water, and Wherewithal in the Time of Crossings

1. Section 136 (s136) of the Mental Health Act of 1983 permits the removal by police in a public place of a person who appears in immediate need of "care or control" owing to their apparent mental state.

2. Demography is significant in propelling young Afghan men to migrate to Europe. In 2015, 85 percent of Afghanistan's population was reportedly under twenty-four years of age (UNHCR 2015). Michael Winterbottom's 2002 docudrama *In This World* tells of two boys from Kacha Garai camp who make the dangerous overland journey to London, which typifies the journeys of many others.

3. Taken from the video "Meena Raka Rasha Meena Dar Karwoma" ("Give Me Love, Come I Will Give You Love"), available on YouTube, https://youtube.com/watch?v=1r9davpWE3I, accessed November 7, 2017.

4. Tagore's 1892 story about the itinerant Afghan trader, "Kabuliwala," concerns an impoverished door-to-door trader selling dried fruits and nuts in Calcutta. Tagore deployed stereotypes of hotheadedness, violence, innocence, and naiveté to engage a critique of the suspicion of foreigners in Bengali society as well as early marriage customs.

5. The tribal agencies were merged with the province of Khyber-Pakhtunkhwa in 2018.

6. For example, 63 percent between 2016 and 2017.

5. Barth in Sussex

1. Regarding the epigraphs, *gul,* meaning flower, has positive connotations of humility and modesty.

2. Briefly, these are as follows: (1) The presence of a persisting opposition of interests between wards occupied by collaterals in the agnatic descent system (i.e., persisting direct opposition between some units of the system). (2) The recognition by Yusufzai Pathans of patron–client relations (so that no person is limited to agnatic relatives as potential supporters) and unrestricted freedom for units of the system to form coalitions from strategic choices. (3) Recognition is accorded the chief of a ward and leader of a party alliance in a set of indivisible "bonuses," whose distribution is the subject of understandings between persons.

3. *Gul* is a flower, or rose; *shin* is green, associated with Islam; *zai* and *zada* are suffixes denoting patrilineal grouping—*zai* is exclusively Pashto, and *zada* occurs in regions of greater Pashtun/Tajik ethnic and linguistic mixing. Gulzai is the singular case, Gulzi the plural.

4. There is little point tracing lineage back too far because ultimately all Pashtuns are considered related, and differentiation is lost.

5. Poignantly captured in the father–son relationship in Benjamin Gilmour's 2007 film *Son of a Lion.*

6. See Barth (1959b, 11) regarding the negative charge on structural relationships between close agnatic collateral segments in Yusufzai Pashtun kinship terminology.

7. For a discussion on the parallel rise of the Afghan cricket team alongside the settlement of Afghan migrant communities in Britain, see Khan (2013). The rise of the Afghan national cricket team has been exponential since 2009. In 2017 they were ranked ninth worldwide in the International Twenty20 cricket format. The national cricket team, originating with refugees from Peshawar's Kacha Garai camp, symbolizes an arena for Pashtun dominance.

8. The 2011 census numbers 3,635 Muslims in the city, constituting 1.47 percent of its population. There are three mosques within city limits.

BIBLIOGRAPHY

Abraham, Karl. 1979. "Dreams and Myths: A Study in Folk Psychology." In *Clinical Papers and Essays on Psychoanalysis*, 47–63. New York: Brunner/Mazel.

Adey, Peter. 2006. "If Mobility Is Everything Then It Is Nothing: Towards a Relational Politics of (Im)mobilities." *Mobilities* 1 (1): 75–94.

Adey, Peter. 2010. *Aerial Life: Spaces, Mobilities, Affects*. Oxford, UK: Wiley-Blackwell.

Agamben, Giorgio. 1994. "We Refugees." Translated by Michael Rocke. http://www.faculty.umb.edu/ (accessed July 2, 2017).

Agnew, Vijay, ed. 2005. *Diaspora, Memory, and Identity: A Search for Home*. Toronto: University of Toronto Press.

Ahmad, Aijaz. 1992. *In Theory: Classes, Nations, Literatures*. London: Verso.

Ahmad, Ali Nobil. 2011. *Masculinity, Sexuality and Illegal Migration: Human Smuggling from Pakistan to Europe*. Farnham, UK: Ashgate.

Ahmed, Akbar. 1980. *Pukhtun Economy and Society: Traditional Structure and Economic Development in a Tribal Society*. London: Routledge.

Ahmed, Akbar. 2004. *Resistance and Control in Pakistan*. London: Routledge.

Akhter, Majed. 2015. "Infrastructure Nation: State Space, Hegemony, and Hydraulic Regionalism in Pakistan." *Antipode* 47 (4): 849–70.

Alam, Anwar. 2012. "Barriers to Repatriation of Afghan Refugees (A Case Study of Afghan Community at Shah and Khusar Colony Board Area Peshawar)." *International Journal of Academic Research in Business and Social Sciences* 2 (3): 59–69.

Ali, Mohammed. 1964. *A Cultural History of Afghanistan.* Kabul: Punjab Educational Press.

Alimia, Sanaa. 2014. "Who Counts as a Refugee: The Geopolitics of Afghan and Bangladeshi Migrants in Pakistan." *Himal South Asia* 27 (2): 260–69.

Alimia, Sanaa. 2019. "Performing the Afghanistan–Pakistan Border through Refugee ID Cards." *Geopolitics* 24 (2): 391–425.

Allison, Anne. 2013. *Precarious Japan.* Durham, N.C.: Duke University Press.

Anderson, Jon. 1979. "Doing Pakhtu: Social Organization of the Ghilzai Pakhtun, Afghanistan." PhD diss., University of North Carolina.

Anderson, Jon. 1983. "*Khan* and *Khel*: Dialectics of Pakhtun Tribalism." In *The Conflict of Tribe and State in Iran and Afghanistan*, edited by Richard Tapper, 119–49. New York: St. Martin's Press.

Anzaldua, Gloria. 2012. *Borderlands / La Frontera: The New Mestiza.* 4th ed. San Francisco: Aunt Lute Books.

Arbabzadeh, Nushin. 2013. *The Afghan Rumour Bazaar.* London: Hurst & Co.

Arendt, Hannah. 1958. *The Human Condition.* Chicago: University of Chicago Press.

Asad, Talal. 1972. "Market Model, Class Structure and Consent: A Reconsideration of Swat Political Organization." *Man*, n.s., 7 (1): 74–94.

Asad, Talal. 2007. *On Suicide Bombing.* New York: Columbia University Press.

Asad, Talal. 2011. "Thinking about the Secular Body, Pain and Liberal Politics." *Cultural Anthropology* 26 (4): 657–75.

Asdar Ali, Kamran. 2012. "Women, Work and Public Spaces: Conflict and Co-existence in Karachi's Poor Neighborhoods." *International Journal of Urban and Regional Research* 36 (3): 585–605.

Azami, Dawood. 2017. "'Afghan Girl' Sharbat Gula in Quest for New Life." *BBC News*, January 16, 2017. http://www.bbc.co.uk/news/world-asia-38640487 (accessed January 16, 2017).

Babayan, Kathryn, and Afsaneh Najmabadi, eds. 2008. *Islamicate Sexualities: Translations across Temporal Geographies of Desire.* Cambridge, Mass.: Harvard University Press.

Baily, John. 1988a. "Amin-e-Diwaneh: The Musician as Madman." *Popular Music* 7 (2): 133–46.

Baily, John. 1988b. *Music of Afghanistan: Professional Musicians in the City of Herat.* Cambridge, UK: Cambridge University Press.

Baily, John. 2014. "*Wah Wah! Meida Meida!* The Changing Roles of Dance in Afghan Society." In *Music, Culture and Identity in the Muslim World: Performance, Politics and Piety*, edited by Kamal Salhi, 103–21. London: Routledge.

Baily, John. 2015. *War, Exile, and the Music of Afghanistan: The Ethnographer's Tale.* Farnham, UK: Ashgate.

Balibar, Etienne. 2002. *Politics and the Other Scene*. London: Verso.

Banerjee, Mukulika. 2000. *The Pathan Unarmed: Opposition and Memory in the Khudai Khidmatgar Movement*. London: Hurst & Co.

Barad, Karen. 2007. *Meeting the Universe Halfway: Quantum Physics and the Entanglement of Matter and Meaning*. Durham, N.C.: Duke University Press.

Barfield, Thomas. 2010. *Afghanistan: A Cultural and Political History*. Princeton, N.J.: Princeton University Press.

Barth, Fredrik. 1959a. *Political Leadership among Swat Pathans*. London: Athlone Press.

Barth, Fredrik. 1959b. "Segmentary Opposition and the Theory of Games: A Study of Pathan Organization." *Journal of the Royal Anthropological Institute of Great Britain and Ireland* 89 (1): 5–21.

Barth, Fredrik. 1969a. "Introduction." In *Ethnic Groups and Boundaries: The Social Organization of Culture Difference*, edited by Fredrik Barth, 9–38. London: George Allen & Unwin.

Barth, Fredrik. 1969b. "Pathan Identity and Its Maintenance." In *Ethnic Groups and Boundaries: The Social Organization of Culture Difference*, edited by Fredrik Barth, 117–34. London: George Allen & Unwin.

Basso, Ellen. 1987. "The Implications of a Progressive Theory of Dreaming." In *Dreaming: Anthropological and Psychological Interpretations*, edited by Barbara Tedlock, 86–104. Cambridge, UK: Cambridge University Press.

Batnitzky, Adina, Linda McDowell, and Sarah Dyer. 2012. "Remittances and the Maintenance of Dual Social Worlds: The Transnational Working Lives of Migrants in Greater London." *International Migration* 50 (4): 140–56.

Battaglia, Deborah. 1995. "On Practical Nostalgia: Self-Prospecting amongst Urban Trobrianders." In *Rhetorics of Self-Making*, edited by Deborah Battaglia, 77–97. Berkeley: University of California Press.

Battiscombe, Georgina. 1949. *English Picnics*. London: Harvill Press.

Baumann, Gerd. 1995. "Managing a Polyethnic Milieu: Kinship and Interaction in a London Suburb." *Journal of the Royal Anthropological Institute* 1 (4): 725–41.

Bayly, Martin. 2016. *Taming Their Imperial Imagination: Colonial Knowledge, International Relations, and the Anglo-Afghan Encounter, 1808–1878*. Cambridge, UK: Cambridge University Press.

BBC News. 2013. "More Than Seven Million Refugees Displaced in 2012—UN." June 19, 2013. http://www.bbc.co.uk/news/world-22963060 (accessed January 29, 2017).

BBC News. 2019. "Greece Migrant Crisis: 'Horrible' Camps to Shut Amid Influx." November 20, 2019. https://www.bbc.co.uk/news/world-europe -50486209 (accessed December 3, 2019).

Beard, James. 1965. *Menus for Entertaining*. New York: Delacorte Press.

Beattie, Hugh. 2002. *Imperial Frontier: Tribe and State in Waziristan.* London: Routledge.

Bedi, Tarini. 2016. "Mimicry, Friction and Trans-Urban Imaginaries: Mumbai Taxis / Singapore-Style." *Environment and Planning A: Economy and Space* 48 (6): 1012–29.

Bell, Sandra, and Simon Coleman, eds. 1999. *The Anthropology of Friendship.* Oxford, UK: Berg.

Benjamin, Walter. (1937) 1968. "Theses on the Philosophy of History." In *Illuminations,* 253–64. Translated by Harry Kohn. New York: Schocken Books.

Benjamin, Walter. 1999. *The Arcades Project.* Translated by Rolf Tiedemann. Cambridge, Mass.: Belknap Press of Harvard University Press.

Berger, John. 2007. *Hold Everything Dear: Dispatches on Survival and Resistance.* London: Verso.

Bergson, Henri. 2002. *The Creative Mind: An Introduction to Metaphysics.* New York: Citadel Press.

Berlant, Lauren. 2011. *Cruel Optimism.* Chicago: University of Chicago Press.

Berlant, Lauren, and Kathleen Stewart. 2019. *The Hundreds.* Durham N.C.: Duke University Press.

Besteman, Catherine. 2016. *Making Refuge: Somali Bantu Refugees and Lewiston, Maine.* Durham, N.C.: Duke University Press.

Bhambra, Gurminder. 2010. "Historical Sociology, International Relations and Connected Histories." *Cambridge Review of International Affairs* 23: 127–43.

Biao, Xiang. 2014. "The Would-Be Migrant: Post-Socialist Primitive Accumulation, Potential Transnational Mobility, and the Displacement of the Present in Northeast China." *Trans-Regional and National Studies of Southeast Asia* 2 (2): 183–99.

Biehl, João. 2005. *Vita: Life in a Zone of Social Abandonment.* Berkeley: University of California Press.

Billaud, Julie. 2015. *Kabul Carnival: Gender Politics in Postwar Afghanistan.* Philadelphia: University of Pennsylvania Press.

Bloch, Maurice. 2005. "Commensality and Poisoning." In *Essays on Cultural Transmission,* 45–60. Oxford, UK: Berg.

Bolognani, Marta. 2014. "Visits to the Country of Origin: How Second-Generation British Pakistanis Shape Transnational Identity and Maintain Power Asymmetries." *Global Networks* 14 (1): 103–20.

Borges, Jorge Luis. (1944) 1998. "Circular Ruins." In *Fictions,* 44–50. Translated by Andrew Hurley. New York: Penguin.

Borneman, John. 2011. "Daydreaming, Intimacy, and the Intersubjective Third in Fieldwork Encounters in Syria." *American Ethnologist* 38 (2): 234–48.

Bose, Sugata. 2006. *A Hundred Horizons: The Indian Ocean in the Age of Global Empire.* Cambridge, Mass.: Harvard University Press.

Bourdieu, Pierre. 1977. *Outline of a Theory of Practice*. Translated by Richard Nice. Cambridge, UK: Cambridge University Press.

Bourdieu, Pierre. 1984. *Distinction: A Social Critique of the Judgement of Taste*. Translated by Richard Nice. Cambridge, Mass.: Harvard University Press.

Bourdieu, Pierre. 1990. *The Logic of Practice*. Translated by Richard Nice. Cambridge, UK: Polity Press.

Bourdieu, Pierre. 2001. *Masculine Domination*. Translated by Richard Nice. Stanford, Calif.: Stanford University Press.

Brewin, Chris, Ruth Lanius, Andrei Novac, Ulrich Schnyder, and Sandro Galea. 2009. "Reformulating PTSD for *DSM-V*: Life after Criterion A." *Journal of Traumatic Stress* 22 (5): 366–73.

Broadfoot, James S. 1886. "Reports on Parts of the Ghilzi Country." *Royal Geographical Society Supplementary Papers* 1: 341–400.

Brown, Derek. 2000. "Asylum Seekers' Vouchers." *The Guardian*, September 28, 2000. https://www.theguardian.com/world/2000/sep/28/qanda.immigration andpublicservices (accessed November 21, 2017).

Burdsey, Daniel. 2016. *Race, Place, and the Seaside: Postcards from the Edge*. London: Palgrave-Macmillan.

Burnes, Alexander. 1834. *Travels into Bokhara: Being an Account of a Journey from India to Cabool, Tartary and Persia*. London: John Murray.

Büscher, Monika, and John Urry. 2009. "Mobile Methods and the Empirical." *European Journal of Social Theory* 12: 99–116.

Butler, Judith. 1997. *The Psychic Life of Power*. Stanford, Calif.: Stanford University Press.

Candea, Matei, and Giovanni da Col. 2012. "The Return to Hospitality: Strangers, Guests, and Ambiguous Encounters." *Journal of the Royal Anthropological Institute* 18 (S1): S1–19.

Canfield, Robert. 1988. "Afghanistan's Social Identities in Crisis." In *Le fait ethnique en Iran et en Afghanistan*, edited by Jean-Pierre Digard, 185–99. Paris: CNRS.

Canfield, Robert. 2010 "Introduction." In *Ethnicity, Authority, and Power in Central Asia: New Games Great and Small*, edited by Robert Canfield and Gabriele Rasuly-Paleczek, 1–16. New York: Routledge.

CAR (Commissionerate for Afghan Refugees). 2016. "Khyber-Pakhtunkhwa: Urban Refugees Cell." http://kpkcar.org/carnewsite/CAR/index.php/ shortcodes/urban-refugees-cell-cdu (accessed March 3, 2016).

Caroe, Olaf. (1958) 2006. *The Pathans*. 15th ed. Karachi: Oxford University Press.

Caron, James. 2009. "Cultural Histories of Pashtun Nationalism, Public Participation, and Social Inequality in Monarchic Afghanistan, 1905–1960." PhD diss., University of Pennsylvania.

Caron, James. 2013. "Ambiguities of Orality and Literacy, Territory and Border Crossings: Public Activism in Pashto Literature in Afghanistan, 1930–2010." In *Afghanistan in Ink*, edited by Nile Green and Nushin Arbabzadah, 113–40. London: Hurst & Co.

Caron, James. 2016. "Borderland Historiography in Pakistan." *South Asian History and Culture* 7 (4): 327–45.

Caron, James. 2019. "Pashto Border Literature as Geopolitical Knowledge." *Geopolitics* 24 (2): 444–61.

Cassidy, Rebecca. 2002. *Sport of Kings: Kinship, Class and Thoroughbred Breeding in Newmarket*. Cambridge, UK: Cambridge University Press.

Centlivres, Pierre, and Micheline Centlivres-Demont. 2012. "Retours en Afghanistan: Un nouveau regard sur un terrain revisité." *Anthropology of the Middle East* 7 (1): 1–17.

Chandrasekaran, Rajiv. 2012. *Little America: The War within the War for Afghanistan*. New York: Vintage Books.

Chatwin, Bruce. 1990. "A Lament for Afghanistan." In *What Am I Doing Here?* 286–96. London: Penguin.

Clifford, James. 1997. *Routes*. Cambridge, Mass.: Harvard University Press.

Coburn, Noah. 2011. *Bazaar Politics: Power and Pottery in an Afghan Market Town*. Stanford, Calif.: Stanford University Press.

Coburn, Noah. 2016. *Losing Afghanistan: An Obituary for the Intervention*. Stanford, Calif.: Stanford University Press.

Coburn, Noah, and Anna Larson. 2014. *Derailing Democracy in Afghanistan: Elections in an Unstable Political Landscape*. New York: Columbia University Press.

Collective for Social Science Research. 2006. *Afghans in Peshawar: Migration, Settlements, and Social Networks*. Kabul: Afghanistan Research and Evaluation Unit. http://www.unhcr.org/43e754da2.pdf (accessed May 11, 2009).

Connolly, Arthur. 1838. *Journey to the North of India, Overland from England, through Russia, Persia, and Afghanistan*. 2 vols. London: Richard Bentley.

Constable, Pamela. 2017. "Opium Use Booms in Afghanistan, Creating a Silent Tsunami of Addicted Women." *Washington Post*, June 19, 2018. https://www.washingtonpost.com/world/asia_pacific/opium-use-booms-in-afghanistan-creating-a-silent-tsunami-of-addicted-women/2017/06/19/6c5b16f2-3985-11e7-a59b-26e0451a96fd_story.html (accessed July 11, 2019).

Crapanzano, Vincent. 1975. "Saints, Jnun, and Dreams: An Essay in Moroccan Ethnopsychiatry." *Psychiatry* 38: 145–59.

Cresswell, Tim. 2006. *On the Move: Mobility in the Modern Western World*. London: Routledge.

Curry, Steve. 2007. *In the Shadow of Mountains*. New York: Phaidon Press.

Daniel, E. Valentine. 1996. "Crushed Glass, or, Is There a Counterpoint to Culture?" In *Culture/Contexture: Explorations in Anthropology and Literary Studies,* edited by E. V. Daniel and J. M. Peek, 357–75. Berkeley: University of California Press.

Das, Veena. 2006. *Life and Words: Violence and the Descent into the Ordinary.* Berkeley: University of California Press.

Das, Veena. 2015. *Affliction: Health, Disease, Poverty.* New York: Fordham University Press.

Das, Veena. 2018. "Ethics, Self-Knowledge, and Life Taken as a Whole." *HAU: Journal of Ethnographic Theory* 8 (3): 537–49.

Daulatzai, Anila. 2006. "Acknowledging Afghanistan: Notes and Queries on an Occupation." *Cultural Dynamics* 18: 293–311.

Dean, Bartholomew. 2016. "Freedom." In *Keywords of Mobility: Critical Anthropological Engagements,* edited by Noel Salazar and Kiran Jayaram, 55–72. New York: Berghahn Books.

De Certeau, Michel. 1984. *The Practice of Everyday Life.* Translated by Steven Rendall. Berkeley: University of California Press.

De Genova, Nichola. 2017. *The Borders of "Europe": Anatomy of Migration, Tactics of Bordering.* Durham, N.C.: Duke University Press.

De Lauri, Antonio. 2013. "Access to Justice and Human Rights." *Crime, Law, and Social Change* 60 (3): 261–85.

De Lauri, Antonio. 2014. "Law as an Anti-Value: Justice, Violence and Suffering in the Logic of Becoming." *Anthropology Today* 30 (3): 261–85.

De Leon, Jason. 2015. *The Land of Open Graves: Living and Dying on the Migrant Trail.* Berkeley: University of California Press.

Deleuze, Gilles, and Félix Guattari. 2004. *A Thousand Plateaus: Capitalism and Schizophrenia.* Translated by Brian Massumi. London: Continuum.

DelVecchio Good, Mary-Jo, Paul Brodwin, Byron Good, and Arthur Kleinman, eds. 1994. *Pain as Human Experience: Anthropological Perspectives.* Berkeley: University of California Press.

Derrida, Jacques. 1987. *The Post Card: From Socrates to Freud and Beyond.* Translated by Alan Bass. Chicago: University of Chicago Press.

Derrida, Jacques. 2000. *Of Hospitality.* Translated by Rachel Bowlby. Stanford, Calif.: Stanford University Press.

Desjarlais, Robert. 2016. *Subject to Death.* Chicago: University of Chicago Press.

Devereux, George. 1951. *Reality and Dream: Psychotherapy of a Plains Indian.* New York: International Universities Press.

Dietler, Michael. 2001. "Theorising the Feast: Rituals of Consumption, Commensal Politics and Power in African Contexts." In *Feasts: Archaeological and Ethnographic Perspectives on Food, Politics and Power,* edited by Michael

Dietler and Brian Hayden, 65–114. Washington, D.C.: Smithsonian Institution Press.

Donnan, Hastings. 2015. "The Anthropology of Borders." In *International Encyclopedia of the Social and Behavioral Sciences,* 2nd ed., edited by James D. Wright, 760–65. Oxford, UK: Elsevier.

Donnan, Hastings, Carolin Leutloff-Grandits, and Madeleine Hurd, eds. 2017. *Migrating Borders and Moving Times: Temporality and the Crossing of Borders in Europe.* Manchester, UK: Manchester University Press.

Doubleday, Veronica. 1985. *Three Women of Herat.* London: Johnathon Cape.

Doubleday, Veronica. 2015. "Spiritual Dimensions of Female Lullaby Singing in Afghanistan and Beyond." Paper presented at the conference Music, Art and Spirituality in Central Asia, Venice, Italy, October 29–31.

Douglas, Mary. 1972. "Deciphering a Meal." *Daedalus* 101: 61–81.

Dupree, Louis. 1973. *Afghanistan.* Princeton, N.J.: Princeton University Press.

Dwyer, Peter. 2009. "Worlds of Waiting." In *Waiting,* edited by Ghassan Hage, 15–26. Melbourne: University of Melbourne Press.

Edgar, Iain. 2011. *The Dream in Islam: From Qur'anic Tradition to Jihadist Inspiration.* New York: Berghahn Books.

Edwards, David B. 1994. "Afghanistan, Ethnography, and the New World Order." *Cultural Anthropology* 9 (3): 345–60.

Edwards, David B. 1996. *Heroes of the Age: Moral Fault Lines on the Afghan Frontier.* Berkeley: University of California Press.

Edwards, David B. 1998. "Learning from the Swat Pathans: Political Leadership in Afghanistan, 1978–97." *American Ethnologist* 25 (4): 712–28.

Edwards, David B. 2002. *Before Taliban: Genealogies of the Afghan Jihad.* Berkeley: University of California Press.

Edwards, David B. 2017. *Caravan of Martyrs: Sacrifice and Suicide Bombing in Afghanistan.* Berkeley: University of California Press.

Eggan, Dorothy. 1949. "The Significance of Dreams for Anthropological Research." *American Anthropologist* 51 (2): 177–98.

Elphinstone, Mountstuart. (1815) 1992. *An Account of the Kingdom of Caubul, and Its Dependencies in Persia, Tartary, and India.* 2 vols. Karachi: Indus Publications.

Elyachar, Julia. 2010. "Phatic Labor, Infrastructure, and the Question of Empowerment in Cairo." *American Ethnologist* 37 (3): 452–64.

Eriksen, Thomas Hylland. 2015. *Fredrik Barth: An Intellectual Biography.* London: Pluto Press.

Eurostat. 2016a. "Record Number of Over 1.2 Million First Time Asylum Seekers Registered in 2015." March 4. https://ec.europa.eu/eurostat/documents/2995521/7203832/3-04032016-AP-EN.pdf/790eba01-381c-4163-bcd2-a54959b99ed6 (accessed May 9, 2020).

Eurostat. 2016b. "EU Member States Granted Protection to More Than 330,000 Asylum Seekers in 2015." April 20. https://ec.europa.eu/eurostat/documents/2995521/7233417/3-20042016-AP-EN.pdf/34c4f5af-eb93-4ecd-984c-577a5271c8c5 (accessed May 9, 2020).

Eurostat. 2017. "1.2 Million First Time Asylum Seekers Registered in 2016." March 16. https://ec.europa.eu/eurostat/documents/2995521/7921609/3-16032017-BP-EN.pdf/e5fa98bb-5d9d-4297-9168-d07c67d1c9e1 (accessed May 9, 2020).

Eurostat. 2018. "EU Member States Granted Protection to More Than Half a Million Asylum Seekers in 2017." April 19. https://ec.europa.eu/eurostat/documents/2995521/8817675/3-19042018-AP-EN.pdf/748e8fae-2cfb-4e75-a388-f06f6ce8ff58 (accessed May 9, 2020).

Evans-Pritchard, Edward Evan. 1940. *The Nuer: A Description of the Modes of Livelihood and Political Institutions of a Nilotic People.* Oxford, UK: Clarendon Press.

Evans-von Krbek, Jeffrey. 1977. "The Social Structure and Organization of a Pakhto Speaking Community in Afghanistan." PhD diss., Durham, UK: Durham University.

Ewing, Katherine. 1994. "Dreams of a Saint: Anthropological Atheism and the Temptation to Believe." *American Anthropologist* 96 (3): 571–83.

Farmer, Paul 1996. "On Suffering and Structural Violence: A View from Below." *Daedalus* 125: 261–83.

Fog Olwig, Karen. 2012. "The 'Successful' Return: Caribbean Narratives of Migration, Family, and Gender." *Journal of the Royal Anthropological Institute* 18 (4): 828–45.

Fortes, Meyer, and Edward Evan Evans-Pritchard, eds. 1940. *African Political Systems.* Oxford, UK: Oxford University Press.

Foucault, Michel. 1985. "Dream, Imagination, and Existence." *Review of Existential Psychology and Psychiatry* 19 (1): 25–78.

Freud, Sigmund. (1913) 2013. *Totem and Taboo: Some Points of Agreement between the Mental Lives of Savages and Neurotics.* Translated by James Strachey. London: Routledge Classics.

Freud, Sigmund. (1914) 2013. *On Narcissism: An Introduction.* Vancouver: Read Books.

Freud, Sigmund. (1917) 2005. "Mourning and Melancholia." In *On Murder, Mourning and Melancholia,* 201–19. Translated by Shaun Whiteside. London: Penguin.

Freud, Sigmund. 1919. "The 'Uncanny.'" In *The Standard Edition of the Complete Psychological Works of Sigmund Freud, Volume XVII (1917–1919): An Infantile Neurosis and Other Works,* 217–56. Translated by James Strachey. London: Hogarth Press.

Freud, Sigmund. (1929) 2002. *Civilization and Its Discontents*. Translated by David McLintock. London: Penguin.

Freud, Sigmund. (1953) 1975. *The Interpretation of Dreams*. Translated by James Strachey. London: Penguin.

Gay y Blasco, Paloma. 2011. "Agata's Story." *Journal of Royal Anthropological Institute* 17 (3): 445–61.

Gedalof, Irene. 2007. "Unhomely Homes: Women, Family and Belonging in UK Discourses of Migration and Asylum." *Journal of Ethnic and Migration Studies* 33 (1): 77–94.

Gell, Alfred. 1999. "The Technology of Enchantment and the Enchantment of Technology." In *The Art of Anthropology: Essays and Diagrams*, edited by Eric Hirsch, 159–86. London: Athlone Press.

Gilsenan, Michael. 1996. *Lords of the Lebanese Marches: Violence and Narrative in an Arab Society*. London: I. B. Tauris.

Giustozzi, Antonio. 2000. *War, Politics, and Society in Afghanistan, 1978–1992*. Washington, D.C.: Georgetown University Press.

Giustozzi, Antonio. 2012. *Empires of Mud: Wars and Warlords in Afghanistan*. London: Hurst & Co.

Glatzer, Bernt. 1983. "Political Organization of Pashtun Nomads and the State." In *The Conflict of Tribe and State in Iran and Afghanistan*, edited by Richard Tapper, 212–32. New York: St. Martin's Press.

Gommans, Jos. 1994. *The Rise of the Indo-Afghan Empire, c. 1710–1780*. London: Brill's Indological Library.

Good, Byron. 2012. "Theorising the 'Subject' of Medical and Psychiatric Anthropology." *Journal of the Royal Anthropological Institute* 18 (3): 515–35.

Green, Matthew. 2016. "Is Pakistan Expelling Hundreds of Thousands of Afghan Refugees?" *Newsweek*, November 14, 2016. https://www.newsweek.com/2016/11/25/pakistan-expelling-afghanistan-refugees-520821.html (accessed January 11, 2017).

Green, Nile. 2013. "The Afghan Afterlife of Phileas Fogg: Space and Time in the Literature of Afghan Travel." In *Afghanistan in Ink: Literature between Diaspora and Nation*, edited by Nile Green and Nushin Arbabzadah, 67–90. London: Hurst & Co.

Green, Nile. 2015a. "Introduction: A History of Afghan Historiography." In *Afghan History through Afghan Eyes*, edited by Nile Green, 1–51. New York: Oxford University Press.

Green, Nile. 2015b. *The Love of Strangers: What Six Muslim Students Learned in Jane Austen's London*. Princeton, N.J.: Princeton University Press.

Green, Nile, and Nushin Arbabzadah, eds. 2013. *Afghanistan in Ink: Literature between Diaspora and Nation*. London: Hurst & Co.

Greenblatt, Stephen, ed. 2009. *Cultural Mobility: A Manifesto.* Cambridge, UK: Cambridge University Press.

Greenwood, Joseph. 1844. *Narrative of the Late Victorious Campaign in Afghanistan, under General Pollock.* London: H. Colburn.

Gregorian, Vartan. 1969. *The Emergence of Modern Afghanistan: The Politics of Reform and Modernization, 1880–1946.* Stanford, Calif.: Stanford University Press.

Grima, Benedicte. 1992. *The Performance of Emotion among Paxtun Women.* Austin: University of Texas Press.

Griswold, Eliza. 2015. *I Am the Beggar of the World: Landays from Contemporary Afghanistan.* New York: Farrar, Straus and Giroux.

Gupta, Akhil. 2004. "Imagining Nations." In *A Companion to the Anthropology of Politics,* edited by David Nugent and Joan Vincent, 267–81. Malden, Mass.: Blackwell.

Hage, Ghassan, ed. 2009a. *Waiting.* Melbourne: Melbourne University Press.

Hage, Ghassan. 2009b. "Waiting Out the Crisis: On Stuckedness and Governmentality." In *Waiting,* edited by Ghassan Hage, 97–107. Melbourne: University of Melbourne Press.

Hanifi, Mohammed Jamil. 2000. "Anthropology and Representations of Recent Migrations from Afghanistan." In *Rethinking Refuge and Displacement: Selected Papers on Refugees and Immigrants,* edited by Elzbieta Godziak and Dianna J. Shandy, 291–321. Arlington: American Anthropological Association.

Hanifi, Mohammed Jamil. 2001. "Ghalzi." *Encyclopaedia Iranica* 10 (6): 670–72.

Hanifi, Shah Mahmoud. 2006. "Material and Social Remittances to Afghanistan." In *Converting Migration Drains into Gains: Harnessing the Resources of Overseas Professionals,* edited by C. Wescott and J. Brinkerhoff, 98–126. Manila: Asian Development Bank.

Hanifi, Shah Mahmoud. 2011. *Connecting Histories in Afghanistan: Market Relations and State Formation on a Colonial Frontier.* Stanford, Calif.: Stanford University Press.

Hanifi, Shah Mahmoud. 2013. "A History of Linguistic Boundary Crossing within and around Pashto." In *Beyond Swat: History, Society and Economy along the Afghanistan–Pakistan Frontier,* edited by Magnus Marsden and Ben Hopkins, 63–76. New York: Columbia University Press.

Hanifi, Shah Mahmoud. 2016. "The Pashtun Counter-Narrative." *Middle East Critique* 25 (4): 385–400.

Hanifi, Shah Mahmoud, ed. 2019. *Mountstuart Elphinstone in South Asia: Pioneer of British Colonial Rule.* London: Hurst & Co.

Hansen, Thomas Blom. 2006. "Sounds of Freedom: Music, Taxis, and Racial Imagination in Urban South Africa." *Public Culture* 18 (1): 185–208.

Hansen, Thomas Blom. 2012. *Melancholia of Freedom: Social Life in an Indian Township in South Africa*. Princeton, N.J.: Princeton University Press.

Hardt, Michael, and Antonio Negri. 2004. *Multitude: War and Democracy in the Age of Empire*. New York: Penguin.

Harvey, David. 2000. *Spaces of Hope*. Berkeley: University of California Press.

Hassan, Ahmed Mohamed. 2014. "Sending Remittance as Transnational Kinship Practices: A Case Study of Somali Refugees in London." DPhil diss., University of London. https://research.gold.ac.uk/11156/1/SOC_thesis _HassanAM2015.pdf (accessed May 9, 2020).

Hemingway, Ernest. (1964) 2000. *A Moveable Feast*. London: Vintage Books.

Herzfeld, Michael. 1987. "As in Your Own House: Hospitality, Ethnography, and the Stereotype of Mediterranean Society." In *Honor and Shame and the Unity of the Mediterranean*, edited by David Gilmour, 75–89. Washington D.C.: American Anthropological Association.

Holbraad, Martin. 2012. "Truth beyond Doubt." *HAU: Journal of Ethnographic Theory* 2 (1): 81–109.

Hollan, Doug. 2003. "The Cultural and Intersubjective Context of Dream Remembrance and Reporting." In *Dream Travelers: Sleep Experiences and Culture in the Western Pacific*, edited by Roger Ivar Lohmann, 169–88. New York: Palgrave Macmillan.

Holtzman, Jon. 2006. "Food and Memory." *Annual Review of Anthropology* 35: 361–78.

Hopkins, Benjamin. 2008. *The Making of Modern Afghanistan*. London: Palgrave Macmillan.

Hopkins, Benjamin. 2011. "Managing 'Hearts and Minds': Sandeman in Balochistan." In *Fragments of the Afghan Frontier*, edited by Magnus Marsden and Benjamin Hopkins, 49–70. Oxford, UK: Oxford University Press.

Hopkirk, Peter. 2006. *The Great Game: On Secret Service in High Asia*. London: John Murray.

Hsu, Elisabeth. 2008. "The Senses and the Social: An Introduction." *Ethnos* 73 (4): 433–43.

Hurd, Madeleine, Hastings Donnan, and Carolin Leutloff-Grandits. 2017. "Introduction: Crossing Borders, Changing Times." In *Migrating Borders and Moving Times: Temporality and the Crossing of Borders in Europe*, edited by Hastings Donnan, Carolin Leutloff-Grandits, and Madeleine Hurd, 1–25. Manchester, UK: Manchester University Press.

Husain, Farrukh. 2018. *Afghanistan in the Age of Empires: The Great Game for South and Central Asia*. London: Silk Road Books.

Ingold, Tim. 2007. *Lines: A Brief History*. New York: Routledge.

Ingold, Tim. 2011. *Being Alive: Essays on Movement, Knowledge, and Description*. New York: Routledge.

Jackson, Michael. 2008. "The Shock of the New: On Migrant Imaginaries and Critical Transitions." *Ethnos* 73 (1): 57–72.

Jackson, Michael. 2009. *The Palm at the End of the Mind*. Durham, N.C.: Duke University Press.

Jackson, Michael. 2013. *Lifeworlds: Essays in Existential Anthropology*. Chicago: University of Chicago Press.

Jayaram, Kiran. 2016. "Capital." In *Keywords of Mobility: Critical Anthropological Engagements*, edited by Noel Salazar and Kiran Jayaram, 13–32. New York: Berghahn Books.

Jedrej, M. C., and Rosalind Shaw, eds. 1992. *Dreaming, Religion and Society in Africa*. Leiden: E. J. Brill.

Kalra, Virinder. 2000. *From Textile Mills to Taxi Ranks: Experiences of Migration, Labor and Social Change*. Aldershot, UK: Ashgate.

Kalra, Virinder, Umber Ibad, and Navtej Purewal. 2013. *Diasporic Shrines: Transnational Networks Linking South Asia through Pilgrimage and Welfare Development*. London: Palgrave Macmillan.

Kapferer, Bruce. 2013. "How Anthropologists Think: Configurations of the Exotic." *Journal of the Royal Anthropological Institute* 19 (4): 813–37.

Kaplan, Caren. 1996. *Questions of Travel: Postmodern Discourses of Displacement*. Durham, N.C.: Duke University Press.

Khan, Ghani. (1947) 2010. *The Pathans*. Peshawar: University Book Agency.

Khan, Ijaz. 2016. "The Question of Afghan Refugees." July 9, 2016. http://ijazk .blogspot.co.uk/2016/07/the-question-of-afghan-refugees.html (accessed December 2, 2016).

Khan, Nichola. 2010. *Mohajir Militancy in Pakistan*. New York: Routledge.

Khan, Nichola. 2013. "A Moving Heart: Querying a Singular Problem of 'Immobility' in Afghan Migration to the UK." *Medical Anthropology: Cross-Cultural Studies in Health and Illness* 32 (6): 518–34.

Khan, Nichola. 2014. "The Taste of Freedom: Commensality, Liminality, and Return amongst Afghan Transnational Migrants in the UK and Pakistan." *Journal of the Royal Anthropological Institute* 2 (3): 466–85.

Khan, Nichola. 2016. "Immobility." In *Keywords of Mobility: Critical Anthropological Engagements*, edited by Noel Salazar and Kiran Jayaram, 93–112. New York: Berghahn Books.

Khan, Nichola, ed. 2017a. *Cityscapes of Violence in Karachi: Publics and Counterpublics*. London: Hurst & Co.

Khan, Nichola. 2017b. *Mental Disorder: Anthropological Insights*. Toronto: University of Toronto Press.

Kipling, Rudyard. (1888) 2013. *The Man Who Would Be King*. London: Penguin. Amazon Kindle.

Kipling, Rudyard. (1901) 1993. *Kim*. London: Wordsworth Classics.

Kleinman, Arthur. 2014. "How We Endure." *Lancet* 383 (9912): 119–20.

Knoema. 2015. "Migration and Remittances Factbook: Afghanistan." https://knoema.com/WBRIO2014/migration-and-remittances-factbook-2015 (accessed January 2, 2016).

Kracke, Waud. 2003. "Afterword: Beyond Mythologies: A Shape of Dreaming." In *Dream Travelers: Sleep Experiences and Culture in the Western Pacific,* edited by Roger Lohmann, 211–36. New York: Palgrave Macmillan.

Laidlaw, James. 2002. "For an Anthropology of Ethics and Freedom." *Journal of the Royal Anthropological Institute* 8 (2): 311–32.

Lakha, Salim. 2009. "Waiting to Return Home: Modes of Immigrant Waiting." In *Waiting,* edited Ghassan Hage, 121–35. Melbourne: University of Melbourne Press.

Lambek, Michael. 2003. "Rheumatic Irony: Questions of Agency and Self-Deception as Refracted through the Art of Living with Spirits." *Social Analysis* 47 (2): 40–59.

Lambek, Michael, ed. 2010. *Ordinary Ethics: Anthropology, Language and Action.* New York: Fordham University Press.

Leader, Darian. 2011. *What Is Madness?* London: Penguin.

Leake, Elisabeth. 2017. *The Defiant Border: The Afghan–Pakistan Borderlands in the Era of Decolonization, 1936–65.* Cambridge, UK: Cambridge University Press.

Leonard, Robert. 2006. *Yellow Cab.* Albuquerque: University of New Mexico Press.

Levinas, Emmanuel. 1987. *Time and the Other.* Translated by Richard A. Cohen. Pittsburgh: University of Duquesne Press.

Lévi-Strauss, Claude. (1955) 2011. *Tristes Tropiques.* Translated by John Weightman and Doreen Weightman. London: Penguin Classics.

Lewis, Herbert S. 2017. "'Fredrik Barth' by Thomas Hylland Eriksen." *History of Anthropology Newsletter* 41. https://histanthro.org/reviews/fredrik-barth/ (accessed July 17, 2018).

Lindholm, Charles. 1982. *Generosity and Jealousy: The Swat Pukhtun of Northern Pakistan.* New York: Columbia University Press.

Lindisfarne, Nancy. 2006. *Bartered Brides: Politics, Gender and Marriage in an Afghan Tribal Society.* Cambridge, UK: Cambridge University Press.

Lohmann, Roger, ed. 2003. *Dream Travelers: Sleep Experiences and Culture in the Western Pacific.* New York: Palgrave Macmillan.

Lovell, Anne, Stefania Pandolfo, Veena Das, and Sandra Laugier. 2013. *Face aux désastres: Une conversation à quatre voix sur la folie, le care et les grandes détresses collectives.* Paris: Les Editions d'Ithaque.

Loyn, David. 2009. *In Afghanistan: Two Hundred Years of British, Russian and American Occupation.* New York: Palgrave Macmillan.

Maghbouleh, Neda. 2017. *The Limits of Whiteness: Iranian Americans, and the Everyday Politics of Race.* Stanford, Calif.: Stanford University Press.

Maimbo, Samuel Munzele. 2003. "The Money Exchange Dealers of Kabul." World Bank Working Paper 13, World Bank, Washington, D.C.

Maira, Sunaina. 2002. *Desis in the House: Indian American Youth Culture in New York City.* Philadelphia: Temple University Press.

Majumder, Atreyee. 2016. *Field of Dreams: An #amanth2016 Panel Review.* December 16. https://culanth.org/fieldsights/1009-field-of-dreams-an-amanth2016-panel-review (accessed April 9, 2017).

Malik, Iftikhar. 2016. *Pashtun Identity in Pakistan.* New York: Anthem Press.

Malinowski, Bronislaw. 1922. *Argonauts of the Western Pacific.* London: Routledge and Kegan Paul.

Malinowski, Bronislaw. 1954. *Magic, Science, and Religion, and Other Essays.* Garden City, N.Y.: Doubleday.

Mapril, Jose Manuel Fraga. 2011. "The Patron and the Madman: Migration, Success, and the (In)visibility of Failure among Bangladeshis in Portugal." *Social Anthropology* 19 (3): 288–96.

Marcus, George. 1995. "Ethnography in/of the World System: The Emergence of Multi-Sited Ethnography." *Annual Review of Anthropology* 24: 95–117.

Marcus, George. 2013. "Experimental Forms for the Expression of Norms in the Ethnography of the Contemporary." *Hau: Journal of Ethnographic Theory* 3 (2): 197–217.

Marsden, Magnus. 2008. "Muslim Cosmopolitanisms? Transnational Life in Northern Pakistan." *Journal of Asian Studies* 67: 213–47.

Marsden, Magnus. 2011. "Muslim Cosmopolitans? Transnational Village Life on the Frontiers of South and Central Asia." In *Fragments of the Afghan Frontier,* edited by Magnus Marsden and Benjamin Hopkins, 137–76. Oxford, UK: Oxford University Press.

Marsden, Magnus. 2012. "Fatal Embrace: Trading in Hospitality on the Frontiers of South and Central Asia." *Journal of the Royal Anthropological Institute* 18 (S1): S117–30.

Marsden, Magnus. 2015. *Trading Worlds: Afghan Merchants across Modern Frontiers.* New York: Oxford University Press.

Marsden, Magnus, and Benjamin D. Hopkins, eds. 2011. *Fragments of the Afghan Frontier.* Oxford, UK: Oxford University Press.

Martin, Emily. 2007. *Bipolar Expeditions: Mania and Depression in American Culture.* Princeton, N.J.: Princeton University Press.

Mascelloni, Enrico. 2009. *War Rugs: The Nightmare of Modernism.* Milan: Skira Editore.

Masood, Salman, Mujib Mashal, and Zia ur Rehman. 2019. "'Time Is Up':

Pakistan Army Targets Protest Movement, Stifling Dissent." *New York Times,* May 28, 2019.

Massumi, Brian. 2002. *Parables for the Virtual: Movement, Affect, Sensation.* Durham, N.C.: Duke University Press.

Mathew, Biju. 2008. *Taxi! Cabs and Capitalism in New York City.* Ithaca, N.Y.: Cornell University Press.

Mauss, Marcel. 1990. *The Gift: The Form and Reason for Exchange in Archaic Societies.* London: Routledge.

Meeker, Michael. 1980. "The Twilight of a South Asian Heroic Age: A Rereading of Barth's Study of Swat." *Man,* n.s., 15: 682–701.

Misdaq, Nabi. 2006. *Political Frailty and External Interference.* New York: Routledge.

Mishra, Pankaj. 2011. *Temptations of the West: How to Be Modern in India, Pakistan and Beyond.* London: Picador.

Mitchell, Stephen A. 1993. *Hope and Dread in Psychoanalysis.* New York: Basic Books.

Mitra, Diditi. 2012. "Social Capital Investment and Immigrant Economic Trajectories: A Case Study of Punjabi American Taxi Drivers in New York City." *International Migration* 50 (4): 67–84.

Monroe, Kristin. 2011. "Being Mobile in Beirut." *City and Society* 23 (1): 91–111.

Monsutti, Alessandro. 2005. *War and Migration: Social Networks and Economic Strategies of the Hazaras of Afghanistan.* Translated by Patrick Camiller. London: Routledge.

Monsutti, Alessandro. 2010a. "Afghan Migratory Strategies and the Three Solutions to the Refugee Problem." In *Beyond the Wild Tribes,* edited by Ceri Oeppen and Angela Schlenkhoff, 173–88. London: Hurst & Co.

Monsutti, Alessandro. 2010b. "Food and Identity among Young Afghan Refugees and Migrants." In *Deterritorialized Youth: Sahrawi and Afghan Refugees at the Margins of the Middle East,* edited by Dawn Chatty, 213–47. New York: Berghahn Books.

Monsutti, Alessandro. 2010c. "The Transnational Turn in Migration Studies and the Afghan Social Networks." In *Dispossession and Displacement in the Middle East,* edited by Dawn Chatty and Bill Finlayson, 45–67. Oxford, UK: Oxford University Press.

Monsutti, Alessandro. 2012. "A Strategic Dispersion: The Remittance System of Afghan Refugees and Migrants." Middle East Institute. http://www.mei.edu/content/strategic-dispersion-remittance-system-afghan-refugees-and -migrants (accessed April 20, 2012).

Monsutti, Alessandro. 2013. "Anthropologising Afghanistan: Colonial and Postcolonial Encounters." *Annual Review of Anthropology* 42: 269–85.

Monsutti, Alessandro. 2018. *Homo itinerans: La planète des Afghans*. Paris: Presses Universitaires de France.

Napolitano, Valentina. 2007. "Of Migrant Revelations and Anthropological Awakenings." *Social Anthropology* 15 (1): 75–93.

Napolitano, Valentina. 2015. *Migrant Hearts and the Atlantic Return: Transnationalism and the Roman Catholic Church*. New York: Fordham University Press.

Nations, Marilyn. 2013. "Dead-Baby Dreams, Transfiguration and Recovery from Infant Death Trauma in Northeast Brazil." *Transcultural Psychiatry* 50: 662–82.

Navaro-Yashin, Yael. 2003. "Life Is Dead Here: Sensing the Political in 'No Man's Land.'" *Anthropological Theory* 3 (1): 107–25.

Navaro-Yashin, Yael. 2007. "Make-Believe Papers, Legal Forms and the Counterfeit: Affective Interactions between Documents and People in Britain and Cyprus." *Anthropological Theory* 7 (1): 79–98.

Navaro-Yashin, Yael. 2009. "Affective Spaces, Melancholic Objects: Ruination and the Production of Anthropological Knowledge." *Journal of the Royal Anthropological Institute* 15 (1): 1–19.

The New Humanitarian. 2017. "Afghan Refugees in Greek Camp: 'If You Kept Animals in This Situation, They Would Die.'" June 2, 2017. https://www.thenewhumanitarian.org/feature/2017/06/02/afghan-refugees -greek-camp-if-you-kept-animals-situation-they-would-die (accessed May 6, 2019).

Nguyen, Mimi. 2011. "The Biopower of Beauty: Humanitarian Imperialisms and Global Feminisms in an Age of Terror." *Signs* 36 (2): 359–84.

Nguyen, Mimi. 2012. *The Gift of Freedom: War, Debt, and Other Refugee Passages*. Durham, N.C.: Duke University Press.

Nojumi, Neamatollah. 2002. *The Rise of the Taliban in Afghanistan: Mass Mobilization, Civil War, and the Future of the Region*. New York: Palgrave Macmillan.

Notar, Beth. 2012. "'Coming Out' to 'Hit the Road': Temporal, Spatial and Affective Mobilities of Taxi Drivers and Day Trippers in Kunming, China." *City and Society* 24 (3): 281–301.

O'Ballance, Edgar. 1993. *Afghan Wars 1839–1992: What Britain Gave Up and the Soviet Union Lost*. London: Brassey's.

Oeppen, Ceri. 2010. "The Afghan Diaspora and Its Involvement in the Reconstruction of Afghanistan." In *Beyond the Wild Tribes*, edited by Ceri Oeppen and Angela Schlenkhoff, 141–56. London: Hurst & Co.

Oeppen, Ceri, and Angela Schlenkhoff, eds. 2010. *Beyond the Wild Tribes: Understanding Modern Afghanistan and Its Diaspora*. London: Hurst & Co.

Office for National Statistics. 2018. "Suicides in the UK: 2018 Registrations."

https://www.ons.gov.uk/peoplepopulationandcommunity/birthsdeathsand marriages/deaths/bulletins/suicidesintheunitedkingdom/2018registrations (accessed May 10, 2020).

Olszewska, Zuzanna. 2007. "A Desolate Voice: Poetry and Identity among Young Afghan Refugees in Iran." *Iranian Studies* 40: 203–24.

Olszewska, Zuzanna. 2012. "Editorial: An Overview of the Contemporary Ethnography of Afghanistan." *Anthropology of the Middle East* 7 (1): v–vii.

Olszewska, Zuzanna. 2015. *The Pearl of Dari.* Bloomington: Indiana University Press.

Omidian, Patricia. 1996. *Aging and Family in an Afghan Refugee Community: Traditions and Transitions.* New York: Garland.

Omidian, Patricia, and Nina Joy Lawrence. 2007. "A Community-Based Approach to Focusing: The Islam and Focusing Project of Afghanistan." *Folio: A Journal for Focusing and Experiential Therapy* 20 (1): 152–64.

Ortner, Sherry. 1978. *Sherpas through Their Rituals.* Cambridge, UK: Cambridge University Press.

Ossman, Susan. 2013. *Moving Matters: Paths of Serial Migration.* Stanford, Calif.: Stanford University Press.

Oustinova-Stjepanovic, Galina. 2017. "A Catalogue of Vice: A Sense of Failure and Incapacity to Act among Roma Muslims in Macedonia." *Journal of the Royal Anthropological Institute* 23 (2): 338–55.

Pajhwok News. 2016. "Over 2,000 Afghan Families Return Home from KP in a Week." August 3, 2016. http://www.pajhwok.com/ (accessed August 5, 2016).

Pandolfo, Stefania. 1997. *Impasse of the Angels: Scenes from a Moroccan Space of Memory.* Chicago: University of Chicago Press.

Pandolfo, Stefania. 2008. "The Knot of the Soul: Postcolonial Conundrums, Madness and the Imagination." In *Postcolonial Disorders,* edited by Mary-Jo DelVecchio Good, Sarah Hyde, Sarah Pinto, and Byron Good, 329–58. Berkeley: University of California Press.

Pandolfo, Stefania. 2016. "Field of Dreams: Ethnographic Dreaming as Evidence, Accident, Discovery." Panel discussion at the American Anthropological Association Annual Meeting, Minneapolis, November 19, 2016.

Pardy, Maree. 2009. "The Shame of Waiting." In *Waiting,* edited by Ghassan Hage, 195–209. Melbourne: University of Melbourne Press.

Paul, Robert. 1989. "Psychoanalytic Anthropology." *Annual Review of Anthropology* 18: 177–202.

Phillips, Adam. 2012. *Missing Out: In Praise of the Unlived Life.* London: Hamish Hamilton.

Pitt-Rivers, Julian. 1968. "The Stranger, the Guest and the Hostile Host: Introduction to the Study of the Laws of Hospitality." In *Contributions to Medi-*

terranean Sociology: Mediterranean Rural Communities and Social Change, edited by John George Peristiany, 13–30. Paris: Mouton.

Poirier, Sylvie. 2003. "'This Is Good Country. We Are Good Dreamers: Dreams and Dreaming in the Australian Western Desert." In *Dream Travelers: Sleep Experiences and Culture in the Western Pacific*, edited by Roger Lohmann, 107–26. New York: Palgrave Macmillan.

Potamianou, Anna. 1997. *Hope: A Shield in the Economy of Borderline States*. London: Routledge.

Prieur, Annick. 1998. *Mema's House, Mexico City: On Transvestites, Queens, and Machos*. Chicago: University of Chicago Press.

Quigley, Jeff. 2014. "Pakistan: The Most Heroin-Addicted Country in the World." *The Diplomat*, March 24, 2014. https://thediplomat.com/2014/03/pakistan-the-most-heroin-addicted-country-in-the-world/ (accessed July 11, 2019).

Qureshi, Kaveri. 2010. "Sickness, Dreams and Moral Selfhood among Migrant Pakistani Muslims." *Anthropology and Medicine* 17 (3): 277–88.

Qureshi, Kaveri. 2014. "Culture Shock on Southall Broadway: Re-thinking 'Second Generation' Return through 'Geographies of Punjabiness.'" *South Asian Diaspora* 6 (2): 161–77.

Qureshi, Kaveri. 2016. *Marital Breakdown amongst British Asians: Conjugality, Legal Pluralism and New Kinship*. Basingstoke, UK: Palgrave Macmillan.

Rabinow, Paul. 2007. *Marking Time: The Anthropology of the Contemporary*. Princeton, N.J.: Princeton University Press.

Radcliffe-Brown, Alfred Reginald. 1950. "Introduction to African Systems of Kinship and Marriage." In *African Systems of Kinship and Marriage*, edited by Alfred Reginald Radcliffe-Brown and Daryll Forde, 1–66. Oxford, UK: Oxford University Press.

Rana, Junaid. 2011. *Terrifying Muslims: Race and Labor in the South Asian Diaspora*. Durham, N.C.: Duke University Press.

Rashid, Ahmed. 2000. *Taliban: Militant Islam, Oil and Fundamentalism in Central Asia*. 2nd ed. London: I. B. Tauris.

Rashid, Ahmed. 2009. *Descent into Chaos: The U.S. and the Disaster in Pakistan, Afghanistan, and Central Asia*. New York: Random House.

Rashid, Amjad, and G. M. Arif. 2014. "Analysing the Impact of Overseas Migration and Workers' Remittances in Khyber Pakhtunkhaw (KP): Suggested Measures for Maximising Development Benefits." Working Paper F-37108-PAK-1, International Growth Centre, London.

Rehman, Zia. 2017. "Karachi: A Pashtun City?" In *Cityscapes of Violence in Karachi: Publics and Counter-Publics*, edited by Nichola Khan, 63–84. London: Hurst & Co.

Rivers, William Halse Rivers. 1910. "The Genealogical Method of Social Inquiry." *Sociological Review* 3 (1): 1–12.

Rivers, William Halse Rivers. 1923. *Conflict and Dream*. New York: Harcourt, Brace and Co.

Robbins, Joel. 2003. "Dreaming and the Defeat of Charisma: Disconnecting Dreams from Leadership among the Urapmin of Papua New Guinea." In *Dream Travelers: Sleep Experiences and Culture in the Western Pacific*, edited by Roger Lohmann, 19–42. New York: Palgrave Macmillan.

Robbins, Joel. 2013. "Beyond the Suffering Subject: Toward an Anthropology of the Good." *Journal of the Royal Anthropological Institute* 19 (3): 447–62.

Roden, Claudia. 1984. *Everything Tastes Better Outdoors*. New York: Knopf.

Rogaly, Ben. 2015. "Disrupting Migration Stories: Reading Life Histories through the Lens of Mobility and Fixity." *Environment and Planning D: Society and Space* 33 (3): 528–44.

Rohlof, Hans, Jeroen Knipscheer, and Rolf Kleber. 2014. "Somatization in Refugees: A Review." *Social Psychiatry and Psychiatric Epidemiology* 49 (11): 1793–1804.

Rosaldo, Renato. 2014. *The Day of Shelly's Death: The Poetry and Ethnography of Grief*. Durham, N.C.: Duke University Press.

Rose, Gillian. 1992. *The Broken Middle*. Oxford, UK: Blackwell.

Rose, Jacqueline. 2017. "From the Inside Out." *London Review of Books*, September 22, 2017.

Rosenblat, Alex. 2019. *Uberland: How Algorithms Are Rewriting the Rules of Work*. Berkeley: University of California Press.

Roy, Olivier. 1985. *Islam and Resistance in Afghanistan*. Cambridge, UK: Cambridge University Press.

Rubin, Barnett. 1995. *The Fragmentation of Afghanistan: State Formation and Collapse in the International System*. New Haven, Conn.: Yale University Press.

Ruskin, John. (1866) 2015. *Traffic*. London: Penguin Classics.

Ruttig, Thomas. 2017. "Pressure and Peril: Afghan Refugees and Europe in 2017." *Afghan Analysts Network*. https://www.afghanistan-analysts.org/ (accessed March 14, 2018).

Sadiq, Kamal. 2009. *Paper Citizens: How Illegal Immigrants Acquire Citizenship in Developing Countries*. Oxford, UK: Oxford University Press.

Saeed, Aamir, and Jared Ferrie. 2017. "UN under Fire Even as Pakistan Lifts Deportation Order." *New Humanitarian*, February 13, 2017. http://www.thenewhumanitarian.org/news/2017/02/13/un-under-fire-even-pakistan-lifts-afghan-deportation-order (accessed February 13, 2017).

Said, Edward. 1987. *Orientalism*. London: Penguin.

Salazar, Noel. 2012. "Imagining (Im)mobility at the 'End of the World.'" In

Technologies of Mobility in the Americas, edited by Phillip Vannini, Paola Jiron, Ole Jensen, Lucy Budd, and Christian Fisker, 237–54. New York: Peter Lang.

Salazar, Noel. 2013. "Anthropology." In *The Routledge Handbook of Mobilities,* edited by Peter Adey, David Bissell, Kevin Hannam, Peter Merriman, and Mimi Sheller, 55–63. London: Routledge.

Salazar, Noel, and Kiran Jayaram, eds. 2016. *Keywords of Mobility: Critical Anthropological Engagements.* New York: Berghahn Books.

Salazar, Noel, and Alan Smart. 2011. "Anthropological Takes on (Im)mobility." *Identities: Global Studies in Culture and Power* 18: i–ix.

Scarry, Elaine. 1985. *The Body in Pain: The Making and Unmaking of the World.* New York: Oxford University Press.

Schiller, Nina Glick, and Noel B. Salazar. 2013. "Regimes of Mobility across the Globe." *Journal of Ethnic and Migration Studies* 39 (2): 183–200.

Schlenkhoff, Angela. 2010. "Challenges to Research in Afghanistan and Its Diaspora." In *Beyond the Wild Tribes,* edited by Ceri Oeppen and Angela Schlenkhoff, 9–25. London: Hurst & Co.

Sengupta, Kim. 2008. "Butcher and Bolt, by David Loyn." *The Independent,* October 24, 2008. https://www.independent.co.uk/arts-entertainment/books/reviews/butcher-and-bolt-by-david-loyn-970614.html (accessed October 24, 2008).

Shahrani, Nazif. 2002. "War, Factionalism and the State in Afghanistan." *American Anthropologist* 104 (3): 715–22.

Shyrock, Andrew. 2004. "The New Jordanian Hospitality: House, Host, and Guest in the Culture of Public Display." *Comparative Studies in Society and History* 46: 35–62.

Shyrock, Andrew. 2012. "Breaking Hospitality Apart: Bad Hosts, Bad Guests, and the Problem of Sovereignty." *Journal of the Royal Anthropological Institute* 18 (S1): S20–33.

Singh, Bhrigupati. 2015. *Poverty and the Quest for Life: Spiritual and Material Striving in Rural India.* Chicago: University of Chicago Press.

Sopranzetti, Claudio. 2017. *Owners of the Map: Motorcycle Taxi Drivers, Mobility, and Politics in Bangkok.* Berkeley: University of California Press.

Steele, Jonathon. 2011. *Ghosts of Afghanistan: The Haunted Battleground.* London: Portobello Books.

Stevens, Christine. 1989. *Tin Mosques and Ghantowns: History of Afghan Camel Drivers in Australia.* Melbourne: Oxford University Press.

Stoler, Laura Ann. 2008. "Imperial Debris: Reflections on Ruins and Ruination." *Cultural Anthropology* 23 (2): 191–219.

Stoller, Paul. 1989. *The Taste of Ethnographic Things.* Philadelphia: University of Pennsylvania Press.

Stoller, Paul. 2007. "Ethnography/Memoir/Imagination/Story." *Anthropology and Humanism* 32 (2): 178–91.

Street, Brian. 2006. "Autonomous and Ideological Models of Literacy: Approaches from New Literacy Studies." *Media Anthropology Network* 17: 1–15.

Strick van Linschoten, Alex, and Felix Kuehn, eds. 2012. *Poetry of the Taliban.* London: Hurst & Co.

Subrahmanyam, Sanjay. 2004. *Explorations in Connected History: Mughals and Franks.* Delhi: Oxford University Press.

Suhrke, Astri. 2011. *When More Is Less: The International Project in Afghanistan.* London: Hurst & Co.

Sutton, David. 2001. *Remembrance of Repasts: An Anthropology of Food and Memory.* London: Berg.

Szakolczai, Arpad. 2009. "Liminality and Experience: Structuring Transitory Situations and Transformative Events." *International Political Anthropology* 2: 141–72.

Tagore, Rabindranath. (1892) 1991. "Kabuliwala." In *Selected Stories of Rabindranath Tagore,* 113–20. London: Penguin.

Tapper, Richard, and Nancy Tapper. 1986. "Eat This, It'll Do You a Power of Good: Food and Commensality amongst Durrani Pakhtuns." *American Ethnologist* 13: 62–78.

Taussig, Mick. 1989. "Terror as Usual: Walter Benjamin's Theory of History as a State of Siege." *Social Text* 23: 3–20.

Tedlock, Barbara. 1987. "Dreaming and Dream Research." In *Dreaming: Anthropological and Psychological Interpretations,* edited by Barbara Tedlock, 1–30. Cambridge, UK: Cambridge University Press.

Thangaraj, Stanley. 2015. *Desi Hoop Dreams: Pickup Basketball and the Making of Asian American Masculinity.* New York: NYU Press.

Thomassen, Bjorn. 2009. "The Uses and Meanings of Liminality." *International Political Anthropology* 2: 5–27.

Thompson, Edwina. 2011. *Trust Is the Coin of the Realm: Lessons from the Money Men in Afghanistan.* Karachi: Oxford University Press.

Truitt, Alison. 2008. "On the Back of a Motorbike: Middle-Class Mobility in Ho Chi Minh City, Vietnam." *American Ethnologist* 35 (1): 3–19.

Turner, Victor. 1967. *The Forest of Symbols: Aspects of Ndembu Ritual.* Ithaca, N.Y.: Cornell University Press.

Turner, Victor. (1969) 2011. *The Ritual Process.* London: Aldine Transaction.

Turner, Victor. 1974. "Passages, Margins, and Poverty: Religious Symbols of Communitas." In *Dramas, Fields, and Metaphors: Symbolic Action in Human Society,* edited by Victor Turner, 231–71. Ithaca, N.Y.: Cornell University Press.

Tylor, Edward B. (1871) 1877. *Primitive Culture: Researches into the Development of Mythology, Philosophy, Religion, Language, Art, and Custom.* 2 vols. New York: Henry Holt and Company.

UNHCR (UN Refugee Agency). 2005. *Statistical Summary Overview: Census of Afghans in Pakistan.* Geneva: UNHCR.

UNHCR (UN Refugee Agency). 2012. *Population Profiling, Verification and Response Survey of Afghans in Pakistan 2011.* Geneva: UNHCR.

UNHCR (UN Refugee Agency). 2015. *Afghanistan Refugee and Returnee Overview.* Geneva: UNHCR.

UNHCR (UN Refugee Agency). 2017. "UNHCR Welcomes New Government Policy for Afghans in Pakistan." February 7, 2017. https://unhcrpk.org/ (accessed July 1, 2017).

UNODC (United Nations Office on Drugs and Crime). 2017. *World Drug Report, 2017.* Vienna: United Nations Office on Drugs and Crime. https://www.unodc.org/wdr2017/index.html (accessed July 22, 2019).

UNODC (United Nations Office on Drugs and Crime). 2018. "Last Year's Record Opium Production in Afghanistan Threatens Sustainable Development, Latest Survey Reveals." May 21, 2018. https://www.unodc.org/unodc/en/frontpage/2018/May/last-years-record-opium-production-in-afghanistan-threatens-sustainable-development-latest-survey-reveals.html (accessed July 1, 2019).

Urry, John. 2004. "The 'System' of Automobility." *Theory, Culture and Society* 21 (4–5): 25–39.

Urry, John. 2007. *Mobilities.* Cambridge, UK: Polity Press.

Vanore, Michaella, Melissa Siegel, Katie Kuschminder, Nassim Majidi, Michaella Vanore, and Carla Buil. 2014. *Afghanistan Migration Profile.* Kabul: International Organization for Migration Afghanistan.

Virgil. 1956. *The Aeneid.* Translated by W. F. Jackson Knight. London: Penguin.

Von Grunebaum, Gustave, and Roger Callois. 1966. *The Dream and Human Societies.* Berkeley: University of California Press.

Vulliamy, Elsa. 2016. "Refugees Who Cannot Pay Smugglers Being Sold for Organs." *The Independent,* July 4, 2016. https://www.independent.co.uk/news/world/europe/refugee-crisis-sold-for-organs-people-smugglers-trafficker-a7119066.html (accessed December 4, 2019).

Wagner, Roy. 1981. *The Invention of Culture.* Chicago: University of Chicago Press.

Wallace, Anthony. 1958. "Dreams and the Wishes of the Soul: A Type of Psychoanalytic Theory among Seventeenth Century Iroquois." *American Anthropologist* 60: 234–48.

Wallace, Christopher Julian. 2014. "'Masterly Inactivity': Lord Lawrence, Britain and Afghanistan, 1864–1879." PhD diss., King's College London.

Walle, Thomas. 2007. "Making Places of Intimacy: Ethnicity, Friendship and Masculinities in Oslo." *Nora: Nordic Journal of Women's Studies* 15 (2): 144–57.

Wide, Thomas. 2013a. "Around the World in 29 Days: The Travels, Translations, and Temptations of an Afghan Dragoman." In *On the Wonders of Land and Sea: Persianate Travel Writing,* edited by Roberta Micallef and Sunil Sharma, 89–113. Boston: Ilex.

Wide, Thomas. 2013b. "Demarcating Pashto: Cross-Border Literature and the Afghan State, 1880–1930." In *Afghanistan in Ink: Between Diaspora and Nation,* edited by Nile Green and Nushin Arbabzadah, 91–112. New York: Columbia University Press.

Wide, Thomas. 2014. "The Refuge of the World: Afghanistan and the Muslim Imagination, 1880–1922." PhD diss., University of Oxford.

Widmark, Anders. 2011. "Voices at the Borders, Prose on the Margins: Exploring the Contemporary Pashto Short Story in a Context of War and Crisis." PhD diss., Uppsala University.

Williams, Francis Edgar. 1936. "Papua Dream Interpretations." *Mankind* 2 (2): 29–39.

Williams, Maynard Owen. 1933. "Afghanistan Makes Haste Slowly." *National Geographic* 64: 71–269.

Wilson, Thomas, and Hastings Donnan, eds. 2012. *A Companion to Border Studies.* Oxford, UK: Wiley-Blackwell.

Wool, Zoe. 2015. *After War: The Weight of Life at Walter Reed.* Durham, N.C.: Duke University Press.

Wulff, Helena. 2008. *Dancing at the Crossroads: Memory and Mobility in Ireland.* New York: Berghahn Books.

Žižek, Slavoj. 1999. "Fantasy as a Political Category: A Lacanian Approach." In *The Žižek Reader,* edited by Elizabeth Wright and Edmund Wright, 89–101. Oxford, UK: Blackwell.

Žižek, Slavoj. 2004. *Organs without Bodies: On Deleuze and Consequences.* New York: Routledge.

Zylinska, Joanna. 2004. "The Universal Acts: Judith Butler and the Biopolitics of Immigration." *Cultural Studies* 18 (4): 523–37.

INDEX

281

NICHOLA KHAN is a reader in anthropology and psychology at the University of Brighton. She is author of *Mohajir Militancy in Pakistan* and *Mental Disorder: Anthropological Insights* and editor of *Cityscapes of Violence in Karachi: Publics and Counterpublics.*